JEAN-HENRY D'ANGLEBERT AND THE SEVENTEENTH-CENTURY CLAVECIN SCHOOL

Music: Scholarship and Performance
Thomas Binkley, General Editor

JEAN-HENRY D'ANGLEBERT AND THE SEVENTEENTH-CENTURY CLAVECIN SCHOOL

BEVERLY SCHEIBERT

INDIANA UNIVERSITY PRESS · BLOOMINGTON

This book was brought to publication with the assistance of a grant from the Andrew W. Mellon Foundation.

Manufactured in the United States of America

Library of Congress Cataloging in Publication Data
Scheibert, Beverly.
Jean-Henry D'Anglebert and the seventeenth-century clavecin school.

Bibliography: p.
Includes index.
1. Anglebert, J. Henry d' (Jean Henry d'), 1628–1691.
2. Composers—France—Biography.   3. Keyboard music—France—17th century—History and criticism.   I. Title.
ML410.A635S3   1985   786.1'092'4 [B]   84-43069
ISBN 0-253-38823-6

1   2   3   4   5   90   89   88   87   86

To David and Marie

CONTENTS

PREFACE

The reign of Louis XIV in France (1643–1715) coincided with a remarkable development in the arts. Was it happenstance that so many brilliant minds were active at the same time? Or did music, theater, and the visual arts flourish because Louis supported them so handsomely? The arts not only enhanced the king's image but were an important source of stability for a society burdened by the costs of a series of wars during the Sun King's reign. Moreover, Louis genuinely enjoyed beautiful furnishings and elegant surroundings, and he loved the theater, dance, and music in all its forms.

Jean-Henry D'Anglebert played a leading role at court as the king's harpsichordist from 1662 to 1691. One of the most significant musicians of the seventeenth century, D'Anglebert not only composed music reflecting an imaginative harmonic vocabulary and a gift for melody but also pioneered in such areas as ornamentation and notation for the unmeasured prelude. He holds his own with François Couperin and Jean-Philippe Rameau from the next generation but, for some reason, he has not received much attention. Perhaps D'Anglebert has been overlooked because he left only a modest amount of keyboard music, in contrast to the larger *oeuvres* from Couperin and Rameau. Jean-Baptiste Lully and his operas dominated the late seventeenth century so completely that other musicians seem mere background figures despite the fact that keyboard music was vigorous and healthy during this period.

Little French harpsichord music has survived from the first half of the seventeenth century, so our history really begins with the editions by Jacques Champion de Chambonnières, published in 1670, near the end of his life, and Louis Couperin's pieces in manuscript from the 1650s. Both D'Anglebert and Couperin were students of Chambonnières, so the three musicians may have exchanged the lively ideas that produced the literature we have today. D'Anglebert's music is found in an autograph manuscript from the 1660s–1670s, in his *Pièces de clavecin*, published in 1689, and in eleven other manuscripts containing miscellaneous pieces. Kenneth Gilbert's carefully executed modern edition of D'Anglebert's works has enabled harpsichordists to explore this *trésor*. In discussing D'Anglebert's harpsichord and organ music, as well as his important contributions to ornamentation and transcription, I have included, where appropriate, examples from works of other key figures of the period—Chambonnières, L. Couperin, Nicolas-Antoine Lebègue, and Elisabeth-Claude Jacquet de La Guerre. Several chapters are devoted to ornamentation and tempo in late seventeenth-century France in order to demonstrate the wide variety of performance practice at this time. After Frederick Neumann's work with the trill and the one-note grace broke new ground, I pursued the matter by translating the early treatises without recourse to his work. My initial orientation centered around "traditional" present-day ornament performance practice, but I found these ideas undergoing alteration as I worked with the treatises and the internal evidence in D'Anglebert's music itself.

Biographical information about D'Anglebert in the existing literature is often contradictory and erroneous. Moreover, some of the documentation for the scanty biographical information compiled in the nineteenth century by Auguste Jal and Léon de Laborde was destroyed in the fire at the Hôtel de Ville in Paris on 24 May 1871. It is especially vexing that even D'Anglebert's date of birth cannot be established; fire and the Revolution seem to have wiped out the sources. A search through nearly illegible baptismal records in Bar-le-Duc has thus far been fruitless. I am indebted to Jean Guinard of the Cercle Généalogique de Lorraine for assisting me in this effort.

The major encyclopedias contain relatively brief articles about D'Anglebert (and they are not reliable in all respects), while articles and books on French keyboard music of the seventeenth century generally award him only a few lines. A notable exception is the commentary by Willi Apel, in *The History of Keyboard Music to 1700*,

> With d'Anglebert French clavier music reaches its highest point of Baroque magnificence and fulness. His skill in continuing a melody, contrapuntally interweaving voices, concatenating harmonies by way of suspensions, and always using meaningful figures as ornaments brings to a final culmination and maturity what his teacher, Chambonnières, began—and certainly his was no mere beginning. The music that follows begins to show the traits of the Rococo *style galant*.

The following libraries, institutions, and publishers have graciously permitted me to reproduce material from their holdings: Bibliothèque nationale (Paris), Archives nationales (Paris), Newberry Library (Chicago), Bibliothèque municipale (Troyes), Carl Dolmetsch Library (Haslemere), Staatsbibliothek Preussischer Kulturbesitz, Musikabteilung (Berlin), Conservatorio di Musica Benedetto Marcello (Venice), Houghton Library and Eda Kuhn Loeb Music Library of Harvard University (Cambridge), Music Library of Boston University (Boston), Music Library of Yale University (New Haven), Broude Bros. Ltd., and Éditions Minkoff. I thank Pierre Hardouin for his generous sharing of data relating to the D'Anglebert family and the executor of the estate of the late Thurston Dart for permitting me to examine the manuscript of clavecin music from Dart's personal collection.

I gratefully acknowledge assistance from, among others, William Dowd, David Fuller, Bruce Gustafson, Edward Higginbottom, John Hsu, Helen La Fleur, Kenneth La Fleur, Nancy Orton, Barbara Owen, William Parsons, Robert Schuneman, and members of the Alliance of Independent Scholars, Cambridge.

JEAN-HENRY
D'ANGLEBERT
AND THE
SEVENTEENTH-CENTURY
CLAVECIN SCHOOL

I

THE TIMES

The late seventeenth century in France, a time of political stability at home, wars abroad, and great productivity in the arts, was dominated by the overwhelming personality of Louis XIV (1638–1715). Jean-Henry D'Anglebert's tenure at court from 1662 to 1691 coincided with the height of the *grand siècle*. When Cardinal Mazarin, the first minister during Louis's minority, died in 1661, young Louis assumed the reins of government himself, rather than seek a replacement. *L'état, c'est moi* sums up his approach to government, for the king was supreme by divine and natural right. Louis was determined above all to impose order on a disordered world—witness the symmetry of Versailles. The original chateau, greatly enlarged by the Sun King, became the principal court and the seat of government in 1682. Its construction was directed by the architects Louis Le Vau and Jules Hardouin Mansart, the painter and decorator Charles Le Brun, and the gardener André Le Nôtre. During Louis's reign, architecture and the arts, like nearly everything else in France, centered around the crown.

Louis sought control in other areas too, and mindful of the *Fronde* rebellion (1648–1653), he strove to reduce the powers of the nobles and other groups. He waged war almost continuously from 1667 to the end of his reign, attempting to acquire territories to which France at one time had a claim. His wars depleted the treasury, and an overtaxed peasantry and poor grain harvests led to rebellion during his last years. Nevertheless, after the Peace of Utrecht in 1713, Louis still held all the territorial gains he considered essential.

The many years of war did not curtail the extravagance of the *divertissements* (entertainments, balls, masquerades, and the like) until much later in Louis's reign. In 1690 the *Mercure galant* could remark that, unlike other countries during a war, France continued its entertainments and artistic life as before because of Louis's strong leadership. Even in 1708, the *Mercure* reported on an ample supply of money, healthy industrial production, and extravagant balls, despite the heavy military losses, as Robert Isherwood notes:

> Thus, the *divertissements* were useful beyond their obvious purpose; they kept the nobility occupied, passive, and even submissive, and they offered a constant show of the affluence of the realm even, and perhaps especially, in time of war. In an age of wars of attrition, the regular presentation of costly *divertissements* was a useful psychological weapon which could be justified by reason of state.[1]

In the literary world, Pierre Corneille and Jean Racine were writing superb drama and Molière brilliant, ironic comedy; while Marie de La Fayette published the popular novel *La Princesse de Clèves*. Other notable works include the letters of Marie de Rabutin-Chantal, Marquise de Sévigné, *Réflexions, ou sentences et maximes morales* of François de La Rochefoucauld, and *Les Fables* of the poet Jean de La Fontaine.

Jean-Baptiste Lully's operatic successes overshadowed the accomplishments of all other French musicians, but some did have distinguished careers, among them D'Anglebert and the other clavecinistes of this book, the lutenist Denis Gaultier, the gambist Marin Marais, the organists Guillaume-Gabriel Nivers and André Raison, and the composers Marc-Antoine Charpentier and Michel-Richard de Lalande.

Louis XIV developed an interest in music under the influence of his father, Louis XIII, who was an accomplished amateur musician and composer. Young Louis studied the lute with Germain Pinel, the guitar (which became his favorite instrument) with the Spaniard Bernard Jourdan de La Salle, and the harpsichord with Étienne Richard. But more than anything else, Louis loved to dance—particularly branles and courantes—and participated in some of Lully's ballets in the 1660s, as Jacques Bonnet (1715) describes:

> Since the king knew music to perfection and danced better than all the lords of the court, he ordered Lambert and Lully to compose a grand ballet for which Sieur de Benserade furnished the text and Beauchamp the *entrées*. Together with the most astonishing machines invented by the Marquis de Sourdiac and de la Grille, it was performed at the Louvre in 1663 with a magnificence that surpassed all that one can imagine of the Venetian opera. The king danced masked

in several *entrées*. One can say that, with his grand manner and beautiful grace, he eclipsed all the most famous dancers of the court who appeared in this royal performance.[2]

Music at court was divided into three main categories: court musicians of the *Chapelle* provided sacred music; those of the *Chambre* furnished music for the king's dinner, *coucher*, balls, ballets, and various entertainments; and those of the *Écurie* (stables) supplied pomp and pageantry for outdoor and other ceremonies. Versailles became the center of court life in 1682, but the court frequently moved around, taking its musicians to other locations such as the Louvre, Fontainebleau, St. Germain-en-Laye, Vincennes, Marly, Meudon, the Tuileries, or Compiègne. Scarcely a day passed without some performance or use of music. According to the 1686 *État de la France* (a yearly chronicle of events and people), the *grande bande* of 24 violins was paid 365[lt] to play at the king's dinner, at ballets, and at comedies. The 21 *petits violons* received 600[lt] for accompanying His Majesty to his country homes and playing for the king's supper, dances, entertainments, and ballets.[3] Music surrounded the king, accompanying daily activities as well as special occasions, and forming an important part of religious services. The musicians of the *Chambre* were also called upon to assist at grand ceremonies with members of the *Chapelle* or the *Écurie*.

Written accounts from this period describe the accomplishments of those connected with the design, construction, and furnishing of Versailles. Similarly, there are many accounts of those who lived at the grand palace—the royal family, clergy, government officials, army officers, and courtiers. But curiously, musicians are mentioned infrequently; for example, Jean-Baptiste Lully was the only musician listed among 100 leaders from all walks of life in Charles Perrault's *Les Hommes illustres qui ont paru en France pendant ce siècle* (1696).

Music at Versailles must have been splendid, as Mme de Sévigné remarks in her letters: "Il y a toujours quelque musique qu'il [the king] écoute et qui fait un très bon effet"; and "Je reviens de Versailles. Tout est grand, tout est magnifique, et la musique et la danse sont dans leur perfection."[4] Although Mme de Sévigné was a talented singer as well as a gifted writer, her musical observations give few details. One can gain some idea of the court's musical forces, however, from the payroll accounts for Lully's splendid ballet *Le*

Triomphe de l'Amour (1680–1681). They list eight soloists, 48 *musitiens* (probably singers and continuo players), 18 dancers, 25 *grands violons du Roy*, 22 *petits violons*, and 21 flutes and oboes.[5]

Court musicians purchased or inherited their titles, a custom about which Marcelle Benoit provides interesting information.[6] The date on which a musician received an appointment (*charge*) was not a reliable indication of the time he joined the court. Often he had been esteemed long before his nomination (for example, François Couperin, who never did attain the title), so the new position did not necessarily add new duties to the honor. Titles could be sold, subject to the king's pleasure, so naming a successor was a way of profiting financially from one's post, with the added advantage of having the new person available to deputize. A simple reversion (*survivance*) entailed assigning one's office to another, with the reversion taking effect on the death or voluntary resignation of the incumbent. Other types of reversion could be implemented during the life of the incumbent or allow for the sharing of duties.

Musicians' titles signified their rank. The *musicien ordinaire* was second only to the *musicien-officier, ordinaire* indicating that the individual served at the court regularly and with a frequency determined by the nature of his employment. Musicians of lesser rank, whose services were needed on a more-occasional basis, were termed *musiciens extraordinaires* and *musiciens suivant la Cour*.

His Majesty's singers and instrumentalists provided chamber music and dance music for the social events that took place in the royal apartments three evenings a week during the winter. A valuable first-hand account is given in a letter of 6 December 1682 written by Elizabeth Charlotte ("Liselotte," wife of the king's brother, "Monsieur") to her sister-in-law, Wilhemine Ernestine:

> Every Monday, Wednesday and Friday is *jour d'appartement*. All the gentlemen of the Court assemble in the King's antechamber, and the women meet in the Queen's rooms at 6 o'clock. Then everyone goes in procession to the drawing-room. Next to it there is a large room, where fiddles play for those who want to dance. Then comes the King's throne-room, with every kind of music, both played and sung. Next door in the bed-chamber there are three card tables, one for the King, one for the Queen and one for Monsieur. Next comes a large room—it could be called a hall—with more than twenty tables covered in green velvet with golden fringes, where all sorts of games

can be played. Then there is the great antechamber where the King's billiard table stands, and then a room with four long tables with re-freshments, all kinds of things—fruit-tarts, sweetmeats, it looks just like the Christmas spread at home. Four more tables, just as long, are set out in the adjoining room, laden with decanters and glasses and every kind of wine and liqueur. People stand while they are eating and drinking in the last two rooms, and then go to the rooms with the tables and disperse to play. It is unbelievable how many games there are: *lansquenet*, backgammon, *piquet, reversi, ombre*, chess, *Trou Madame, Berlan, summa summarum*, everything you can think of. If the King or Queen comes into the room, nobody has to rise. Those who don't play, like myself and many others, wander from room to room, now to the music, now to the gamblers—you are allowed to go wher-ever you like. This goes on from six to ten, and is what is called *jour d'appartement*. If I could describe the splendour with which all these rooms are furnished, and the amount of silver there is everywhere, I should go on for ever. It really is worth seeing.[7]

Other writers have remarked about the king's beneficence and infor-mality at these evening gatherings, where the largesse and convivi-ality served to keep the nobles occupied in harmless pursuits, while at the same time impressing foreign visitors with the affluence of the French court. The 1687 *État de la France* reported that the rooms were illuminated by an infinite number of crystal chandeliers, branched candlesticks, and silver torches, and that at the beginning of the *Apartemens* [sic], "His Majesty's Singers perform part of an opera, but not in costume."[8]

An engraving by Antoine Trouvain depicts a chamber concert—perhaps for one of these *jour d'appartements*—in the "fourth room" of the king's *appartements*, attended by the Duc de Bourgogne, Ma-dame, the Duchesse de Chartres, the Duc de Chartres (the future regent), Mademoiselle (his sister), the Duchesse du Maine, and the Princesse de Conty. Another engraving by Trouvain portrays a con-cert in the "fifth room," also with a gallery. A character in Made-leine de Scudéry's celebrated novel *Le Grand Cyrus* mentions that the musicians are placed in a gallery to spare the audience the fuss and bother of having them underfoot—moreover, one is obliged to pay them compliments when they are nearby.[9]

Bonnet gives accounts of some splendid fetes during the Sun King's reign; e.g., music was prominent in the celebration of his brother's first marriage:

Trouvain. *Concert in the Fourth Room of the
Royal Apartments.* Courtesy of the Cabinet
des estampes, Bibliothèque nationale, Paris.

But it must be acknowledged that nothing approached the magnificence or the pomp of the fetes that the king gave at Versailles in 1665
to honor the marriage of Monsieur with the Princess Henrietta of
England. After tilting at the ring, the *Comédie,* the ballets, and fire-
works, a light meal was served, accompanied by *récits de Musique,* in
a place appropriately illuminated. A company of thirty musicians
sang as they entered, followed by the four Seasons, who carried the
most delicious food to serve before their Majesties and the lords
invited to this fete. The Seasons danced a ballet *entrée,* the most
unique that one had yet seen. Spring appeared mounted on a beautiful Spanish horse, with a green costume embroidered with silver and
fresh flowers. Summer followed him on an elephant with a richly
embroidered cover spread with pearls. Autumn was mounted on a
very ornate camel, and Winter wore the coat of a bear. Their entou-
rage was composed of forty-eight persons who carried on their heads
large bowls for the meal, which they placed on the steps while they
were dancing. . . . The gods Pan and Diane appeared at the end of
all this spectacle, accompanied by a large group of musicians [male

and female] from the court of these two divinities playing a pleasant piece for flutes and musettes. They appeared forthwith on a boulder shaded by several trees that seemed to be floating in air, although one could not perceive any contrivance. These Seasons and Divinities performed their *récits* to the Queen and to the wedding couple. . . . This feast was continually accompanied by different concerts, such that it would be difficult to make a fete more superb, more magnificent, or better received. One can also say that never has a court been more elegant or more prosperous than that of France at this time.[10]

Music was also a part of His Majesty's elaborate bedtime ceremony. Lully wrote numerous instrumental trios for Louis's *coucher*, two of which D'Anglebert transcribed for harpsichord. If one were a courtier at Versailles, it was prudent not only to arise early each morning to attend the king's *lever* ceremony but to be present late each evening for his *grand coucher*. The nobles had to live at Versailles, where Louis could keep an eye on them; to be banished to live on one's estate in the provinces was a dreaded ignominy. The 1687 *État de la France* lists the various individuals who attended the *lever* ceremony. The musician Lully was included in this august list "par une grace particuliere attachée à sa persone."[11] The same men also attended Louis's *grand coucher* ceremony, consisting of prayers and an undressing sequence.[12] Amazing importance was attached to minutiae—for example, being chosen to hold the candlestick was a signal honor. According to the *État de la France*, "It is always the highest ranking Prince or Officer who gives the chemise to the King." Details of who does what and exactly when were orchestrated with utmost precision: "And when His Majesty puts on a night jacket, the Grand Master of the Wardrobe takes this jacket from the hands of a Valet of the Wardrobe, and puts it on the King, who then takes his dressing gown, held up by two Valets of the Chamber who are always behind the armchair of His Majesty." After Louis bowed and dismissed the courtiers, the Criers called out loudly: "*Allons, Messieurs!*"

Now followed the *petit coucher du Roy*, with the highest ranking individuals and "some others to whom the King gave the grace of being present." Formerly in Paris on certain days of the week, one could hear the *musique du petit-coucher*, composed of some voices or at times only of instruments. The king's toilette included trimming and combing his hair, as well as washing: "To all the Princes of the

Blood and *Légitimes*, the Grand Chamberlain or the First Nobleman of the Chamber yields the honor of giving the King the towel with which he wipes his hands and face." His Majesty's nightcap and handkerchiefs were offered to him ceremoniously, after which at times a fortunate courtier might importune the king for a favor. By bestowing great significance on the slightest favors or honors, Louis controlled his nobles and helped ensure that he would never face a rebellion such as the *Fronde* of his youth.

An inventory of the furniture in the king's residence in 1673 included two *épinettes* (small spinets) and four clavecins, of which two were *grands* (presumably meaning double harpsichords); two theorbos; two guitars; one violin; one lute; and three viols.[13] The lute, popular in early seventeenth-century France, declined in importance as the portable *épinette* and the clavecin came into their own. Only the rich could own clavecins, but a wide variety of people purchased *épinettes*. Marin Mersenne's *Harmonie universelle* (1636) includes an engraving of a single-keyboard clavecin that resembles the Flemish instruments (with a chromatic range of C–c‴ and two sets of strings at 8' and 4' pitch) and an illustration of an *épinette*.[14] According to Jean-Baptiste-Charles de La Rousselière (1679), the *épinette* derived its name from the thorns (*épines*) that were used for quills in the jacks before feather quills were adopted.[15]

Most of the few surviving clavecins from seventeenth-century France have two keyboards (double harpsichord),[16] but single-keyboard instruments also seem to have been common; e.g., D'Anglebert's posthumous inventory includes only single harpischords, and one with a transposing keyboard. Unlike some of Chambonnières's and Louis Couperin's works, none of D'Anglebert's pieces requires a double harpsichord or the short-octave keyboard that makes it possible to play large intervals in the bass register with ease.[17] St.-Lambert (1702) shows a drawing of a harpsichord keyboard with a short-octave compass of GG to c‴. The two lowest accidental keys are split and produce C♯ and E♭ when struck at the rear of the keys, but AA and BB when struck in front. The apparent BB key sounds GG.[18]

The harpsichord joined the other continuo instruments in large ensembles to play music connected with the stage—opera, ballet, and musical comedy—but it also participated in chamber music with voices and/or instruments. Members of the nobility took their cue

Épinette in Mersenne's *Harmonie universelle.*
Courtesy of Éditions Minkoff.

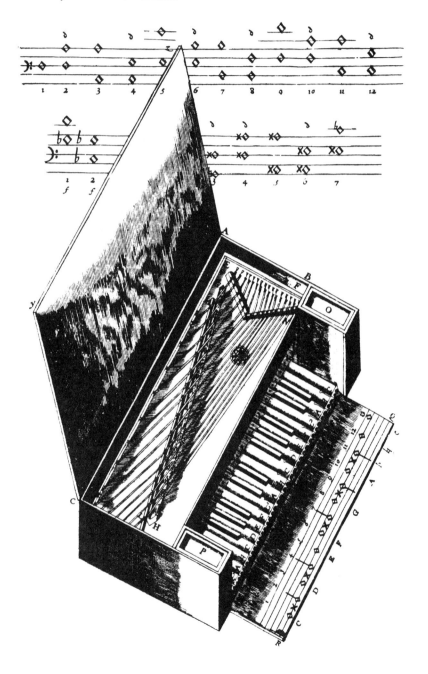

from the king and made music an important part of their lives, for it was the socially acceptable thing to do. Mme de Sévigné and many others sponsored concerts, as salons in private homes became fashionable, while Molière wittily portrayed the bourgeoisie's aping of their betters in *Le Bourgeois gentilhomme*. An eighteenth-century gentleman, Mr Ancelet, gives a less than enthusiastic account of these concerts:

> Each house has its favorite musician. There are those, the fashion pacesetters, whose pupils are infatuated with their productions, with which all the music stands are furnished. The head of the house is only busy with bragging about their works, and in getting copies for those good-natured enough to buy them. The concert ends with a worn-out clavecin piece; the audience suffers and boredom prevails as we yawn, we bow, and we leave.[19]

Perhaps the seventeenth century fared better, as well-known artists inaugurated concerts; e.g., Pierre Chabançeau de La Barre (one of the king's organists) and some colleagues began the *Concerts spirituels* in the mid-1600s, and in 1641 Jacques Champion de Chambonnières founded a series of private concerts that later came to be called the *Assemblée des honnestes curieux*.[20]

In D'Anglebert's milieu, the greatest minds in France clustered around one of the most magnificent courts in history. Members of the upper class may have been bored with their endless round of *plaisirs*, as writers such as Mme de La Fayette indicate: "Toujours les mêmes plaisirs, toujours aux mêmes heures, et toujours avec les mêmes gens,"[21] but artists and intellectuals must have found it a wonderfully stimulating time to be alive. They were not always justly rewarded for their efforts—but the company must have been fascinating!

II

D'ANGLEBERT—LIFE AND WORKS

D'Anglebert spent the last 29 years of his life serving the Sun King in various splendid settings. Although little is known of D'Anglebert's private life, we have some documents concerning his marriage, the birth of some of his children, and his professional life, as well as a posthumous inventory. Conflicting information given by Auguste Jal in 1872 leads to a birth date of 1628 or 1635. Jal wrote that D'Anglebert was 63 at the time of his death in 1691, but "about" 24 when he married in 1659.[1] Under a separate category of "ÉPI-NETTE, JOUERS D'," Jal reported that the reversion of Jacques Champion's post was given to the child D'Anglebert in 1633; that is, D'Anglebert would assume the post after Champion's death or voluntary resignation.[2] D'Anglebert's tender age, however, would make that unlikely unless he were a blood relative. Jal may have confused this reversion with that of D'Anglebert's son in 1672, but this too is implausible because none of the other elements fit. All efforts to verify Jal's entry have proved fruitless, and a 1633 document lists Chambonnières (Champion's son) as holding the reversion of his father's post.[3] Jal's entry therefore seems incorrect, and the source for his statements remains a mystery. The year 1628 may be the correct birth date if Jal took D'Anglebert's age at death from the burial document (now lost). F.-J. Fétis (1878) also gave D'Anglebert's age at death as 63.[4]

The D'Anglebert family was from Bar-le-Duc, but Jean-Henry is first heard of in Paris, where he studied the harpsichord with Chambonnières. On 12 October 1659 at the church of Saint-Germain l'Auxerrois, across from the Louvre, D'Anglebert was married to Magdelaine Champagne, sister-in-law of the well-known composer

François Roberday. According to the marriage contract, the groom was the son of Claude-Henry D'Anglebert, a surgeon from Bar-le-Duc. (D'Anglebert's sister Anne married M^r de La Bruyère, Lord of Mauvière and Secretary of Finances for the king's brother.)

Jean-Henry and Magdelaine had two daughters and eight sons. The first six children were baptized at St.-Germain l'Auxerrois (the first and fifth sons have similar names):[5]

Magdelaine Renée, baptized 19 September 1660—perhaps the child who died on 11 February 1693 at the age of 23.

Jean-Baptiste Henry, born 5 September 1661, baptized 26 March 1662 (a curiously long delay), and named for his godfather Lully. He was to succeed his father as *Ordinaire de la musique de la chambre du roy pour le clavecin* until his death c.1735.

d'Alexandre-Marie, born 14 September 1662 and baptized two days later, became a priest in Bar-le-Duc and spent the rest of his long life there (apparently he was still alive in 1747).

François-Henry, baptized 2 March 1664, died a bachelor in 1733.

Nicolas-Henry, baptized 8 April 1665. His godmother was D'Anglebert's sister-in-law Charlotte Champagne, wife of François Roberday.

Jean-Henry, baptized 14 July 1666—probably the master of the clavecin who was buried at St.-Sauveur on 11 March 1747 at the age of 80.

A document of 8 May 1691, which names guardians for the minor children—the mother, Magdelaine Champagne; the eldest son, Jean-Baptiste Henry; and a first cousin, Henry-Henri d'Anglebert—also lists four other D'Anglebert children:[6] Claude-Nicolas Henry, born c.1671 (died before 1724); Antoine-Henry, born c.1676 (died 13 April 1700); Louis-Henry, born c.1678 (died before 1724); and Catherine-Magdelaine Henry, born c.1683 (still alive in 1747 after the death of her brother Jean-Henry). Jean-Henry, who was 24 years old in 1691, is also described as a minor child, and his name heads this list. The existing baptism records name godparents from the upper classes.[7]

Quite possibly there were other children who did not survive infancy. Indeed, the fact that so many D'Anglebert children lived well past early childhood suggests that musicians, being of a lower social class than members of the court, were blessedly free of the ministrations of the doctors, whose blood-letting, purges, and potions seem to have killed more patients than they cured. His Majesty had a misplaced faith in his doctors. Madame, the king's sister-in-law, relates that "the doctors have repeated the mistake they made with Mme la Dauphine, because when the little Dauphin [Louis, the third Dauphin and heir-apparent] was red from the measles and in a sweat they bled him and gave him an emetic, and during this operation the poor child died." The future Louis XV was then hidden away by his ladies to prevent his being bled for the same illness. If the doctors had had their way, "He would have died too."[8]

Early in his career, D'Anglebert held important posts as organist to the Jacobins, an order of Dominicans on rue Saint-Honoré (c.1660), and to the Duc d'Orléans (the king's brother) at the time of Jean-Baptiste Henry's baptism in 1662. These positions and his study with Chambonnières must have earned him a good deal of visibility in Paris.

A key event occurred on 23 October 1662 when Chambonnières sold D'Anglebert the reversion of his *charge, Ordinaire de la musique de la chambre du roy pour le clavecin.*[9] The price was 2,000 *livres,* of which 500 were paid in cash. In the document Chambonnières reserved his rights to the annual wages and included protective clauses. Documents through 1689 show Chambonnières (or his estate, after 1672) and D'Anglebert each receiving the rather trifling annual sum of 600[lt], while Chambonnières received additional payment from another account. This amount was customary for *musiciens ordinaires,* but each also received 900[lt] as a maintenance (*nourriture*) allowance and 80 *écus* for transportation. For comparison, Mme de Sévigné, together with her daughter and son-in-law, paid 1,800 *livres* per year for their lease on the family mansion called the Hôtel Carnavalet, and sublet apartments for 400 and 250 *livres* per year.[10] In his new position, D'Anglebert was "to perform the function and duties in the place of the said Mr. Chambonnières, all that he had performed and currently performs, and to commence carrying out the said exercise and function from this day forward."[11]

Chambonnières relinquished his post because he either could not or would not play from figured bass. The story is related by Jean Rousseau in a letter he wrote during his dispute with the violist

Demachy in 1688.[12] It is likely that Lully was at the center of this episode. The "figured bass" may have been the official reason for removing Chambonnières, but one suspects that Lully did not want to deal with another star performer as proud and stubborn as himself. The fact that Chambonnières had been forced to sell his reversion was an event that the musical world was not likely to forget for decades to come. Indeed, in 1732 Titon du Tillet mentions that Chambonnières's position at court had first been offered to Louis Couperin.[13]

A few years after assuming his post at court, D'Anglebert had to settle another matter with Chambonnières in connection with a position that was thought to have become obsolete. The *charge* of *porte-épinette* involved an additional sum to be paid to the *joueur d'épinette* for expenses incurred in moving the instrument, but it became unnecessary when the clavecin supplanted the *épinette*. D'Anglebert, however, discovered that the post had not been discontinued, and that Sieur d'Aligré, treasurer of the Petty Funds of His Majesty, had simply "la tiroit à neant par faute de fond depuis l'année MVI soixante deux" (withdrawn the fee for lack of funds since 1662).[14] According to a document of 25 October 1668, Chambonnières sold this post to D'Anglebert for 900 *livres* to keep D'Anglebert from bringing action against him. They agreed to share the sum due from 1662, on the condition that D'Anglebert continue to assume the costs of moving instruments where necessary in the service of the king. A receipt from Chambonnières, dated 19 July 1670, indicates that the certificate of the post of *porte-épinette* had been drawn up under the name of D'Anglebert.

The 1668 document names D'Anglebert as the "ordinaire de la musique de la Chambre du Roy et de Monsieur, frère unique de Sa Maiesté, pour le clavessin." Thus he was still in the service of the king's brother, for holding more than one post was common. Monsieur's musical establishment in 1686 comprised *Un Maître & Intendant de Musique* (paid 1000[lt]) and twelve *Musiciens Ordinaires* (600[lt] each), including nine singers, two string players, and the claveciniste D'Anglebert.[15] D'Anglebert also served the Dauphin's wife, Marie-Anne de Bavière, after her marriage in 1680. Her accounts for 1686 list D'Anglebert and Le Sieur Lambert (*Maître à Chanter*) as the musicians on her staff, each with a salary of 400[lt].[16]

The position of *Ordinaire de la musique de la chambre du roy pour le clavecin* must have been demanding, so one can only guess why the king named but one incumbent (whereas the chapel had four organists, each of whom served a quarter year for a salary of 600[lt]). The claveciniste took part in most secular musical events except those involving wind instruments outdoors. Benoit suggests that the chapel organists, who were also harpsichordists, may have assisted.[17] During all of Louis XIV's reign, only three men held the *charge* for the clavecin: Chambonnières, D'Anglebert, and D'Anglebert's son Jean-Baptiste Henry. D'Anglebert was named to succeed Chambonnières in 1662 (with duties beginning immediately), and the reversion of this post was given to D'Anglebert's son in 1674. Jean-Baptiste Henry took the title in 1691, on the death of his father, and retained it until his own death around 1735. Since Jean-Baptiste Henry suffered from failing eyesight, for many years most of his duties were probably performed by François Couperin. The reversion was given to Couperin in 1717, whose ill health caused him to relinquish it in 1730 to his daughter Antoinette Marguerite. Alas, the Couperin family never gained possession of the title *Ordinaire pour le clavecin*, but only held the reversion, for a royal decree in 1736 abolished the position after Jean-Baptiste Henry's death ("et ne jugeant pas cette charge necessaire à notre service nous avons resolu de la suprimer . . .").[18] Antoinette Marguerite continued to play at court under the terms of a *commission* that apparently did not carry all the emoluments of a standard *charge*.

The reversion from 1674 designates that D'Anglebert be succeeded by his son, but the father's rights are guaranteed until his death or his voluntary consent:

> His Majesty granted him [Jean-Baptiste Henry] the said *charges* of *ordinaire de la musique de sa chambre pour le clavessin* and *porte Espinette*, to engage jointly and separately with his father, the said D'Anglebert, in enjoying and using the honors, exemptions, liberties, wages, fees, benefits, profits, income and emoluments inured, belonging and similar to those currently enjoyed by the said D'Anglebert, father. And so long as it pleases His Majesty, he enjoins the treasurer of petty cash and household affairs to continue to pay the said D'Anglebert, father, the same fees, and after his death or his consent during his lifetime, to the said D'Anglebert, son, in the customary terms. . . .[19]

What duties Jean-Baptiste Henry actually performed are not known; he probably acted as his father's apprentice and assistant. On 4 January 1681, a *Mémoire de pain, vin, verres et bouteilles* listed "M. Danglebert *père*" and "M. Danglebert *fils*" among the group accompanying the *récits* on the clavecin, theorbo, gamba, flute, and *basse de violon* for Lully's *Le Triomphe de l'Amour*. Each participant was given bread and wine on the occasion of this splendid event.

The similarity of names within the D'Anglebert family has led to considerable confusion; e.g., Auguste Jal's brief biography erroneously refers to both father and son as Jean-Baptiste Henry.[20] Jal maintains that the father signed his name "J. H. d'Anglebert" while the son signed only "d'Anglebert." The document with D'Anglebert's posthumous inventory, however, shows that Jean-Baptiste Henry consistently signed his full name. Examples of the handwriting of D'Anglebert *père* indicate that he always signed his name with a capital *D*, as did the other members of his family. The capital letter may have indicated a noble lineage; indeed, a document after his death describes the deceased as *noblehomme*.

D'Anglebert wrote music for keyboard only—organ in the first part of his career and harpsichord after his appointment at court. In 1689, two years after Lully's death and just two years before his own death, D'Anglebert published his only edition, *Pièces de clavecin*. It contains 57 harpsichord pieces (including original pieces and transcriptions), six organ pieces, and five lessons on keyboard accompaniment:

No.	
1–16	Pieces in G major
17–37	Pieces in G minor
38–49	Pieces in D minor
50–57	Pieces in D major
58–62	Organ fugues
63	Organ *quatuor*
64	*Principes de l'accompagnement*

Each key grouping has the general order of prelude, allemande, courante, sarabande, gigue, gaillarde, other dances, and transcriptions from Lully (but three dance transcriptions from Lully alternate with D'Anglebert's own pieces in the G-minor set). Four short arrangements from anonymous sources are also included. The exer-

J.-H. D'Anglebert, *Pièces de clavecin*, title
page.[21] Reprinted by arrangement with
Broude Brothers Limited.

Pièces de Clavecin
Composées par J. Henry. d'Anglebert
Ordinaire de la Musique de la Chambre du Roy
Avec la maniere de les Joüer.
Diverses Chaconnes, Ouvertures, et autres Airs
de Monsieur de Lully mis sur cet Instrum.ᵗ
Quelques Fugues pour l'Orgue.
Et
les Principes de l'accompagnement.
Livre premier.
AVEC PRIVILEGE DU ROY.
A Paris Chez l'Autheur Rüe St Honoré près St Roch

cises in the *Principes de l'accompagnement*, a short self-instruction
guide, are valuable for achieving facility in playing from figured or
unfigured bass.

D'Anglebert dedicated this edition to a student, Marie-Anne, the
Princesse de Conty (1666–1739). She must have occupied a special
place among his pupils because of her position as the king's legiti-
mated daughter by Louise de La Vallière, his first mistress. When
Marie-Anne was a baby, the king offered her as a wife for William of
Orange in order to gain cooperation with the Dutch, but William
made a humiliating reply about marrying only legitimate daughters of
royalty. Apparently that did not crush Marie-Anne, for she seems to
have had a normal amount of youthful spunkiness. Nancy Mitford re-

lates that the king once encountered a letter written by Marie-Anne in which she said "that she was obliged to drive out with Mme de Maintenon and an old freak called the Princesse d'Harcourt, day after day. 'Judge what fun this must be for me.' The king sent for Marie-Anne and blasted her with his terrifying tongue."[22] Mme de Maintenon, a rather severe woman who became Louis's second wife, never forgave the princess this youthful indiscretion. Marie-Anne married Louis Armand de Bourbon (1661–1685), the Prince de Conty. He returned safely from fighting the Turks only to contract smallpox from his wife and die, leaving her a widow at the age of nineteen. Beautiful Marie-Anne refused all offers of marriage after her early widowhood. She inherited her father's love of dancing, and was also known for her pleasant and agreeable nature. Jacques Bonnet (*Histoire générale de la danse*, 1723) says that Madame la Princesse de Conty was "one of the principal ornaments of the ball." D'Anglebert's dedication to the princess is couched in the customary humble tone:

A Son Altesse Serenissime

Madame la Princeße de Conty

Fille du Roy

Madame

    I am presenting you with a collection of my pieces for harpsichord. There has never been a more justifiable homage. I have composed nearly all of them for your Most Serene Highness. And I can say that they owe their greatest beauty to you. The natural graces which accompany all you do have extended themselves to the manner in which you have played since your earliest childhood. And when I had the honor of showing you some of these pieces, you would mix some qualities into their execution that gave me new inspiration, and helped me create the most beautiful of what one will find here. All the teachers who have had the honor of contributing to your education have experienced the same thing, and have improved themselves through instructing you. The Heavens have let us see in you,

Madame, a perfect combination of all that can be accomplished by persons of your class. As much elevated by the qualities of spirit and body as you are by your noble birth, you make one sense, from the moment one sees you, that you were born to be above others. It would be thus, Madame, that I would begin your praise, but such a purpose is too great and too far beyond my capability. I must only try to let you know how grateful I am for the kindnesses with which you have always honored me. It is also primarily to have an opportunity to make this known that I have decided to have my works appear. And if I am desirous of their being passed on to posterity, it is only to extend beyond the duration of my lifetime the most respectful gratitude with which I am

Madame

De Votre Altesse Serenissime

Letres humble & tres obeissant serviteur
D'Anglebert.

The fact that D'Anglebert composed most of his pieces for Marie-Anne, who would have been only 23 in 1689, indicates that he chose mainly his later works for his edition. The princess, an apt and talented pupil, continued her lessons with François Couperin after D'Anglebert's death. With a lifelong interest in music, she regularly held salons at her home in which the finest musicians performed.

The dedication of D'Anglebert's edition to a student calls attention to the fact that teaching was a principal resource for musicians (Du Pradel's *Livre commode des adresses de la ville de Paris*, 1692, gives addresses of various *maîtres*). François Couperin explained that one of the reasons his first book of *Pièces de clavecin* (1713) was so late in appearing was his heavy teaching load:

A few of the occupations that have caused me delay are too glorious to complain about. For twenty years, I have had the honor of being with the King, and of teaching at the same time the Dauphin, the Duc de Bourgogne, and six princes or princesses of the royal household.[23]

Mignard/Vermeulen, portrait of D'Anglebert. Reprinted by arrangement with Broude
Brothers Limited.

D'Anglebert's edition includes an engraving by C. Vermeulen of a
portrait by Pierre Mignard, an artist known for his many paintings
of the king, the royal family, and various nobility. The portrait
clearly shows D'Anglebert's crossed eyes.

The Preface of the edition furnishes some interesting information
and gives explicit instructions for the performance of the organ *quatuor:*

I have included in this collection pieces in only four keys, although I have composed in all the others. I hope to present the remainder in a second book. I have added to them some compositions of Mr. Lully, for it must be acknowledged that the works of this incomparable man are of a taste far superior to any other. As they succeed even more admirably on the harpsichord, I thought that my giving several of different character would be appreciated. I have added a few *Vaudeviles* [sic], principally to fill up the bottoms of pages that would have been useless otherwise. It is, however, true to say that these small airs are of an extraordinary *finesse*, and have a noble simplicity that has always pleased everyone.

I also wanted to give a sample of what I formerly wrote for the organ, so that is why I have included only five fugues on the same subject, varied with different *mouvemens*, and I have ended with a *Quatuor* on the Kyrie of the mass. As this piece is more contrapuntal than the others, its effect can only be achieved on a large organ with four different keyboards—I mean three keyboards for the hands and one for the pedals, with stops of equal weight and different timbre in order to distinguish the entries of the voices.

I have often been asked for some instructions for accompaniment. I thus give here the principles condensed into five lessons, which contain all that seems necessary to know in order to be able to acquire this skill on one's own.

An important complement to the *Pièces de clavecin* is D'Anglebert's manuscript, F-Pn Rés. 89ter. As Kenneth Gilbert points out, it is an autograph,[24] as can be seen by comparing the signature with that in the document of 23 October 1662 in which D'Anglebert purchased his *charge* from Chambonnières.

Rés. 89ter, one of the few extant seventeenth-century keyboard autographs, contains fourteen pieces found in D'Anglebert's *Pièces de clavecin* and five other original pieces (plus one *double*, or variation). Also included are a few more transcriptions from Lully, *doubles* of works by other keyboard composers (J. C. de Chambonnières, L. Couperin, and E. Richard), and transcriptions from a number of lute works by E. and D. Gaultier, R. Mesangeau, and Pinel. No original

XLV, 213. Courtesy of the Archives nationales de France, Paris.

Rés. 89ter, l52v. Courtesy of the Département de la musique, Bibliothèque nationale,
Paris.

has been found for a sarabande bearing the name of (Marin) Marais,
but it is probably another transcription. The miscellaneous pieces
and fragments in other hands are later additions.

Bruce Gustafson dates Rés. 89ter between 1677 and 1680 because it
includes a transcription from Lully's *Isis*, performed in 1677, but
lacks one from *Proserpine*, of 1680, which D'Anglebert included in
his 1689 edition.[25] A good part of the manuscript may have been
compiled much earlier, since D'Anglebert does not use the symbol
for the turn that appeared in Chambonnières's book of 1670, but
writes out the turns in conventional notation. Thus the manuscript
might have been begun in the 1660s, with additions being made
over the years. The overture from *Isis* is one of the last pieces.

Rés. 89ter contains 48 pieces and twelve *doubles* in D'Anglebert's
hand. They are grouped by key as follows:

No.	
1–18	Pieces in C major
20–22	Miscellaneous pieces
23–30	Pieces in D minor
32–42	Pieces in G major
42a–44	Pieces in G minor

The largest key grouping in this manuscript that does not appear in
the edition of 1689 is that in C major. Since these pieces use no pitch
lower than C, they were probably written for an instrument lacking
the short octave notes down to GG. The additional original pieces by
D'Anglebert are all in C major except for the Gaillarde in A minor
(No. 20). Variants between the *Pièces de clavecin* and Rés. 89ter are of

relatively minor significance, the most substantive of which concern different ornamentation symbols, the use of written-out ornaments in the manuscript, and changes in rhythmic values in melodic lines (see chapter 4). This manuscript is especially valuable for the three preludes in a variant notation.

Appendix 1 contains a list of D'Anglebert's harpsichord pieces and their sources, as well as information about miscellaneous pieces and transcriptions from eleven other manuscripts. The Oldham Manuscript (c.1650s) includes two pieces in D'Anglebert's hand. One is a Courante in C major (found in no other source), which remains unpublished at this time. Three previously unknown pieces by D'Anglebert—a Courante, Sarabande (with *Double*) and Gigue in A minor—are given in Appendix 2. These unattributed pieces in an English household manuscript are clearly in D'Anglebert's unique and engaging style. A C-major Sarabande attributed to D'Anglebert in a manuscript from Troyes is a weaker piece and does not resemble his other writing.

D'Anglebert's works received fairly wide circulation, since they are also found in two English and two German manuscripts—one from the late eighteenth century, the other a large manuscript from the Bach circle. J. G. Walther's *Musikalisches Lexikon* (1732) includes a brief paragraph about D'Anglebert's edition, and refers to his ornament table in several separate entries. One hundred years after his death, D'Anglebert earned a listing in E. L. Gerber's *Historisch-biographisches Lexikon der Tonkünstler.*[26]

D'Anglebert died on 23 April 1691 at rue St.-Anne and was buried at St.-Roch. In the posthumous inventory, his widow claimed "there is due the said estate the sum of 600 *livres* for the said deceased having taught Mademoiselle to play the harpsichord last year, 1690. . . ."[27] The inventory included the following possessions:

> Fourteen paintings and seven engravings, among them a large painting on canvas by Monsieur Mignard that depicts the Virgin holding the child Jesus and St. Joseph at her side, together with a sculpted gilt wooden frame, green taffeta draperies, and a gilt iron curtain rod: 600[lt].
> A clavecin with one keyboard and three registers: 90[lt].
> An *épinette* with two registers on a footpiece of walnut, painted in the Chinese style: 60[lt].
> A clavecin of one keyboard and three registers (with a transposing keyboard), painted inside and out, on a walnut base: 200[lt].

A small Flemish clavecin by Ruckers with one keyboard and two registers, on a walnut base: 100^{lt}.

An old lute in its case.

An *ardoize* for composing music [perhaps a type of blackboard that could be cleaned after use].

Forty-one copies of *Pièces de clavecin,* composed by the deceased, bound in leather.

Clasp trimmed with diamonds: 280^{lt}.

Brillant (a jewel): 150^{lt}.

Wife's necklace with 62 pearls: 250^{lt}.[28]

Although D'Anglebert did not achieve Lully's fame, he was well respected, for his children's godparents include some illustrious names. He resided at a fashionable address, and the inventory suggests that he had modest wealth. However, contemporary accounts of D'Anglebert seem to be lacking, and Titon du Tillet's biography of writers and musicians inexplicably omits him. Perhaps there is material waiting to be uncovered, or maybe D'Anglebert was a reserved figure content to remain in Lully's shadow. Possibly the claveciniste owed his position at court to Lully's intervention, for he seems to have had a close connection with the famous Italian. D'Anglebert named his first son after Lully (who served as godfather), transcribed and published many of his pieces, and praised his work in the Preface to his own edition.

It is tempting to speculate that D'Anglebert is absent from contemporary chronicles because he did nothing to attract special attention or notoriety, in contrast, for example, to François Couperin *le grand*'s uncle François, whose taste for wine was legendary. Titon du Tillet relates that a student could easily make him lengthen his lessons by providing a carafe of wine and a crust of bread—a lesson ordinarily lasted as long as the student continued to refill the carafe.[29] On the contrary, D'Anglebert appears to have been a sober family man who had at least ten children by the same wife over a period of 23 years. Perhaps his visual handicap made him reticent and retiring. Maybe the sophistication of D'Anglebert's music was beyond the taste of the period, but without a contemporary judgment, who can say? It would appear that D'Anglebert, unlike Chambonnières before him and François Couperin after, was not a prominent performer. He may have found it politic to keep a low profile where Lully was concerned and to stay out of his way.

Other major composers of seventeenth-century clavecin literature include Jacques Champion de Chambonnières (c.1601–1672) and his pupils Louis Couperin (c.1626–1661) and Nicolas-Antoine Lebègue (c.1631–1702). Étienne Richard (c.1621–1669), a Parisian organist and harpsichordist, is assumed to be the composer of the few keyboard works ascribed to Richard. Much later in the century, Elisabeth-Claude Jacquet de La Guerre (c.1669–1729) began a celebrated career as a child prodigy and published her first book of harpsichord pieces around 1687. The major sources for the music of these composers are given in Appendix 1. Not included in this discussion of seventeenth-century clavecin music is the large manuscript presumably by the organist Jean-Nicolas Geoffroy (d.1694). Bruce Gustafson notes that "the pieces are a peculiar combination of a traditional idiom with a harmonic vocabulary which is sometimes so mannered as to seem bizarre."[30]

Chambonnières, a well-known and influential figure praised by such notables as Marin Mersenne, Constantijn Huygens, and Johann Jakob Froberger, is considered to be the founder of the seventeenth-century clavecin school. Called *gentilhomme ordinaire de la Chambre du Roy* in his father's will of 1632, Chambonnières's name appears in payment records for 1643 as *joueur d'espinette,* but his fortunes declined in his last decade, after he was forced to sell the reversion of his post to D'Anglebert. In 1670, Chambonnières published two books containing 60 of his approximately 145 harpsichord pieces.

Louis Couperin had a brief but outstanding career after coming to Paris around 1651. He began the family dynasty as organist at St. Gervais in 1653. After refusing Chambonnières's post at court, he was given another position as a treble viol player. He wrote approximately 215 pieces, most of which are for organ and harpsichord, and a few for instrumental ensemble. All exist only in manuscript form, including one autograph.

Lebègue published two books for harpsichord (1677 and 1687) and three for organ. His works had a wide currency and appear in a great number of foreign manuscripts. Their popularity perhaps resulted from their simple texture and ornamentation and their easily grasped formulas. Organist at St. Merry from 1664 to his death, Lebègue also held a post at the royal chapel for a quarter of each year from 1678.

La Guerre presents a colorful contrast to the other composers, for she was praised in the *Mercure galant* in 1677, when she was ten years old (?), and she was encouraged by the king himself. After her death, Titon du Tillet awarded her a substantial biography, which comments on her great reputation for improvisation.[31] In contrast to the composers cited here, she published a good deal of stage, vocal, and instrumental ensemble music, in addition to two books of clavecin pieces. The first is undated, but was announced in the *Mercure galant* of March 1687; the second appeared in 1707. In 1754 Antoine de Léris wrote a brief biography of La Guerre:

> LA GUERRE (Elisabeth-Claude JACQUET de), born in Paris in 1669 and died in 1729 at the age of about 70 years, was noted from her earliest youth for her musical style and for her art of playing the harpsichord. She had, moreover, a wonderful genius for composition, and left us the opera *Céphale & Procis*, three books of cantatas, some clavecin pieces, some sonatas, and a *Te Deum*. She married Marin de LA GUERRE, organist of Saint Severin and of Saint Gervais, by whom she had a single son who at the age of eight years played the clavecin in an astonishing manner, but he died in his tenth year.[32]

III

STYLE AND TEMPO

French harpsichord literature of the late seventeenth century* consists largely of dances and preludes. Only occasionally do titles suggest the character pieces that became so popular in the eighteenth
century. The clavecinistes naturally appropriated dance forms as the
structure for their works, for this era was the grand period of the
dance: "All Europe knows what a Capacity and Genius the French
have for dancing, and how universally it is admired and followed."[1]
Their allemandes, courantes, sarabandes, gigues, gaillardes, gavottes, and menuets are generally in binary form, while the chaconnes and passacailles are constructed in the form of a rondeau or
with a ground bass. According to St.-Lambert, "the second half of a
piece is called the REPRISE," and each half of a binary piece is to be
repeated,[2] although his own example lacks the dots for the repetition of the second strain (as do a few of D'Anglebert's small pieces).
These repetitions are necessary to preserve the balance and symmetry intended in such short forms. An additional short repeat of the
piece's final measures, called the *petite reprise*, is often added at the
end. Many of D'Anglebert's dances have a symbol (*renvoy*) to play
the entire piece again without repeats, as recommended by St.-
Lambert, after the normal repeats have been taken. This penchant
for using the same material is perhaps a reflection of the seventeenth-century French leisurely mindset.

*Styles and customs change dramatically from one generation to the next, so the
conclusions drawn here about France in the second half of the seventeenth century
may not apply to a later time or to other countries. Translations of French and German
texts, which generally tend more toward a paraphrase, are mine unless they are drawn
from a modern edition (as indicated in the Notes). Accents in quoted material conform
to the grandly inconsistent original French when possible, but capitalization and accents in titles have been standardized.

The only clue from D'Anglebert regarding the performance order of pieces and their *doubles* (variations) is found in his transcription of Chambonnières's sarabande *O beau jardin,* which is constructed so that the *double* can serve as the repeat for each section. Nevertheless, each section of the sarabande ends with a measure that enables one to perform the piece without the *double.*

An important characteristic of D'Anglebert's composition is the use of broken chords. Manfred Bukofzer's apt description of the lutenists' *style brisé* or *style luthé*—a technique that exploits the rapid decay of tone—applies equally to the works of the clavecinistes:

> The "broken style" of lute music . . . may be called the glorification of the simplest lute figure: the arpeggio. The broken style is characterized by rapidly alternating notes in different registers that supply, in turn, melody and harmony. Seemingly distributed in arbitrary fashion over the various registers, the notes produced in their composite rhythm a continuous strand of sound.

And in a reference to Gaspard Le Roux's *Courante luthée* for clavecin, J. G. Walther (1732) characterizes the lute style as "arpeggiando" or "gebrochen."[3]

The many written-out examples of *style luthé* and the widespread use of the arpeggio symbols indicate the importance of this technique in French harpsichord music (see pp. 77–83). D'Anglebert frequently employs the written-out as well as the arpeggio-symbol form of *style luthé.* The close of his Gigue in G minor, for example, illustrates a broken style that results in a rhythmically active cadential treatment. François Couperin added the designation *Luthé, et lié* to *Les Charmes* (*Ordre* 9) and *Luthé–mesuré* to *La Mézangére* (*Ordre* 10).

D'Anglebert's music is distinguished from that of his keyboard contemporaries by his skillful use of harmony and dissonance (see p. 172). His adept handling of seventh chords and inversions, suspensions and other nonharmonic tones, communicates across 300 years with a profound depth of expression. But joy and gaiety are not absent from his music: D'Anglebert's gigues, menuets, and chaconnes, with their correspondingly simpler harmonic treatment, are charming and vivacious. Nevertheless, the bulk of D'Anglebert's *oeuvre* profits from a relaxed tempo that allows the listener to savor its luxuriant harmonies.

Several sources of the period provide information about the tempo of various dances, among them the *dictionaires* of Sébastien de Brossard (1703) and Jacques Ozanam (1691), and the treatises of Jean Rousseau (1678–1710 and 1687), Charles Masson (1699), and St.-Lambert (1702). A generation later, Abbé Demoz de la Salle (1728) lists some Italian equivalents for the French terms of tempo:

> *Adagio = Lent*
> *Allegro = Gay & Léger*
> *Vivace = Vif*
> *Presto = Vite*
> *Prestissimo = Très-vite*
> *Andante = Allant* or *Rondement* [walking briskly]
> *Largo = Large* or *à grand trait d'Archet* [full bow]
> *Affettuoso = Affectueux*[4]

Among the harpischord dances by Louis Couperin, Chambonnières, Lebègue, La Guerre, and D'Anglebert, covering a period of about 30 years, pieces carrying the same title are often in such disparate styles as to suggest differing tempi. The sarabande's simple texture, for example, became much more intricate and required a slower tempo to allow the fine detailing to be heard, but the allemande experienced a reversal of this process. Since dissimilar forms of the same dance type are often found within the works of one composer, the more unusual examples are sometimes given a tempo marking to distinguish them from the conventional dances. Louis Couperin's works, dating from the mid-seventeenth century, are found only in manuscript form and thus contain very few tempo markings. Chambonnières's *oeuvre* contains perhaps two tempo indications. Lebègue's first book (1677), however, makes it clear that tempos are marked when they deviate from the norm, and the same is true of D'Anglebert's edition. La Guerre's c.1687 imprint gives no tempo indications.

To understand tempo in seventeenth-century French music, one must first grasp the significance of the time signature. According to St.-Lambert:

> The sign that one places at the beginning of a piece signifies these three things at the same time: how many notes there must be in each measure, the number of beats into which they must fall, and what *mouvement*, i.e., the quickness or slowness, one must give the piece.[5]

These signatures should convey the following *mouvements:*

Measures composed of four notes:

Major	C	4 quarter notes & 4 beats/m.	Very slow
Minor	₵	4 quarter notes & 2 beats/m.	Faster than Major
Binary	2	4 quarter notes & 2 beats/m.	Faster than Minor
Four-eight	4/8	4 eighth notes & 2 beats/m.	Faster than Binary

Measures composed of three notes:

Three-two (*Triple double*)	3/2	3 half notes & 3 beats/m.	Very slow: half note = quarter note of C time.
Ternary (*Triple simple*)	3	3 quarter notes & 3 beats/m.	Faster than 3/2
Three-eight	3/8	3 eighth notes & 1 beat/m.	Faster than Ternary

Measures composed of six notes:

Six-four	6/4	6 quarter notes & either 2 or 6 beats/m.	Different degrees of "Lively"
Six-eight	6/8	6 eighth notes & 2 beats/m.	Faster than 6/4

St.-Lambert attempts to explain the difference between C and ₵:

> The two motions that one's hand makes in beating ₵ time must be similar in their duration to those of a measure with four beats; i.e., neither slower nor more hurried. By this, it must be understood that in pieces with a ₵ signature, the notes are half again as fast [*une fois plus vîte*] as in those marked with a C signature, since in the same duration of a beat one performs two quarter notes instead of one.

These two sentences appear contradictory, but perhaps the first sentence means that there is not a dramatic difference between the quarter-note beat of C time and the half-note beat of ₵ time. A similar contradiction appears in Rousseau's treatises (see p. 35). I suspect that these writers were more concerned with presenting to musical neophytes the concept of the half-note beat unit than with conveying an exact tempo. St.-Lambert consistently uses the phrase *une fois plus vîte* to describe the increments in speed from one time signature to the next faster one. This usage probably does not indicate an exact mathematical proportion but simply a modest increase in speed from the previous signature. Differences among signatures are relative, not absolute.

To clarify what he means by either two or six beats in a 6/4 measure, St.-Lambert notes that:

Ex. 1. St.-Lambert's two manners of 6/4
time. Courtesy of Éditions Minkoff.

PREMIERE MANIÈRE.

SECONDE MANIÈRE.

Although the measure always has the value of six quarter notes,
they are distributed in two manners. In some airs, there is nearly
always an eighth note between two quarter notes, and in other airs
there are several consecutive quarter notes and several consecutive
eighth notes, mixed indiscriminately with some half notes [Ex. 1].

When the notes are distributed in the measure in the way that I
call the first manner . . . the measure is beat in two beats, each of
which has three quarter notes or their value. But when the notes are
distributed in the way that I call the second manner, the measure is
beat in three beats—not in three slow beats by placing two quarter
notes on each beat as in 3/2 time, but in three *gais* beats, similar in
length to those of 2 [3*] time, placing only one quarter note on each
beat, and thus making two measures in one, since there are six
quarter notes in the measure.

. . . when one beats the measure only in two, the notes are performed much faster [than those beat in six] for these two beats must
be at least as rapid as those of 2 time.

In contrast to the rather lively tempi of St.-Lambert's 6/4 time, Michel L'Affilard (1705) refers to 6/4 time as having six beats *graves*.

---

*St.-Lambert probably means 3 time here, since elsewhere he compares this
quarter note of 6/4 time to that of 3 time.

Brossard notes the dual usage of the 6/4 signature and adds that it is used "very improperly" for lively pieces.[6]

Signatures employing an 8 were not generally used until late in the seventeenth century, and D'Anglebert provides perhaps the earliest examples of 6/8 and 12/8 time in keyboard dances (although the Bauyn Manuscript contains a gigue in 3/8 time by Hardel). According to St.-Lambert, "the signature of 6/4 prescribes a *fort gay* tempo for pieces, especially when the measure is beat in two, but 6/8 time gives them a tempo half again as fast; i.e., very fast (*tres vîte*). Here he is probably comparing 6/8 time to 6/4 time beat in the second manner, so that the eighth note of 6/8 time would be half again as fast as the quarter note of 6/4 time and would equal that of 3/8 time (see note 5 above).

Since St.-Lambert is writing primarily for the public (i.e., harpsichord students, according to his Preface), which had decreed the clavecin a fashionable instrument at this time, he searches for a way to communicate a sense of the beats and their equality. He compares the length of quarter notes to the steps of a man walking five quarters of a league in an hour (about three miles), but hastens to add:

> But this is not a rule that must be applied to all sorts of pieces, for if it were, they would have too great a uniformity of movement among them since the notes would all be performed at the same speed. But there are several kinds of *mouvements;* thus it is necessary that quarter notes (and the other notes in proportion) be performed in certain pieces with one speed and in other pieces with another speed.

In St.-Lambert's view, the quarter notes of ¢, 3, and 6/4 time (second manner), all of which he compares to a man's walking pace, have approximately the same value. He speaks of the disagreement among musicians regarding not only the time signatures but also their understanding of various terms of tempo, and of the difficulty in communicating his views via the written page. He acknowledges that his illustration of a man's walking pace is inadequate:

> All men are not the same height. A tall man will walk less quickly to cover five quarters of a league in an hour than another who is shorter. Thus the steps of the first will be much slower than those of the second. . . . Also, I have not so much claimed by this comparison to give the true measure of the duration of quarter notes as I have

hoped to give an idea of the equality that they must have. That is the most essential element of the *mouvement*.

St.-Lambert then lists the most frequently used signatures:

₵   2 beats, *Graves* or *lents*
2   2 beats, *Gais* or *legers*
3   3 beats, *Legers*

The *graves* or *lents* of ₵ time are taken to mean that the beats themselves are slow—not necessarily a *grave* tempo, although this signature is also used for the first part of overtures and other slower pieces.

> When musicians speak of an *air à deux temps*, they always mean one with a signature of ₵ or 2, and never one with signatures of 4/8, 6/4, or 6/8, although these are also beat in two. In the same manner, when they speak of an *air à trois temps simplement*, it refers to one with a signature of 3; but when they say *trois temps lents*, it signifies 3/2 time.

Although musicians give common time (C) a movement of *lent & grave*, and binary (2) and ternary (3) a movement of *gay*, St.-Lambert cautions that composers often find it necessary to add a clarifying tempo description, such as *Lentement, Gravement, Legerement, Gayement, Vîte, Fort vîte*, etc., to make up for the inability of the time signature to express their intention.

"Composers themselves do not use the proper signature consistently," St.-Lambert observes. For example, "Lully conducts the *reprise* of the overture from *Armide* very fast and the Air on p.93 [*Les Sourdines*, marked *gravement*, and transcribed for clavecin by D'Anglebert] from this opera very slowly, although both have the same 6/4 signature and a similar distribution of notes." Of course, "Lully is allowed this license because of his art," but the *maître* wishes that "musicians would agree among themselves to correct this imperfection in which theory is contradicted by practice."

St.-Lambert also takes issue with the long-standing practice of using a time signature of 3, instead of 3/2, for courantes. "In order to have three fast beats per bar [which the 3 signature implies], the measures would have to be cut in half. If one truly wants to have three slow beats per measure, the signature should be 3/2" (see note 5 above). While seventeenth-century clavecin composers nearly always retain the old "3" signature for courantes, La Guerre (*Les Pièces de clauessin*, c.1687) employs the 3/2 signature in six courantes, 4/6 [6/4] in one, and 3 in another. Two *Courantes de Mr Delabarre* from the Bauyn Manuscript are barred in 3/4 time, as are some lute courantes transcribed by D'Anglebert, perhaps in order to follow their original barring. For example, the courantes in Perrine's 1680 collection of the Gaultiers' pieces (*Pièces de luth en musique*, some of which D'Anglebert transcribed) are written in keyboard score and are barred in 3/4 time (see pp. 150–152 for a further discussion of courante tempo).

St.-Lambert's tempo system is logical when one understands it as an attempt to indicate the relationship among the signatures. Perhaps in order not to burden his readers, who are after all members of the upper classes and the bourgeoisie, he does not delve into usages such as ₵ beat in four (see p. 36 below). Nowhere does he indicate that his is an inflexible system with mathematical equivalents; on the contrary, he stresses that one must apply his principles with discretion.

Jean Rousseau (1644–c.1700), a noted *maître* of the viol in Paris, wrote two important treatises. One, on singing, was so popular, it went through six editions from 1678 to 1710. It contains a classification of conventional time signatures similar to St.-Lambert's, but Rousseau adds a C3 to indicate a slow tempo for a measure with three quarter notes:

C	Major	4 beats *graves*
₵	Minor	2 beats *lents*
2	Binary	2 beats *vites*
C3	Ternary	3 beats *lents*
3	*Triple simple*	3 beats *légers*
3/2	*Triple double*	3 beats *lents*[7]

In the Preface Rousseau says that many people are unacquainted with the new time signatures, for the following signatures *extraordinaires* had only been in use for a short time:

3/4	faster than 3
3/8	much faster than 3/4
6/4	six quick beats, or two slow beats (like two 3/4 measures in one)
6/8	faster than 6/4 (like two 3/8 measures in one)
4/8	two very fast beats

Other time signatures are used more in Italy, such as 9/3 [*sic,* 9/4] (beat in 3), 12/17 [*sic,* 12/16] (beat in 4), and 3/16 (beat in 3), as well as 12/4, 12/8, and 9/8. . . . Every signature accompanied by a C (as in the ternary C3) must be beat *gravement,* by a ₵ *plus légére,* and by a 2 still faster. It should be further mentioned that every barred signature must be beat half again as fast as usual [*la moitié plus legérement*], as one sees in ₵, which is none other than C in diminished form.

Here is the key to understanding that ₵ is not twice as fast as C, nor is 2 twice as fast as ₵, as has been commonly supposed by modern writers. This interpretation has arisen from translating St.-Lambert's *une fois plus vîte* as "twice as fast," when in reality the French say *deux fois plus vîte* to obtain this meaning.

Rousseau's other treatise, on the viol, offers a chart showing equivalent notes in different time signatures (Ex. 2).[8] It seems to contradict his previous statement, but one might maintain that it presents approximations, not exact mathematical equivalents. Although occasions arise where one C measure is probably equivalent to two ₵ measures, the increment is usually considerably less.

Ex. 2. Rousseau's chart of equivalent values. Courtesy of Éditions Minkoff.

Like Rousseau, Étienne Loulié (1696) speaks of some combination signatures:

> C is sometimes used with other time signatures to indicate that the pieces are to be performed as slowly as those with the C signature; e.g., C2, C3, or C3/2. Likewise, the ₵, indicating four fast (*vistes*) beats or two slow beats, is used with other signatures to convey a tempo as fast as ₵; e.g., ₵2, ₵3, or ₵4/8.[9]

Demoz de la Salle, of the next generation, describes many time signatures, beginning with the old *Signes simples des mesures:*

2   2 beats more or less *vites* according to the style of the different airs
3   3 beats more or less *vites* according to the style of the different airs
C   4 beats [no description]

¢   2 beats *graves ou lents* (when there are more half and quarter notes
     than eighth and sixteenth notes) or 4 beats *légers* (when there are
     more eighth and sixteenth notes than other notes)[10]

Although four beats *légers* in ¢ time seems unusual to modern eyes,
it makes good practical sense, since, for example, the first part of a
Lully overture needs to move more slowly than can be achieved
satisfactorily in two beats per measure. Most modern performances,
it seems to me, fail to capture the sense of aristocratic grandeur and
hauteur inherent in the Baroque overture. Other theorists, such as
Loulié and Jacques Hotteterre,[11] also refer to ¢ time as having two
slow beats or four quick beats. "Quick" beats should be understood
as relatively faster than slow beats, rather than literally fast. Why
then did the French not use C in these instances? It appears that
they were reluctant to use the C signature except for an old form
such as the allemande, but employed the barred ¢ to indicate a
fairly wide range of tempi (similar to their inconsistent use of 6/4
time). This practice may have been tied to the use of *notes inégales*,
for the C time signature indicated that sixteenth notes, rather than
eighths, were to be played unequally in appropriate locations.

Demoz de la Salle continues with the *Signes doubles ou composez:*

2/4	two beats *légers*
4/8	two beats *vites*
4/16	two beats *très-vites*
6/4	two beats, more or less *graves*, according to the character of the airs
6/8	two beats *légers*
6/16	two beats *vites*
3/2	three beats *graves*
3/4	ordinarily three beats *légers*
3/8	three beats *vites*
3/16	three beats *très-vites*
9/4	three beats *graves*
9/8	three beats *légers*
9/16	three beats *vites*
12/4	four beats *graves*
12/8	four beats *légers*
12/16	four beats *vites*

The number of signatures used commonly enough to be included in
a tutorial treatise had increased dramatically in the span of a genera-

tion. Michel-Pignolet de Montéclair (1736), however, barely concealed his exasperation:

> All musicians agree that all time signatures are related to two and to three beats. Why then do they use up to nineteen signatures to designate these two meters? The *mesure* of four beats is none other than the *mesure* of two beats doubled. In certain instances, ₵ produces the same effect as C, and at other times, the same effect as 2. . . . The passacaille and sarabande, which have a movement of *grave*, are marked with 3 or 3/4, just the same as the chaconne and menuet, which have a movement of *gay*. . . .
> If the nineteen signatures are necessary to indicate the different movements of Airs, why don't composers use them correctly? And if they are not necessary, why are they used? These different signatures are not capable of determining absolutely the true degree of slowness or quickness, as shown by the fact that one of the following terms is nearly always found at the beginning of a piece:
>
> Italian. *Grave, Largo, Adagio, Moderato, Allegro, Presto, Prestissimo*
> French. *Grave, Lent, Aisément, Moderé, Gay, Leger, Vite, Tres vite*[12]

Montéclair proposes simplifying signatures by using only a 2 and a 3 for simple duple and triple meter, and a barred ₄ and ₃ for compound meter. In order to specify the correct tempo, he recommends adding one of the following terms: *Tres grave, Grave, Tres lent, Lent, Moderé, Gay, Leger, Vîte, Tres vîte;* and to convey the proper style or expression of the piece, one of these: *Triste or Tristement, Pathetique, Douloureux, Onctueux, Tendrement, Brusquement, Vivement, Detaché, Marqué, Piqué, Mesuré, Louré, etc.* Montéclair has a valid point, for the usage of time signatures in the eighteenth century became hopelessly confused. They were applied more consistently in the late seventeenth and early eighteenth centuries, but not with complete uniformity.

Time signatures were in a state of development during the last part of the seventeenth century in France. Earlier the 3 signature encompassed movement in 3/2, 3/4, and 6/4 time, but a distinction developed by the time of D'Anglebert's *Pièces de clavecin.* D'Anglebert was surely one of the first French keyboard composers to introduce more variety in time signatures, for most pieces of the period use C for allemandes and 3 for courantes, sarabandes, gigues, passacailles, chaconnes, menuets, and gaillardes. D'Anglebert applied the signatures logically (except for retaining the old 3 in courantes), and his edition of 1689 shows a development from his earlier autograph manuscript (c.1660s–1670s). His Gaillarde in G major is written with a signature of 3 in the manuscript, but with 3/2 in the edition. Similarly, the Gigue in G major has a signature of 3 (barred in 3/4) in the manuscript, but 6/4 in the edition. The manuscript version of the Gavotte in G major is in the barred ₵ time, but the edition employs C time, together with a marking of *Lentement*, perhaps to ensure that the piece would be played slowly, since many gavottes were fast by the end of the century.

How carefully did the French follow the precepts of the treatises? St.-Lambert notes that the rules for tempo are observed so inexactly that we must not be overly concerned with his instructions:

> The reader who studies here the principles of the harpsichord must not stop with what I have said on this matter. He can use the musician's privilege and give pieces such movement as pleases him, otherwise having very little regard for its time signature, provided that he does not choose a movement directly opposed to that which the signature requires, one that could remove the grace of the piece. . . .[13]

St.-Lambert's comparison of the beat to a man's walking pace is too vague, as he points out, to be a reliable indication of tempo. It seems hazardous to assign metronome markings for individual signatures, since there appears to have been a great deal of variation in the tempo among pieces with the same signature. Rather, signatures should be understood in a relative sense; e.g., a quarter note in barred ₵ time moves faster than one in C time. The theorists were describing a complex issue to the best of their ability and probably did not intend to prescribe a strict system with mathematical equivalents. To determine a suitable tempo, one can more safely rely on the character of the pieces themselves, together with primary-source descriptions of tempo and signatures.

Other clues to tempo can be obtained from descriptions of various musical forms, such as Charles Masson's (1699), which classifies forms from slow to fast:

> Duple meter:
> *Lent* C, in recitatives of motets and operas, and sometimes in choruses
> *Lent* ₵, airs such as the *Entrée d'Apollon* in *Triomphe de l'Amour* [Lully]

> *Legerement* 2, gavotte and gaillarde
> *Vîte* 2, bourées and rigaudons, marked with *vite*
> *Fort vîte* 8/4 [4/8], such as the *Entrée de[s] bergers & bergeres, Roland*
>   [Lully]
>
> Triple meter:
> *Fort gravement* 3/2
> *Gravement* Sarabande, passacaille, courante
> *Legerement* Chaconne
> *Vîte* Menuet
> *Tres vîte* Passepied[14]

Masson adds that gigues have the same movement as *bourées* and *rigaudons*, and *canaries* are a little faster than gigues. *Loures*, with a signature of 6/4, are beat in two *lentement*. Although he assigns the gaillarde a time signature of 2, the clavecinistes' gaillarde is in triple meter. Louis Pécour explains this difference in *La nouvelle gaillarde*, which contains the steps for a dotted rhythm gaillarde in 2 time.[15] This "new gaillarde" is also seen in Lully's "Un Berger" from *Thesée* (LWV 51/66), in ₵ time, which is called a gaillarde in some sources but a gavotte in another.

Nearly thirty years later, Demoz de la Salle lists the same five degrees of tempo found in Masson's work: *Très-Lent, Grave* or *Lent, Legers, Vite,* and *Três-vite*.[16] He observes that the measure is beat more or less slowly according to its time signature and the character of the different airs. Compare Masson's 1699 tempo classification of various forms (above) with that given by Demoz in 1728:

> Two beats *graves:* march, *l'Entrée de ballet,* the first part of an opera
>   overture, gavotte, *loure,* pavane
> Two beats *légers* (or *gais*): rigaudon, branle, gaillarde, bourée, *villa-
>   nelle, paysane & villageoise,* musette, gigue
> Three beats *graves* (or *lents*): courante, sarabande, passacaille, *folies
>   d'Espagne*
> Three beats *legers* (or *gais*): chaconne, menuet, musette
> Three beats *vites:* passepiéd, canarie[s]
> Four beats *légers* (or *gais*): allemande

Masson and Demoz agree closely for the most part, but it should be noted that the gavotte had both slow and fast identities, while the allemande developed an additional faster form that may have been paramount by 1728 (see chap. 10). The Troyes organist Nicolas Siret gives *lent ou grave* as the tempo of his allemandes, sarabandes, pas-

sacaille, and the first part of overtures; and *vif ou leger* for his courantes, gigues, gavottes, menuets, and overture *reprises*.[17] This one
characterization of the courante as a faster dance is puzzling, since
Siret's courantes (one of which is entitled "La Luthée" and seems to
refer to the famous seventeenth-century French lute courantes) generally employ traditional courante mannerisms and the 3/2 signature
reserved for very slow pieces.

In writings of the period, one often encounters the words *mesure*
(the number and equality of the beats, according to François Couperin, below) and *mouvement* (the slowness or quickness of the beat,
according to Sébastien Brossard[18]). Jean Rousseau explains the difference between *mesure* and *mouvement*:

> For the *Mesure* is a road that has the *mouvement* as its destination. But
> as there is a difference between the road and the destination to
> which it leads, so too is there a difference between the *Mesure* and
> the *mouvement*. Just as the voice must be led by the *Mesure*, the
> *Mesure* must also be led and animated by the *mouvement*. Thus, with
> the same time signature, we often perform the *Mesure* differently, for
> sometimes we hurry and sometimes we retard according to the dif-
> ferent passions that the voice must express. That is why it is not
> sufficient to perform music knowing how to beat according to the
> different signs. One still must enter into the spirit of the composer,
> that is to say, into the different *mouvemens* that the expression of the
> piece demands. That is why few people know how to perform music
> well. . . . One will probably ask how one can know the true *mouve-
> ment* of a piece of music, but this knowledge is above all the dis-
> courses one can make on the subject, for it is the perfection of art
> that one can achieve only by practice and a gift for music. Neverthe-
> less, if one hears a piece of music performed by different persons,
> some of whom use the true *mouvement*, but not others, it is an easy
> matter to determine which *mouvement* is the correct.[19]

Rousseau seems to be suggesting a meaning for *mouvement* that ex-
tends beyond that of tempo. François Couperin (1717) elaborates on
this subject by noting one's obligation to add life to the music, in
contrast to simply playing the beats correctly:

> I find that we confuse the *Mesure* with what one calls *Cadence* or
> *Mouvement* [life, animation]. *Mesure* defines the number and equality
> of the beats, and *Cadence* is properly the spirit and soul that it is
> necessary to add. The sonatas of the Italians are scarcely open to this

Cadence. But all of our airs for violin, etc., designate and seem to want to express some feeling. Thus, not having devised signs or characters for communicating our particular ideas, we attempt to remedy it by marking the beginning of our pieces with words such as *Tendrement, Vivement,* etc.[20]

Couperin's description of *cadence* and *mouvement* resembles that of a much earlier treatise by Bénigne de Bacilly:

Many people confuse *Mouuement* with *Mesure* and believe that, because one ordinarily says *Air de mouuement* to distinguish a piece from a very slow Air, all *Mouuement* of a song consists only of a certain skipping suited to gigues, menuets, and other similar dances.

Mouuement is consequently something completely different from what they imagine. I maintain that it is a certain quality that gives soul to the song, and that it is called *Mouuement* because it stirs up, I may say it excites, the listeners' attention, in the same way as do those who are the most rebellious in harmony . . . it inspires in hearts such passion as the singer wishes to create, principally that of tenderness. How is it that most women never succeed in acquiring this manner of expression, which they imagine is contrary to the modesty of their sex (like the theatre); they sing in a completely inanimate style for lack of wanting to play-act a little.

I don't doubt at all that the variety of *Mesure,* whether quick or slow, contributes a great deal to the expression of the song. But there is certainly another quality, more refined and more spiritual, that always holds the listener attentive and ensures that the song is less tedious. It is the *Mouuement* that makes the most of a mediocre voice, making it better than a very beautiful voice without expression.[21]

Mouvement (or sometimes *Cadence*) then can be more than tempo; it is also the vibrancy and expression that gives life to the notes and communicates to the listener. The words of Couperin, Rousseau, and Bacilly are as relevant today as then, for the beauty of D'Anglebert's preludes, allemandes, courantes, gaillardes, and passacaille has often been blurred by excessive speed and mechanical performance. These pieces reflect the intimacy that Couperin claims is an important characteristic of French music. Rameau seems to corroborate Couperin's views, for he says that it is better to err by playing too slowly than by playing too fast.[22] M^r Le Gallois (1680) too is not pleased with flamboyance:

How many people do we see who are more impressed by playing

that makes a great deal of noise with many *passages* and diminutions (badly done, by the way) than by well-controlled playing; and who admire a man whose hands create great brilliance by some precipitous and muddling tempi (but who observes neither control nor *mesure* in the *mouvemens*). These people, on the contrary, scorn another whose playing is neat, delicate, and correctly observant of the *mesure*.

The writer advocates a playing style sensibly balanced between legato and brilliant (perhaps lyrical and articulated?), as exemplified by that of Chambonnières:

> Everyone knows that this illustrious personage excelled others as much because of the pieces he composed as because of his having been the originator of that beautiful style of playing in which he revealed a brilliance and a legato so well contrived and adjusted one to the other that it would have been impossible to do better.

Le Gallois stresses the tastelessness of excessive ornamentation and rapid execution on the one hand, and the vapidity of excessive legato on the other:

> Those who possess virtuosity are subject to several defects . . . their trills are often too hurried and consequently very rough, being produced with too much energy . . . their tempo is rushed or uneven . . . they strike the keys instead of flowing smoothly from one to another. Finally, one hears nothing in their playing but a perpetual trill, which prevents one from hearing the melody of the piece distinctly. And they continually add *passages*, particularly from one note to its octave, which Chambonnières used to call "tinkering". . . . We see also that the most expert musicians, following a middle path in this, as one must in everything, only use this lightness of hand and rapidity of execution with great moderation, for fear, as I have said, of muddling and confusing what ought to be neat and distinct.
>   But if the brilliant style has its defects, the legato style also has its own, which are easy to observe in those whom affectation causes to slur their playing in an agonizing manner . . . their playing is indeed so very legato that it sounds more like the playing of a hurdy-gurdy . . . because of the slurring the playing has no rhythm. . . .[23]

But three-quarters of a century later, Pierre-Claude Foucquet suggests that the taste of an earlier period was superior to that of his own: "Many play the clavecin, but very few with appropriate taste. Today we esteem a fleet and agile hand, and appear less moved by a graceful, tender, and warm performance."[24] Mr Ancelet too laments the erosion of *bon goût,* as performers and audiences preferred music of a virtuoso nature:

> One must judge a musician's taste by the choice of pieces he plays. A connoisseur is attracted to the beauty of the melody, to the choice of harmony, and not to difficult pieces overloaded with notes, which most often yield only some bizarre sounds without expression. I would prefer likewise clarity, excellence of tone, and accuracy to rapid performance. Ignorant people and mediocre students take as the newest fad the flights of imagination of a composer without talent. For each instrument, one is bent on finding some extraordinary and impractical ideas for those who have not had the patience to practice them. Certain composers of sonatas are the most complete proof of this.[25]

These quotations from 1680 to 1757 tell us that some things never change, for there have always been those concerned with virtuosity for its own sake. Nevertheless, most of the music left by the French masters of the seventeenth and the early eighteenth century reflects a style inimical to displays of technique. A more leisurely outlook will enable us to discover the beauty of these pieces and to understand the attraction that they held for *les gens* of the Splendid Century. Although many eighteenth-century clavecin pieces imitate the Italian style, others are in the best French tradition; e.g., the magnificent *La Forqueray* by Jacques Duphly and *La d'Héricourt* by Claude-Bénigne Balbastre.

The French, concerned with performing music in a tasteful manner, employed various styles listed in Brossard's *Dictionaire:*[26]

Stile gay, enjoüé, fleury (lively, sprightly, florid)
Stile picquant, pathetique, expressif (piquant, full of emotion, expressive)
Stile grave, serieux, majestueux (solemn, serious, majestic)
Stile naturel, coulant, tendre, affectueux (unaffected, flowing, tender, warm)
Stile grand, sublime, galant (grand, lofty, elegant)
Stile familier, populaire, bas, rampant (familiar, popular, low, pedestrian)

Brossard characterizes French compositions as *naturel, coulant, tendre,* etc., but Italian compositions as *picquant, fleury & expressif.* The French and Italian manners appear to have been predominant in Europe throughout the Baroque period, so the observations of

Johann Joachim Quantz (1752) are valuable for representing a foreigner's perception of these two styles:

> The *Italian manner of playing* is arbitrary, extravagant, artificial, obscure, frequently bold and bizarre, and difficult in execution; it permits many additions of graces, and requires a seemly knowledge of harmony; but among the ignorant it excites more admiration than pleasure. The *French manner of playing* is slavish, yet modest, distinct, neat and true in execution, easy to imitate, neither profound nor obscure, but comprehensible to everyone, and convenient for amateurs; it does not require much knowledge of harmony, since the embellishments are generally prescribed by the composer; but it gives the connoisseurs little to reflect upon.[27]

A vigorous controversy over the merits of French and Italian music raged in France around the turn of the eighteenth century, with the principal protagonists being François Raguenet in favor of Italian music (*Parallèle des Italiens et des Français en ce qui regarde la musique et les opéras*, 1702) and Le Cerf de La Viéville defending the French cause (*Comparaison de la musique italienne et de la musique française*, 1705–1706).

François Couperin implies that the French valued musical sensitivity highly:

> The harpsichord is a complete instrument by virtue of its range, and sufficient unto itself. However, as one can neither swell nor diminish its sounds, I shall always be grateful to those who, by consummate skill supported by good taste, are able to render this instrument capable of expression. Such was the task my ancestors set themselves, quite apart from the fine quality of their pieces; I have endeavoured to perfect their discoveries, for their works still appeal to persons of refined taste.[28]

Jean Rousseau too stresses unaffected and graceful playing in French music. For him, playing melodies on the viol is an unpretentious art that requires a great deal of delicacy and sensitivity: "The viol is the closest instrument to the human voice, which all the instruments are obliged to imitate. . . . Playing melodies is most pleasant, and even touching, when one performs them well."[29]

François Couperin *le grand* has often been cited as the quintessential Baroque composer embodying this French style. Laurence Boulay writes:

Because Couperin and Fauré are, more than other composers, musicians of intimacy—I would say even musicians of the spirit—their work is addressed to an elite whose culture and refinement favor a greater receptivity. . . . The sensitivity, the reserve, the inner feeling are, with Couperin as with Fauré, dominant qualities. Need I repeat the celebrated phrase of the great claveciniste? "I will candidly admit to preferring that which moves me to that which amazes me."[30]

Boulay describes Couperin as "delicate, pensive, a little melancholy, and not without nobility or depth." These characteristics seem to apply to much French composition of the period. For example, the greater part of D'Anglebert's *oeuvre* can best be described as *naturel, coulant, tendre, affectueux*—the style Brossard says typifies French music. The French thought of their music as simple and unaffected, touching the soul, as an anonymous poet expressed it in 1714:

> La musique française a l'heureux avantage
> De n'enfanter jamais un son dur, ou sauvage,
> La douceur et la grâce accompagnent ses chants.
> Ils sont tendres, flatteurs, expressifs et touchants.[31]

IV

ORNAMENTATION

The table of 29 ornaments (*agréments*) included with D'Anglebert's *Pièces de clavecin* (1689) greatly expanded the number of ornament symbols used to add grace and elegance to French keyboard music. D'Anglebert played an important role in the development of shorthand symbols for keyboard ornamentation. These symbols were devised primarily in France, during the latter part of the seventeenth century, and were widely copied or varied in other parts of Europe.

Early in the century and before, diminutions affecting the entire melodic line often served as embellishment. Ex. 1, containing three written-out trills with turned endings, is the last of several possibilities given in Marin Mersenne's *Harmonie universelle* (1636) to demonstrate diminutions by *le sieur de la Barre* on the first two measures of "Tu crois o beau soleil", a chanson composed by Louis XIII.[1]

Concurrent with the use of diminutions was the development of *agréments*, which affect only single notes or chords. Mersenne describes the performance of various types of lute *tremblemens* (trills), gives some symbols for them (but no realization), and mentions that these ornaments can also be performed on the harpsichord.[2] The vocal portion of his treatise, however, illustrates a trill preceded by a note of the same pitch and the *port de voix* in its classic seventeenth-century form as a tone that is slurred to the main note and takes its value and its pitch from the preceding note (see p. 85).[3] The *Traité de l'accord de l'espinette* (1650), by Jean Denis, discusses ornaments briefly, but does not include an ornament table.[4]

Early references indicate that performers could add ornamentation; e.g., Jean Titelouze (1624) instructs his readers to use the "common *cadences* [trills] that everyone knows"[5]; and Mersenne notes the extemporaneous ornamentation practiced by Pierre (III) Chabançeau de La Barre (1592–1656): "But it would be necessary to have several

Ex. 1. Diminution given by Mersenne.
Courtesy of Éditions Minkoff.

special symbols to mark the places of the *martelemens,* the *tremblemens,* the *battemens,* and the other graces with which this excellent organist enriches his playing at the keyboard."[6] In 1655 Constantijn Huygens wrote to Henri Du Mont asking to hear him play Huygens's allemande with the "ornaments that can scarcely be expressed in a musical score."[7] Perhaps these writers are referring to ornaments that have the same general shape as the turned trills of the diminution in Ex. 1 but are performed much more freely.

Most French keyboard composers from G.-G. Nivers (1665) to those writing in the first part of the eighteenth century included an ornament table in their editions. Their music is carefully marked, in contrast to vocal and instrumental music, where the performer may be expected to add some of the ornamentation. Some ornaments, such as the *port de voix* and the turn, can be written out in conventional notation; but others, such as the various forms of the trill, can be only approximately realized via notation. The speed and the number of repercussions must have varied with the context. The commonest French ornaments that can be readily translated into English usage include:

Tremblement or *Cadence*	Trill
Pincé	Mordent
Cheute or *Port de voix*	One-note grace (appoggiatura)
Coulé	Slide (later, a one-note grace)
Arpegé or *Harpegement*	Arpeggio

Since *appoggiatura* is an Italian term closely identified with an on-beat ornament, let us adopt Frederick Neumann's "one-note grace" as a generic term to refer to all French ornaments that add a single tone.[8]

The *agréments* were considered an integral part of the melody and not merely decoration, according to Bénigne de Bacilly (1668):

> As in all cases where one makes a distinction between beauty and ornament, it is the same in song, where a piece of music can without a doubt be beautiful, but not please the listener because it has been executed without the necessary ornaments.[9]

Keyboard Ornament Tables in Seventeenth-Century France

Guillaume-Gabriel Nivers, the first keyboard composer to include a table of symbols for his ornaments (1665), calls the mordent approached from below an *agrément* ($\sim$), the trill a *cadence* ($\sim\!\!\sim$), and the trill with a turned ending a *double cadence* ($\sim\!\!\sim\!\!\sim$).[10] The last, a particularly common ornament (its written-out form appears in Ex. 1), was termed a *cadence parfaite* by Denis.[11] There was much confusion of terminology in the seventeenth century, particularly with the *cadence* and the various forms of the one-note grace. Nivers's form of the mordent was followed by the organist Gilles Jullien (1690), while the harpsichordists often included a lower one-note grace with the mordent, making the execution identical. Nivers advises slurring the *port de voix* (one-note grace) to the following note and suggests consulting a singing manual since the organ should imitate the voice. *Port de voix* means literally "carrying the voice," so the notes, indicated by the small lines above, should be connected smoothly (Nivers writes out the *ports de voix* in his music). He also describes the slide, consisting of a third with an oblique line between the notes, which is performed with only the outer notes held (Ex. 2).

Jacques Champion de Chambonnières's *Les Pièces de clauessin*

Ex. 2. Nivers's ornament table. Courtesy of
Bibliothèque municipale de Troyes.

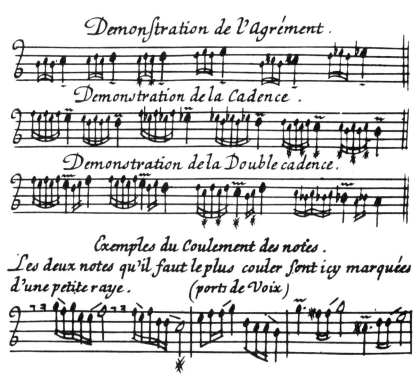

(1670) was the first harpsichord publication to include a table of
ornaments. His realization of the *port de voix* appears to be on the
beat, but its repeated note and rhythmic pattern resembles Nivers's
port de voix. This ornament *is* the same as Nivers's and should be
notated as two sixteenth notes preceding a quarter note (see p. 92
below). The five-note turn beginning on the main note is especially
important in seventeenth-century French literature (see p. 102),

Ex. 3. Chambonnières's ornament table. Reprinted by arrangement with Broude Brothers Limited.

while the remaining ornaments and their symbols became widely used in France and elsewhere (see Ex. 3).

In Nicolas-Antoine Lebègue's table of ornaments (1677) the trill is called a *Cadence ou tremblement* and the symbol is given for the *petite reprise*, the short final repeat found in many French pieces.[12] Otherwise, his table is the same as Chambonnières's, but it lacks the *port de voix* and *double cadence* (see Ex. 4).

Elisabeth-Claude Jacquet de La Guerre's recently discovered first book of *Pièces de clauessin* (c.1687) employs the same ornament symbols as are in Chambonnières's books. In the only extant copy, a leaf has been torn out after the title page, so that the first part of the dedication is missing; and two leaves, which probably contained an ornament table, have been cut out after the dedication. La Guerre's ornaments, except for turns, work well when performed in the man-

Ex. 4. Lebègue's ornament table. By permission of the Houghton Library, Harvard University.

ner of Chambonnières's. Her turns, seldom used in a cadential formula before a trill (see p. 102 below), are usually approached step-
wise from below, so one can speculate that they are to be performed
in the manner of D'Anglebert's four-note turn instead of Chambonnières's five-note version.

André Raison's (1688) table shows the *port de voix*, indicated by a
slur, beginning before the beat.[13] Raison inserts a rest before the
termination of most trills and begins the last trill with a mordent.
His *double cadence* is yet a different rendition of this term, and it
uses two symbols, the first of which is a modified turn symbol.
Noteworthy is the inclusion of the arpeggio in an organ table.
Raison's table (Ex. 5) illustrates a wider variety of possibilities,

Ex. 5. Raison's ornament table. By permission of the Houghton Library, Harvard
University.

Ex. 6. D'Anglebert's ornament table. Reprinted by arrangement with Broude Brothers Limited.

suggesting that ornament performance in France at this time offered many choices.

In D'Anglebert's ornament table, shown in Ex. 6, the basic trill is now termed *tremblement*, rather than *cadence*. Like Jean Denis, D'Anglebert distinguishes between single and double mordents. Several ornaments make their first appearance in this table:

The trill *appuyé*, in which the upper auxiliary is held at the beginning before starting the trill.

The *cadence*, an unusual form of the trill (which can start above or below the main note), apparently not encountered elsewhere in the clavecin tables, but included in J.S. Bach's table in the *Clavier-Büchlein* for Wilhelm Friedemann and used by later German composers.

The *double cadence*, consisting of two ornament symbols—a turn and a *cadence*, with the turn being the same as Chambonnières's five-note turn. When the turn is not followed by a trill (*sans tremblement*), it has four notes and begins on the upper auxiliary—the form that became commonly accepted throughout Europe.

The *coulé sur 2 notes de suitte* (slide on two successive notes), consisting of filler notes between two melodic notes, in contrast to the conventional slide, which adds the inner note between two notes written as the harmonic interval of a third. D'Anglebert's notation indicates precisely that the melodic slide may begin before or on the beat, probably depending on the context. The first note of this type of slide is not held.

The symbol for *cheute* or *port de voix* (one-note grace) placed before a chord, indicating a figured arpeggio with one. or two nonharmonic tones inserted. Also, a unique symbol for the *cheute* can indicate two unusual renditions: *double cheute à une tierce* (double *cheute* on a third) and *idem à une notte seule* (the same on a single note).

The *detaché* (detaching before a trill or mordent), using the seventeenth-century form of the eighth rest (attached to the note head) to indicate a rest before the ornament.

D'Anglebert also inaugurated the use of different signs for previously known *agréments*:

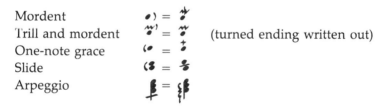

Mordent	•) =	
Trill and mordent	᷍•) = ᷍•	(turned ending written out)
One-note grace	(• =	
Slide	(♦ =	
Arpeggio	♭ = ♭	

D'Anglebert's Influence on the Ornamentation
of Later Composers

The ornament tables of a number of composers of the next generation bear a clear visual resemblance to D'Anglebert's.

"Rules for Graces," printed in both French and English in *Six suittes de clavessin* of Charles (François?) Dieupart (c.1702), was largely modeled after D'Anglebert's table.[14] (The suites were subse-

54

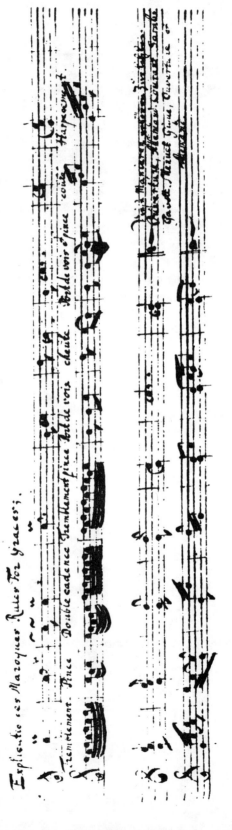

Ex. 7. Ornament table from the Möllersche Manuscript. Courtesy of Berlin, Staatsbibliothek Preussischer Kulturbesitz, Musikabteilung.

quently published in an incomplete form by J. Walsh of London, apparently without the table.) An almost exact copy of Dieupart's table appears in the Möllersche Manuscript (dating perhaps from before 1707),[15] which contains works by J. S. Bach (including an autograph), Georg Böhm, numerous other German composers, and Lebègue (including his ornament table).[16] The table patterned after Dieupart immediately precedes the pages in Bach's hand. The copyist has enlarged the curved lines in the last and third from last examples (see Ex. 7).

French influence extended to Germany through the court at Celle when Georg-Wilhelm, Duke of Braunschweig-Lüneburg, married Eléonore Desmier d'Olbreuse, who was originally from Poitou. Many French musicians were in their service from before 1685, and Georg Böhm became part of this circle. J. S. Bach too was influenced by the Celle court during his student days in Lüneburg, so the Möllersche Manuscript is possibly an outgrowth of relationships formed in this region.

Gaspard Le Roux's ornament table of 1705 (Ex. 8) is patterned after D'Anglebert's, with the exception of the *Autre chute* and the *Separez*.[17] The inclusion of the *Separez* indicates that the diagonal line between two notes a third apart could mean either a slide or a separation of the two notes (see p. 79).

The two tables from Jean-Philippe Rameau's books of clavecin pieces (1706 and 1724) also use many of D'Anglebert's forms for the symbols (see Exx. 9 and 10).[18] In both tables, the mordent is shown

Ex. 8. Le Roux's ornament table. Courtesy of Éditions Minkoff.

Ex. 9. Rameau's ornament table of 1706.
Courtesy of the Département de la musique, Bibliothèque nationale, Paris.

only in multiple repercussions. There are several interesting features in the 1724 table:

1. The *Double cadence* equals a trill with a turned ending.

2. The four-note turn is called a *doublé*.

3. The one-note grace is shown as being tied against the resolution momentarily.

4. The *Coulez* is not a slide but a descending one-note grace.

5. The *Suspension* (a delaying of the melody note—also given by F. Couperin in 1713) is added.

6. The arpeggio illustration at the bottom depicts two figures—one with four notes played as sixteenth notes and one with two notes played as equal eighth notes.

7. "A note slurred to the following trilled note serves as its preparation," so the trill proper begins on the main note (right column).

8. The *Liaison* (slur), a useful bit of shorthand, is used over a group of notes to indicate that they are to be held. (St.-Lambert also discusses this use of the slur.[19])

François Couperin's table in his first book of *Pièces de clavecin* (1713) differs markedly from those of his predecessors. Often unclear rhythmically, it casts doubt on the custom of beginning ornaments on the beat. This table is readily obtained in either the facsimile or the performing editions.[20]

D'Anglebert's *Cadence* appears in J. S. Bach's *Clavier-Büchlein vor Wilhelm Friedemann Bach* of 1720 (in its original form and also with a mordent at the close) for the first time since D'Anglebert's 1689 edition. Bach's table is clearly modeled on D'Anglebert's and on other French sources (see Ex. 11).[21]

Ex. 10. Rameau's ornament table of 1724. Reprinted by arrangement with Broude Brothers Limited.

Ex. 11. J. S. Bach's ornament table. Courtesy of the Music Library, Yale University,
New Haven.

A *Praeludium* of disputed origin from this *Clavier-Büchlein* (No.29,
BWV 931) uses D'Anglebert's symbols for the arpeggio, trill *appuyé*,
one-note grace, and trill with a turned ending. The wavy lines in
front of the first beat in m.1 and the third beat in mm.3 and 4 have
been interpreted as arpeggio symbols.[22] It seems unlikely, however,
that both symbols for the arpeggio would be used in the same piece.
A more probable explanation is that the symbol in front of the first
chord denotes a figured arpeggio, and the symbol in mm.3 and 4 a
slide (see Exx. 7 and 12).

The handling of D'Anglebert's ornamentation symbols is skillful
enough to be his own, but the style of the piece is not like any of
his known works. Nor is it likely that the *Praeludium* was written
by another French composer, for the French considered the prelude an improvisatory form. The brevity of No.29 implies that it
was a didactic example and suggests that the prelude was composed by Bach himself, as a teaching piece in imitation of the
French style. The fact that Bach copied de Grigny's *Livre d'orgue*,
some of Dieupart's clavecin pieces, and D'Anglebert's ornament
table into a manuscript is further evidence of his interest in the
French style.[23]

Ex. 12. Praeludium from the *Clavier-Büchlein.* Courtesy of the Music Library, Yale University, New Haven.

D'Anglebert's Autograph Manuscript
and 1689 Edition Compared

Some clarification of details occurred between D'Anglebert's autograph manuscript (1660s–1670s) and his *Pièces de clavecin* (1689), but there is little change in the overall shape of the pieces. In contrast to the 29 ornaments found in the table of the edition, some basic symbols (primarily the trill, mordent, one-note grace, slide, and arpeggio) are used in the manuscript. The manuscript shows evidence of a transitional stage in the development of some symbols, particularly that of the arpeggio (see p. 64). Some repeated or conjunct notes are written equally in the manuscript but dotted in the print; e.g., all the eighth-note groups in the Gavotte in G major. The ornamental figure in the soprano voice in the Sarabande in D minor is written as an eighth and two sixteenth notes in the manuscript, but as a dotted eighth and two 32nd notes in the edition. The Gail-

Ex. 13. D'Anglebert, Gaillarde in G major,
m.22.

larde in G major (Ex. 13) contains an example of rhythmic alteration
(in this and subsequent examples, a. indicates D'Anglebert's manuscript, b. the edition).

D'Anglebert was careful to indicate the duration of notes in the
edition in order to avoid misunderstanding. For example, the bro-
ken-chord figures (mm.178–191, 218) of the *Variations sur les folies
d'Espagne* are written as simple eighth notes in the manuscript, but
their full duration is given in the edition. This is simply good harpsichord technique written out.

The only instance of a double dot occurs in the manuscript of his
double of a Sarabande by Chambonnières (*Jeunes zéphirs*), an example
that also contains a written-out five-note turn (Ex. 14). Perhaps the
32d note is intended to strike with the one-note grace in the upper
voice (see p.85).

A vertical line is occasionally used in the preludes to mark a concurrence of the upper and lower voices. Ex. 15 shows one that
occurs in a different location in the manuscript from that of the
edition. In the edition, the D in the bass of the first concurrence
comes before the B♭ in the upper voice. D'Anglebert may have
preferred the latter version because the ornament (a *cadence*) actually
begins on the B♭, whereas in the manuscript the bass note occurs in
the middle of this ornament. Might his *cadence* begin after the beat in
some appropriate measured contexts?

Ex. 14. D'Anglebert, *double* of Chambonnières's Sarabande, m.20.

Ex. 15. D'Anglebert, Prelude in G minor
(MS), close.

D'Anglebert's edition substitutes a trill and mordent symbol for a five-note turn (m.2) in the manuscript version of the Gavotte in G major. Conversely, his transcription of Lully's Courante gives a turn (m.2) in the edition, but a trill and mordent in the manuscript. This Courante contains a passage with more difference than usual between the edition and the manuscript (see Ex. 16). Three-note slides appear in the manuscript (mm.13, 15), and the first F in m.16 is a natural in both sources. This courante (m.4) and its *double* (m.13) furnish two more examples of five-note turns written out in the manuscript but indicated by symbol in the edition. Two five-note turns in the *double* are written out in both sources (mm.8 and 16). D'Anglebert's transcription of Lully's *Les Songes agreables* illustrates his differing conceptions between the time of the manuscript and that of the edition (Ex. 17).

An interesting melodic variation occurs in the *Variations sur les folies d'Espagne.* D'Anglebert omits a bar line in the manuscript (probably because of an ornamented note that would tie over the bar), but writes out a five-note turn in the edition (see Ex. 18). A melodic variant occurs in variation 21; each measure opens with alternating

Ex. 16. Lully/D'Anglebert, Courante, mm.
13–16.

Ex. 17. Lully/D'Anglebert, *Les Songes agre-*
ables d'Atys, mm. 28–30.

Ex. 18. D'Anglebert, Variations, mm.175–
177.

forms of the *cadence* in the edition, but with a sixteenth-note pattern
beginning on the upper auxiliary (the same execution as the *cadence*
beginning from above) in the manuscript. The rhythm of the closing
figure of each measure is also different. The fact that D'Anglebert
wrote 32nd notes in the manuscript and sixteenth notes in the edition implies that he changed his mind and meant the sixteenth notes
to be interpreted as written (see Ex. 19).

In several instances a one-note grace, indicated by symbol in the
manuscript, is written out in the edition (e.g., in Ex. 20). Examples

Ex. 19. D'Anglebert, Variations, mm.322–
323.

Ex. 20. D'Anglebert, Sarabande in D minor,
m.26.

Ex. 21. D'Anglebert, Gaillarde in G major,
m.18.

in the edition of written-out one-note graces before the beat occur in
the Gavotte in G major (m.5), the Passacaille (m. 2), and the Gaillarde in G major (Ex. 21).

D'Anglebert's rendition of a one-note grace in the edition, with
the nonharmonic tone sounding alone at the beginning, is at vari-
ance with that given in his ornament table (see Ex. 22, in which c.
indicates my realization). The version in the edition is probably an
exceptional realization that needed to be written out because it could
not be accurately conveyed by a symbol. The performance of a
double *cheute* (figured arpeggio) from the same piece is also at vari-
ance with the ornament table. The manuscript depicts a figured
arpeggio with two one-note grace symbols, but the edition shows
the graces written out first, followed by a simple arpeggio in a
downward direction. This interpretation is stronger, for it introduces
contrary motion between the upper voices and the bass. The use of

Ex. 22. D'Anglebert, Gaillarde in G major,
m.5.

Ex. 23. D'Anglebert, Gaillarde in G major,
m.15.

eighth rather than sixteenth notes can probably be attributed to the
longer duration of the chord as well as the movement in the bass
voice (Ex. 23). The one-note grace in Ex. 24 is replaced with a different rhythm in the edition, perhaps to avoid crowding the arpeggio
on the first beat.

D'Anglebert probably borrowed from the lutenists the oblique line
that denotes the arpeggio. In the manuscript, the diagonal line is
usually placed between the staves instead of on the note stem; e.g.,
the *Double* of the Gaillarde in C major (mm.5 and 6). Sometimes it is
placed between note heads a third apart (*Allemande du Vieux Gautier*,
m.2), giving it the same appearance as Chambonnières's slide.
D'Anglebert often uses his own conventional curved-line symbol for
the slide in these same pieces, so perhaps he means arpeggiation
and not a nonharmonic tone. An oblique line is placed between two
notes a sixth apart in the *Courante du Vieux Gautier* (*La petite bergère*,
m.15), two are found in one chord between note heads in the *Ouuerture d'Isis* (m.8), and one is through the note stem in the *double* of
Couperin's Allemande (m.17). The oblique line of the Gaillarde in G
major (m.1) is placed between the staves in the manuscript, but on
the right-hand note stem in the edition. The diagonal slash in all
these locations, reflecting transitional stages of the arpeggio symbol,
indicates the arpeggiation of chords or intervals.

Ex. 24. D'Anglebert, Gaillarde in G major,
m.20.

A comparison of D'Anglebert's manuscript and edition clarifies the performance of arpeggios, two types of turn, and one-note graces before and on the beat. His meticulous care with rhythmic values suggests that there is little basis for altering note values except for the application of *notes inégales* in appropriate locations.

V

ORNAMENT PERFORMANCE
TREATISES BY ST.-LAMBERT AND ROUSSEAU

Helpful as they are, the ornament tables still leave many unanswered questions. Three treatises from D'Anglebert's period—one for harpsichord by Monsieur de Saint-Lambert and others for voice and viol by Jean Rousseau—are useful for clarifying some of the puzzling aspects of these tables. St.-Lambert, using D'Anglebert's table as his principal source, identifies the most important ornaments:

> If the choice of fingering is arbitrary in playing the harpsichord, the choice of ornaments is no less so. Good taste is the only law to follow. However, there are some essential ornaments that can scarcely be omitted. The most important of these is the trill, while the others are the mordent, the arpeggio, and the slide. But although those of which we shall speak after these first four are not so necessary or so often used, they do not fail to lend a great deal of grace to the pieces, so one should not overlook them.[1]

D'Anglebert's frequent usage of the one-note grace would place it ahead of the slide and possibly ahead of the arpeggio. Indeed, St.-Lambert later describes the *port de voix* as one of the most important ornaments. Nevertheless, the following discussion of the *agréments* follows his order. (It is assumed that the reader is acquainted with the basic tenets of French ornamentation, as described in contemporary books and articles.)

Trills and Mordent

In illustrating D'Anglebert's five trills, St.-Lambert credits D'Anglebert with the definition and probably the invention of the

trill *appuyé* (prepared or supported trill) and the two forms of the
cadence (not the simple trill that earlier composers called *cadence*).
Giving a somewhat different but not inaccurate illustration of Nivers's ornaments, St.-Lambert points out that Nivers's *double cadence*
equals D'Anglebert's trill and mordent combination, and that his
agrément is the same as D'Anglebert's *chutte & pincé* (one-note grace
and mordent; see Ex. 1).[2]

One finds many instances in seventeenth-century clavecin literature that seem to call for a trill other than the commonly accepted
one beginning on the beat with the upper auxiliary. Frederick Neumann presents cogent reasons for beginning some trills on the main
note or before the beat.[3]

While French keyboard players appear to be nearly uniform in
their trill practice as set forth in ornament tables, variants existed in
other idioms. Bénigne de Bacilly says that in vocal music the upper
auxiliary of trills is omitted "very often and very fittingly in a thou-
sand places":

> Those who fancy themselves as great experts of the vocal art would
> not for anything in the world omit that preparation of the trill . . . as
> if it were of its essence, even in the case of the shortest trills. They
> consider it a crime to do otherwise and thereby render the perfor-

Ex. 1. St.-Lambert's illustration of Nivers's
ornaments. Courtesy of Éditions Minkoff.

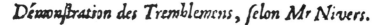

Démonstration des Tremblemens, selon Mr Nivers.

Agrément.   Cadence.   Double Cadence.

Manière de les exprimer.

Agrément.   Cadence.   Double Cadence.

mance dull and monotonous without realizing that the most univer-
sal rules have exceptions which often produce more pleasing results
than the rules themselves. There are even cases of cadential trills
where the preparation is inappropriate and where one plunges immediately into the alternations starting them upward. . . .[4]

Jean Rousseau's treatises for the voice and for the viol are remarkable for their thorough and generally clear treatment of ornamentation issues. Instrumental and vocal music of this period often does
not carry a large number of symbols for ornamentation, in contrast
to clavecin music, so Rousseau discusses in some detail the appropriate locations for adding ornaments. His vocal treatise, which saw
six editions between 1678 and 1710 in Paris and Amsterdam, observes that trills (*cadences*) occur in two forms: prepared (*appuyé*) by
the auxiliary note immediately above the main note, or unprepared.
The value of this preparation note is taken either from the preceding
note or from the main note, while the trill without a preparation "is
made on the natural pitch of the note by a single shake of the
voice."[5] In Rousseau's realizations of prepared trills in his viol treatise, the auxiliary note sometimes begins before the beat and at other
times on the beat. In all cases, a slur connects the auxiliary note to
the trill, which is marked with a +.[6]

In Ex. 2, *A*, *B*, and *C* illustrate trills approached in descending
motion, with notes of differing time values, which are prepared with
the auxiliary note before the beat (Rousseau's text indicates that the
second half of the *A* measure should read as quarter notes in both
the original and its realization). This auxiliary note, sometimes called
a *chute* by Rousseau, is the same one-note grace that can also function by itself, apart from a trill (see p. 86). *D* shows the trill preparation on a note preceded by the same pitch. *C* and *D* dot the note
before the auxiliary note, instead of dividing the time evenly. On the
other hand, *E*, *F*, and *G* demonstrate trills in which the auxiliary
note takes its time from the trilled note.

Apart from the need to have a trilled note long enough to handle
both the preparation and the trill, it is not completely clear why the
preparation note sometimes falls before the beat and sometimes on
it. Perhaps this component was optional and could be determined
by context or by personal taste. According to Rousseau's vocal treatise, a trill whose preparation is made on the beat is employed when
"one descends from a short note to another with more than double

Ex. 2. Rousseau's trills with preparation.
Courtesy of Éditions Minkoff.

its value, such as from an eighth note to a dotted quarter note or a half note, or from a sixteenth note to a quarter note or even a dotted eighth note."[7]

Rousseau's *Traité de la viole* maintains that a trill without preparation (i.e., beginning on the main note) is required on notes approached from below (*A* and *B*) and even on descending notes when their short value hinders the preparation (*C*) (see Ex. 3).[8] *D,E,F,* and *G* demonstrate the use of this trill in passages of conjunct ascending and descending eighth notes. When a passage begins on a beat, the trills are made on the third, fifth, seventh, etc., notes (*D* and *F*), but when the passage begins on the second half of a beat, the trills are made on the second, fourth, sixth, etc., notes (*E* and *G*). Rousseau's list of errata changes the order of examples from *D,E,F,G* to *E,D,G,F* (already taken into account). Passages similar to *D,E,F,* and *G* occur

Ex. 3. Rousseau's trills without preparation.
Courtesy of Éditions Minkoff.

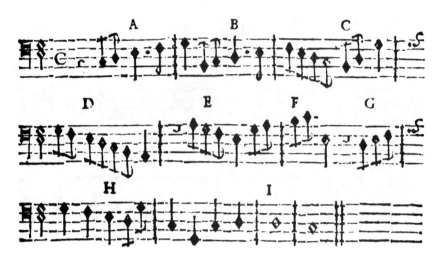

frequently in clavecin music and are more effective when performed in Rousseau's manner, without a preparation note. *H* is similar to the previous four cases, but with quarter notes instead of eighth notes; Rousseau says that a preparation note may be used in this situation if it is played very quickly. *I* shows this trill in a descending cadence in which the preceding note is not above the trilled whole note: "Make the trill on the second half of its value." In a somewhat similar instance, but with an ascending final note, Rousseau advises making "the trill only on the second half of the penultimate note's value, followed by the *port de voix*" (see Ex. 4).[9]

Rousseau's vocal treatise outlines the appropriate use of the trill without a preparation note: "When the notes ascend, when they are on the same degree, and even when they descend (particularly from a fourth, a fifth, or a sixth), when they are short, and when they are not dotted (for every dotted descending note, or note on the same degree, can be trilled with a preparation on the beat, insofar as the rhythm permits)."[10] The unprepared trill is "always used in lively airs such as menuets, and in time signatures such as 3/4, 3/8, and the like. If one uses the preparation, it must be very quick." Rousseau further cautions that "all notes under a slur must be trilled without preparation." His viol treatise also notes, "In all lively

Ex. 4. Rousseau's trill on a whole note
(*Méthode claire*). Courtesy of Éditions Minkoff.

[*légers*] tempi, the trill must be performed without preparation."
Rousseau refers readers who wish to know more about the performance of trills and the *port de voix* to his *Méthode pour la musique*—
presumably his vocal treatise—implying that trill applications are
similar in vocal and instrumental music.

D'Anglebert's transcription of Lully's overture to *Cadmus* provides
an example to substantiate Rousseau's assertion that trills approached by a large leap from above do not require the preparation
note. D'Anglebert wrote out the preparation note of a trill as a
sixteenth note falling on the beat (Ex. 5, soprano, first beat of m.5),

Ex. 5. Lully/D'Anglebert, *Ouuerture de Cadmus*, mm.4–5.

whereas Lully's score utilizes only the unornamented *mi*. Since this pitch is approached by the leap of a fifth from above, the preparation note would not normally have been utilized, so D'Anglebert wrote the preparation as a conventional note to make his intent clear (the slur from *fa*♯ to *mi* indicates that the trill on *mi* begins on the main note, as Rousseau states). Why would D'Anglebert make the effort to write a trill in this manner if the customary trill symbol connoted the very realization that modern performers practice? Nor could he have used the trill *appuyé* symbol, for the preparation of this trill sometimes falls before the beat (see p. 75 below). It appears that the only way D'Anglebert could be certain of beginning the trill with the first auxiliary note on the beat was to write it as he did.

Rousseau explains why both the prepared and the unprepared trill have the same name (*cadence*):

> I use the term of *Cadence* to designate the trill without preparation that is made in ascending motion because there is no particular symbol to distinguish it from the *Cadence* that is made with a preparation in descending motion. Both trills are equally marked by a *t* or + in all books of music. One must, however, distinguish between them. . . . Some, seeing notes marked with the same symbol, incorrectly perform both types in the same manner. That which we call a *Cadence* with preparation is truly a *Cadence* because it is performed in descending motion. But the ornament termed a *Cadence simple* in this book is properly only a flip of the throat, or an unsupported trill. Thus it is correct to say that the term of *Cadence* is badly applied in this instance.[11]

In the middle of the eighteenth century, Pierre-Claude Foucquet sought to remedy this lack of differentiation by using a small eighth note to indicate the preparation of trills that require it. His table gives several varieties of trill that are similar to Rousseau's—some begin on the beat with the main note and others have the grace-note preparation both before and on the beat.[12] The *tremblement subit* described by Michel-Pignolet de Montéclair (1736), indicated by a cross symbol, appears to correspond to Rousseau's trill without preparation.[13] In his 1724 table, J.-P. Rameau gives a trill that he says begins on the main note because the preceding note, to which it is slurred, serves as its beginning (see p. 57, above); and a table by Jean-

Ex. 6. J.-F. Dandrieu's ornament table.
Courtesy of the Carl Dolmetsch Library.

François Dandrieu from the early 1700s (Ex. 6)[14] contains a *tremble-ment lié* with a realization like Rameau's trill.

These composers were probably clarifying an existing situation in which many trills preceded by a note one step higher were begun on the main note. The trill without preparation may have been so familiar in some contexts that the clavecinistes took its use for granted. Seventeenth-century French trills are often called *cadence*, according to Rousseau, because of the cadences from which they are nearly inseparable. Perhaps the trills of the ornament tables were intended primarily as cadential trills, as the many repercussions suggest.

Could there really have been so much difference in trill practice between the clavecin and the other instruments and voice? The main-note trill often makes eminently good sense when approached from above by intervals larger than a third or from below, when short note values hinder a prepared trill in descending movement or when the tempo is lively. It seems logical that musicians would have used a trill that is a mirror image of the popular mordent. Alan Curtis suggests this very interpretation of Jean Denis's *pincement au dessus* (1650).[15]

Evidence from Rousseau presented above indicated that the preparation note of trills could begin before or on the beat. An example in St.-Lambert's treatise shows the upper auxiliary of the trill beginning on the beat, but his text raises doubt: "One must strike these other notes [other voice or voices occurring on the same beat as the trill] precisely when beginning the trill; i.e., as soon as one plays for the first time the auxiliary note that is used to make the trill."[16] Some writers today say that the first auxiliary note of the trill strikes on the beat, along with the other voice or voices. But St.-Lambert may mean that the trill proper (after the preparation note) begins on the beat: "as soon as one plays for the first time the auxiliary note. . . ." The use of "as soon as" instead of "when" seems to imply "after." This interpretation would correspond to Rousseau's trill with a preparation before the beat (Ex. 2).

The French thought of their music as unaffected, simple, graceful, and fluent (see p. 43 above). Interrupting a descending melodic line of eighth or sixteenth notes to repeat an upper auxiliary obscures the beauty of the melody and detracts from its gracefulness (e.g., D'Anglebert's Allemande in G major, m.1). While it is technically possible to start all trills on the upper note, it seems alien to the French character of the period. Virtuosity or composing "difficult" music was foreign to their minds, for they sought grace and elegance. Complicated as D'Anglebert's ornamentation appears, it is not technically demanding. The passage in Ex. 7, from his Courante in G minor, flows easily when the trills are started on the main note.

D'Anglebert often approaches a trill from below, a context in which, as Rousseau points out, it can be awkward to leap to the upper auxiliary to begin the trill. Furthermore, a mordent and a trill are frequently written to be played simultaneously. An unprepared trill in Ex. 8 permits a facile execution of the trill and mordent together (the arpeggio symbol in Gilbert's edition is not in the 1689 edition). In some other contexts in D'Anglebert's works, one could also play the auxiliary before the beat, as illustrated by Rousseau in Ex. 2. Neumann points out that trills are frequently found on a confluence of two voices; therefore a trill beginning on the upper

Ex. 7. D'Anglebert, 2.^e Courante in G minor, mm.19–20.

Ex. 8. D'Anglebert, Chaconne Rondeau in
D major, m.39.

Ex. 9. D'Anglebert, Allemande in G major,
mm.17–18.

auxiliary on the beat would obliterate the identity of the other voice
(see Ex. 9).

The trill *appuyé* also has some puzzling aspects. The first auxiliary
note of this trill in D'Anglebert's table (p. 52, above) is written as a
separate eighth note, which might suggest playing it before the beat.
Some contexts in his pieces seem to require this interpretation,
rather than a prolongation of the initial auxiliary note on the beat.
For example, sometimes a trill and a trill *appuyé* are found simultaneously in different voices. In Ex. 10, one can perform the auxiliary of
the first trill *appuyé* before the beat and the simple trill on the beat

Ex. 10. Lully/D'Anglebert, *Ouverture de la
Mascarade*, mm. 49–50.

Ex. 11. Lully/D'Anglebert, Sarabande. *Dieu
des Enfers*, mm. 10–13; Rousseau, trill
(*Traité*, p.82). Courtesy of Éditions Minkoff.

without an auxiliary, allowing the two trills to be played together in
an easy manner (the second trill *appuyé* might call for a conventional
realization on the beat; this example also contains a simultaneous
mordent and trill).

This technique is also useful when the trill *appuyé* appears with a
simultaneous mordent. In a few instances, D'Anglebert adds a hook
at the end of a trill *appuyé* to signify a turned ending. This ornament
does not often fit easily into the context when it is begun on the
beat. The execution in m.12 of Ex. 11 becomes more fluent when the
preparation is begun before the beat (in contrast to the trills in
mm.11 and 13). The trill *appuyé* in m.12 is approached by leap, a
context that is more graceful when prepared before the beat, as
Rousseau recommends.

An example from Étienne Loulié (1696) gives two trills *appuyé* that
show the eighth-note auxiliary preparation in two manners: the first
begins on the beat; the second, before the beat (Ex. 12). Loulié
defines the trill *appuyé* as one in which the preparation note is held
perceptibly before beginning the trill.[17] It is likely that the lines be-
neath function as both tie and slur, and that these trills are similar to
those of Rousseau in Ex. 2.

D'Anglebert uses the trill *appuyé* several times in his unmeasured

Ex. 12. Loulié, trills *appuyé*. Courtesy of Éditions Minkoff.

preludes, perhaps to ensure that the preparation note is not omitted. The contexts in which this ornament appears are more interesting harmonically when the main note, rather than the upper auxiliary (which is usually consonant with the prevailing harmony), receives the rhythmic stress.

Many clavecin trills should begin on the beat with the upper auxiliary, but one can also consider a main-note start or a pre-beat preparation note in the contexts outlined above. One suspects that the French were not as methodical as we in trying to list every possible variant in their tables. As performers, not pedagogues or scholars, they must have played some ornaments automatically. Chambonnières's ornament table (1670) was possibly a guide for subsequent composers, to which they added more elaborate *agréments* of their own choosing. But because Chambonnières had not included the trill starting on the main note (for whatever reason), for many years no one else thought to add it either, perhaps because of its very simplicity and common use. Therefore, the modern player might be guided by the context to choose the trill performance that produces the most graceful effect.

Arpeggio

The arpeggio (*arpegé, harpegement*), found in nearly all ornament tables in editions of keyboard music from seventeenth- and eighteenth-century France (including the organ works of Raison and Chaumont), was the third of St.-Lambert's four most important ornaments. Its symbols, the wavy vertical line in front of a chord or the diagonal slash through the note stem, are realized with notes distributed throughout the beat. St.-Lambert says that D'Anglebert originated the usage of the slanted stroke [probably derived from the French lutenists] to indicate an arpeggio in keyboard music. The arpeggio is portrayed in the French manner as late as C. P. E. Bach,[18] while James Grassineau's description, "HARPEGGIATO, or HARPEGGIO, signifies to cause the several sounds of one accord to be heard not together, but distinctly one after the other, beginning with either at pleasure, but commonly with the lowest,"[19] seems to indicate that the ornament tables are accurate, with the notes of the arpeggio being separated perceptibly. Perrine's *Pièces de luth en musique*, written in keyboard score, gives precise performance instructions for the arpeggio:

> The oblique line between notes [♪] means that they must be played one after the other. A chord of two notes with the value of one eighth note [♪] must be played as [♪]. A chord of two notes with the value of a dotted eighth note [♪] must be played as [♪]. That of two notes with the value of a quarter note [♪] must be played as [♪]. That of three notes with the value of a dotted eighth note [♪] must be played as [♪]. Three notes with the value of a quarter note [♪] must be played as [♪]. Three notes with the value of a dotted quarter note [♪] must be played as [♪].

The occasional four-note chord with the value of the quarter note can be played as four sixteenth notes, or one can hold the bass for the value of a dotted eighth note and separate the three others for the remainder of the beat.[20]

When possible, one dwells on the first note of the *arpegé* before playing the other notes; thus it is certain that the arpeggio symbol denotes a deliberate separation of the notes. This shorthand symbol saved a good deal of time and paper for the copyist. The keyboard ornament tables show the simple arpeggio as having the following characteristics: It can begin from the bottom or from the top, depending on the direction of the symbol, but most commonly from the bottom; all the notes are held; and the notes appear to be distributed throughout the beat. It also seems that the duration of the notes within a given arpeggio will vary according to the context; i.e., in some cases eighth notes will work better than sixteenths (compare Rameau's two tables, p. 56). The arpeggio is also found in two-note groupings, with the notes generally performed equally, as described by St.-Lambert (and illustrated in the ornament tables by Le Roux's *Separez* and Rameau's 1724 realization):

> In the *Harpegé,* whether plain or figured, the fingers must be applied on the keys so fluently that there does not appear to be any noticeable gap between the notes that alters or breaks the rhythm of the piece. One can exclude the *Harpegé* made on an interval of two notes, however, for when there are several in succession, the notes have more grace by being separated perceptibly, even to the extent that the second ones are reduced to half their value.[21]

Thus the two-note arpeggios in D'Anglebert's Courante might be realized as shown in Ex. 13.

St.-Lambert's text suggests that the arpeggio is to be played with grace and agility, not great speed, so as not to disrupt the rhythmic flow, a description that sounds much like *style luthé.* All chords were

Ex. 13. D'Anglebert, Courante in G minor,
m.5; a. as written, b. realization.

customarily played in a broken manner on the harpsichord, according to Lebègue:

> I have endeavored to notate the preludes with as much clarity as possible, as much for consistency of performance as for the playing style of the harpsichord, in which one separates the notes of chords and strikes them very quickly one after the other, rather than playing them together as on the organ.[22]

Therefore a symbol would not be necessary to indicate that a chord should be rolled. Although Lebègue begins by referring to his preludes, it seems that "the playing style of the harpsichord" is meant to encompass other pieces too, since he contrasts it with the playing style of the organ. Countless chords in this literature carry no symbol to denote an arpeggio, so it appears that the symbol has a special significance. In substantiation of the premise that the arpeggio consisted of broken notes with a determinate value, compare D'Anglebert's manuscript, in which an arpeggio is written out twice (mm.18 and 21), with *Pièces de clavecin*, where it is indicated by symbol (Ex. 14). The arpeggio maintains the rhythmic flow and sustains the tone. By being broken perceptibly, a chord can acquire a melodic function. The frequent use of the arpeggio illustrates the clavecinistes' appropriation of the lutenists' *style luthé* (or *style brisé*— broken style), which is an important part of harpsichord technique.

In a treatise of 1707, St.-Lambert recommends accompanying soloists with broken chords. The chords of *Airs de mouvement* should be struck with their bass note, with this exception: when the bass consists of continuous quarter notes (whether in triple or in duple meter), the player should reserve one note of each chord to be played between the beats. (St.-Lambert provides an example of this technique.[23])

Ex. 14. D'Anglebert, Gigue in G major,
m.18; a. MS, l76 v; b. edition.

Ex. 15. Rameau, *Les Sauvages*, mm.15–16.

Examples from later composers demonstrate how well an arpeggio with determinate values fits into the musical line; e.g., it keeps the eighth-note motion flowing smoothly in Rameau's *Les Sauvages* (in Ex. 15 and subsequent examples, b. is my realization). The pattern in Ex. 16, from François Couperin's *La Tenebreuse*, occurs also at m.12, but none of the many four-part chords in the upper voices in mm.17 and 18 have symbols for arpeggiation.

The arpeggio could also be figured; i.e., have one or more nonharmonic notes (which were not held) inserted between the notes of the arpeggio. D'Anglebert identifies this ornament as *Cheute sur une notte* or a *Cheute sur 2 nottes*; Le Roux, *Chute sur une Notte* and the

Ex. 16. F. Couperin, *La Tenebreuse*, m.16.

Ex. 17. St.-Lambert's explanation of the
Harpegez figurez. Courtesy of Éditions Minkoff.

alternate form an *Autre chute*; Rameau, *Arpegement figuré*; and St.-Lambert, *Harpegez figurez*. St.-Lambert says that this ornament normally begins with the lowest note but may start from the top when the symbol is placed on the highest note. His realization may apply to some instances in D'Anglebert's works where one would expect (from his table) to start the slide from the bottom because the symbol is on the left side instead of the right (Ex. 17).[24]

The notes of the figured arpeggio, like those of the simple arpeggio, are separated perceptibly. While later usage sometimes combined the two forms of arpeggio symbol to indicate a figured arpeggio (e.g., Rameau's table of 1724), only the symbol for the one-note grace (*cheute*) is necessary to indicate that an arpeggio is required (Ex. 18). It follows that a chord in which the nonharmonic tone is indicated by a small note, rather than by a symbol, might be interpreted in the same way (e.g., F. Couperin, *Allemande La Verneüil*, m.1).

Ex. 18. D'Anglebert, Gaillarde in G major,
m.7.

Nearly every French ornament table of the period gives an arpeggio realization in which the notes are separated perceptibly and the harmony notes are held for the duration. The two symbols for the arpeggio, used selectively, denote a special significance. By its continuation of the rhythmic flow, the arpeggio contributes to a graceful performance.

Slides

According to St.-Lambert, D'Anglebert increased the variety of *coulés* (slides—a note or notes to fill in an interval), since "everyone" had previously used only the *coulé sur tierce* (ascending), which is found in each of the ornament tables in chapter 4. D'Anglebert employed a curved line before the notes, instead of a diagonal line between the notes, to indicate the slide. He also created a descending slide by placing the curved line after the notes.

St.-Lambert's observation that D'Anglebert's three slides on two successive melody notes are intended for use in *Pièces graves* (organ pieces in his *oeuvre*) explains why they are given in white notation. These slides connect melodic intervals of a third or a fourth, in contrast to the conventional slide, which fills in the harmonic interval of a third (see ornament table, p. 52). In describing D'Anglebert's slides, St.-Lambert says that "the first example is like the standard slide, except that one repeats the first note and holds only the last note." In the second example, "one repeats the first note, after its value has expired, in order to slide subtly to the second note, passing through all notes in between." The third example is like the second, but "the first note is not repeated."[25]

St.-Lambert seems to ignore the unique feature of D'Anglebert's second slide—the fact that it takes its time value from the first, rather than the second, note. Is he contradicting D'Anglebert when he teaches that this slide begins after the value of the first note has expired ("c'est-à-dire en répétant la première Note, aprés que sa valeur est expirée . . . ")? One might infer that this slide does not begin until after the first note has been held for its full value. Or is St.-Lambert merely instructing the reader to begin the slide at the customary time? D'Anglebert is consistently precise in his directions (although occasionally incomplete), so one can probably assume that he meant what he wrote. St.-Lambert gives another example of a slightly different *coulé* that does fall before the second note.[26]

The *maître* attributes the slides *double cheute a une tierce* and *idem a une notte seule* to D'Anglebert's invention and credits the composer with six or seven types of slide.[27] The terminology is unclear, as D'Anglebert places *cheute* and *port de voix* together, but St.-Lambert groups the *double cheute a une tierce* with the slides.

One-Note Grace (*appoggiatura, port de voix, cheute, accent, coulé*)

The terminology and use of one-note graces in seventeenth- and early eighteenth-century clavecin music can be confusing to the reader. The earliest French term is *port de voix* (Nivers and Chambonnières), then *cheute* (*chutte*) or *port de voix* (D'Anglebert), followed by *port de voix coulé* (F. Couperin). Rameau uses *port de voix* to indicate an ascending one-note grace, but *coulez* (not to be confused with the slide—*coulé*) to designate a descending one. Loulié (1696) makes the same distinction.[28] The one-note graces in J. S. Bach's 1720 ornament table are termed *accent*. Essentially, a *port de voix* indicates an ascending one-note grace and *cheute* (*chutte*) or *coulé* a descending one-note grace, although *port de voix* and *cheute* can also define both functions (e.g., in D'Anglebert, Chaumont, and St.-Lambert). (As mentioned in chapter 4, the generic term "one-note grace" refers to all these *agréments*.)

It has generally been assumed that the French played one-note graces on the beat, taking the value of the grace from the note with the symbol. Numerous ornament tables (most of them derived from D'Anglebert's) depict it this way, and François Couperin says that "the small note of a *port de voix* or of a *coulé* must strike with the harmony: that means at the time in which the following principal note should be played." Frederick Neumann, however, states that Couperin's rule "often did not apply to his own music and consequently cannot be invoked to confirm the exclusive downbeat doctrine"[29]; he gives many examples from Couperin's works to substantiate this premise.

The various terms for the one-note grace could signify different functions. The one most familiar to us occurs when the one-note grace forms a dissonance with the bass on the beat and then resolves gracefully. This practice was antedated by the use of a purely decorative additional note (or, rarely, notes) inserted between the beats; its function was not to create dissonance but to embellish the melodic line and provide a smooth connection to the main note. Nivers's *Livre d'orgue* of 1665 was the first keyboard work to describe this *port de voix* (see p. 48), followed shortly by Bacilly's vocal treatise of 1668. Since Bacilly's work includes an extensive section on ornamentation but no musical examples, Neumann has deduced various types of *port de voix* from the *maître's* none-too-clear descriptions; these solutions are generally in line with information provided by other sources of the period.[30] Austin Caswell, in his translation of this treatise, has located many of the musical examples to which Bacilly refers, but Caswell's realizations of the ornaments may be open to question.[31]

A slender treatise by Danoville (1687) lacks the clarity and thorough treatment of Rousseau's treatises but offers some useful information about the *port de voix*, which

> makes a great liaison in the melody. Without its help, it is impossible to sing or to play with clarity. The *port de voix* is performed by cutting the preceding note in half in order to "carry the voice" by slurring the last half of its value to the main note. You will observe by these examples that one writes it by a small note. Celebrated composers use no other method, in order to leave in its entirety the note that must be divided.

Danoville thus furnishes early evidence for the grace note symbol that takes its time from the preceding note (Ex. 19).[32]

Lambert Chaumont's ornament table (1695) shows a *port de voix* in both ascending and descending movement.[33] It is denoted by a caret placed above and between the notes and is realized in the same

Ex. 19. Danoville's *port de voix*. Courtesy of Éditions Minkoff.

En montant.   *En descendant.*

Ex. 20. Chaumont, *port de voix* and *Récit de cromhorne*, mm.7–9.

manner as those of Nivers and Danoville. Chaumont employs the *port de voix* both alone and as a pre-beat preparation for trills, as can be seen in Ex. 20, from *Récit de cromhorne* (*Septième ton*). Numerous examples of this *port de voix* can be found in Louis Couperin's unmeasured preludes. Although they are written in whole notes, the structure is identical and includes the connecting slur.

The *port de voix* in J.-F. Dandrieu's ornament table, employing D'Anglebert's hook symbol, also is played before the beat (see Ex. 6).

Jean Rousseau's treatises for the voice and for the viol have differing realizations of one-note graces. All the *port de voix* (ascending) and *cheute* (descending) examples in his *Traité de la viole* fall before the main note in the manner shown in Ex. 21.[34] The ascending *port de voix*, slurred to the following main note, normally takes half the value of the preceding note. Rousseau indicates in his examples when it is appropriate to use this grace and advises:

> When the final cadence [G] ends with ascending movement by conjunct degrees and the penultimate note is of less value than a quarter note (and sometimes even a quarter note), one should always finish with a *port de voix*.

The *cheute* generally descends and is slurred to the main note. Unlike the *port de voix*, which usually takes half the value of the preceding note, the *cheute* is played quickly before the main note. Most often it is found in descending thirds, but it also occurs on adjacent notes of the same pitch (C), on a descending fourth (F), on an ascending semitone (G), and on a descending second (I). Rousseau describes the *cheute* on a descending fourth (F) as "very touching and appropriate for tender and languishing airs." The character of G is similar. H is a combination of an *aspiration* (see p. 94, below) and a *cheute*. Rousseau advises that

> in tender and moving pieces, one should often play a *cheute* instead of a trill, in order to render the melody more touching. In pieces that express something frightful and terrible, play the *cheute* in a brusque and precipitous manner.

In contrast, Rousseau's vocal treatise gives one-note graces that fall both before and on the beat (see Ex. 22):

> The *port de voix* using both the value and the pitch of the preceding note [falling before the beat] is made when one ascends by conjunct degrees from one note to another of greater value [a.].
> The *port de voix* using only the pitch of the preceding note [falling on the beat] is made by ascending from a short note to one that has twice the value or more, as from an eighth note or sixteenth note to a dotted quarter note or a half note [b.].
> In airs or *récits de basse*, the *port de voix* is made ascending and descending from a fourth and from a fifth [c.].[35]

In Rousseau's parlance, the one-note grace that falls on the beat is confined to those instances where the main note is at least twice as long as the preceding one. Rousseau does not use this form in a cadence, however, but employs the pre-beat one-note grace in Ex. 21, G. His vocal treatise describes the treatment of a similar cadential context:

> The penultimate note of every perfect cadence must be trilled when its value is not less than a quarter note or a dotted eighth note. But if the cadence is in ascending motion, the penultimate note is shorter than the afore-mentioned, and the preceding note is dotted, one should make the trill on the dotted note in order to finish with a *port de voix*. If this note is not dotted, however, make only the *port de voix*.[36]

Ex. 21. Rousseau's *port de voix* and *cheute*
(*Traité*). Courtesy of Éditions Minkoff.

EXEMPLE.

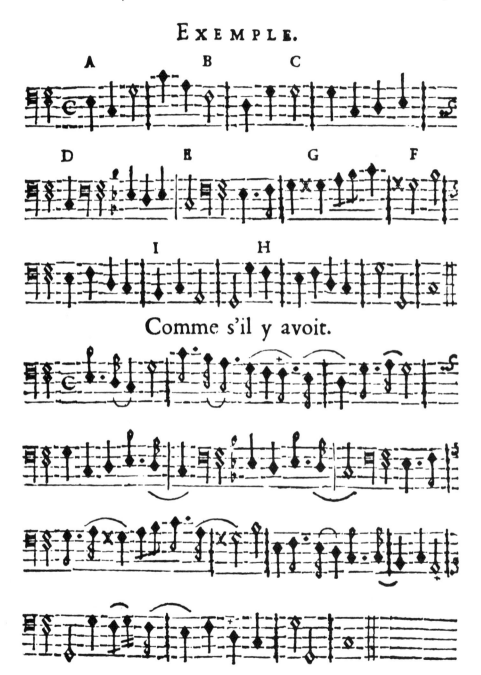

Comme s'il y avoit.

Ex. 22. Rousseau's *port de voix* (*Méthode claire*). Courtesy of Éditions Minkoff.

Ex. 23. Rousseau's cadence with a short penultimate note. Courtesy of Éditions Minkoff.

Thus on the last F♯ in Ex. 23, one would not use a trill but a *port de voix*, playing it as two sixteenth notes with the second slurred to the final G. In similar instances in sevententh-century clavecin music, today's performers take the time of these cadential one-note graces from the main note, but that may not have been the composers' intent.

The one-note grace that takes its value from the note marked with its symbol, seemingly first found in vocal music, began to be described late in the seventeenth century. Some of Loulié's one-note graces for vocal music employ a grace note: "Sometimes the *Petite Notte* takes its time value from the note that precedes it, and at other times from the note that follows."[37] His examples of the *port de voix* are also given in both forms.

Although in D'Anglebert's ornament table examples of the *cheute ou port de voix* clearly fall on the beat, his music contains many instances, as St.-Lambert trenchantly points out, where only a prebeat one-note grace is suitable. (St.-Lambert calls the one-note grace *port de voix* in all instances.) Implying that his own examples are the more customary in France, St.-Lambert suggests that D'Anglebert's realizations of the *port de voix* tend to be aberrations in keyboard music, although they are suitable for vocal music. The following excerpts are a paraphrase of St.-Lambert's section on the *port de voix*:[38]

> The rule of the *port de voix* means that one must play the note preceding the ornament sign twice instead of once when it is a step

Ex. 24. St.-Lambert's *port de voix*. Courtesy
of Éditions Minkoff.

lower or higher than the marked note. However, it has not been
definitely decided whether one should take the value of the added
note from that of the note with the symbol or from the preceding
note. In Mr. d'Anglebert's table, the time of the one-note grace is
taken from the marked note, but I doubt that this, although quite
proper for songs, would be the best manner of performing it in
harpsichord pieces. It is much more fitting to take the value of the
grace from the preceding note, so I would give Mr. d'Anglebert's
ornament as [shown in Ex. 24].

The symbol that Mr. d'Anglebert uses to mark the *port de voix* is
suitable, but one must note its similarity to the symbol for the mordent. They are identical, except that the symbol for the *port de voix*
comes before the note and that for the mordent after. Sometimes Mr.
d'Anglebert uses both symbols on one note, calling it a *chutte & pincé*
since he sometimes calls the *port de voix* a *chutte*. . . . Mr. Chambonnières uses the ascending *port de voix* only, marked with a cross.

Chambonnières's version of the *port de voix* (see p. 49) appears to fall
on the beat. This type of performance rarely produces a musical
effect in his works, however, so a grace like that in Ex. 24 is intended. Moreover, St.-Lambert would have discussed this realization if it were different from his own conception. He continues:

Mr. d'Anglebert does not explain how one performs the *port de voix*
when the preceding note is not on an adjacent scale degree; e.g., his
ports de voix approached by leap. In order to supply information
omitted by Mr. d'Anglebert, we must say that it is essential to distinguish three kinds of graces: the simple *port de voix*, the *port de voix
appuyé*, and the *demy port de voix*. All three are used in descending
movement, but only the first two in ascending movement.

The Descending *Port de voix* [see Ex. 25]
The simple *port de voix* is performed by striking the note that precedes the symbol twice, instead of once, assuming that it is only one

degree higher than the note that bears the symbol. The preceding note is never on the same degree [as the marked note] and is always an eighth or a quarter note.

The *port de voix appuyé* is performed by striking the note before the ornament three times. This ornament is suitable only for slow pieces, when the preceding note is a quarter note, not an eighth.

When the preceding note is two degrees higher than the marked note, one no longer strikes the preceding note twice to perform the grace, but the note that is between the marked note and the preceding note (a borrowing similar to that for the trill!).

The *demy port de voix* is used when the preceding note is two degrees higher than the marked note. It consists of playing the "borrowed" note only once, and is suitable for pieces in a fast duple movement, such as rigaudons or airs that have the same movement [the hook is turned in the opposite direction].

The simple *port de voix*, which calls for striking the note preceding the symbol twice instead of once, is used most frequently. The double symbol for the *port de voix appuyé*, confined to pieces in a slow tempo, is not encountered in D'Anglebert's works, but this ornament may nevertheless be used effectively on occasion. When

Ex. 25. Descending *port de voix*, St.-Lambert. Courtesy of Éditions Minkoff.

EXEMPLE.

Des Ports de Voix en descendant.

Port de Voix simple.　　Autre　　Port de Voix appuyé. Demy Port de Voix.

Manière de les exprimer.

Port de Voix simple.　　Autre　　Port de Voix appuyé. Demy Port de Voix.

the preceding note is a third higher than the main note, the note in between should be added in one of two ways: struck twice before the main note (slow to moderate tempo), or struck once just before the main note (fast tempo).

The Ascending Port de voix [Ex. 26]

    The *demy port de voix* is not used in ascending movement, but the observations for descending movement apply equally well to the remaining two types. The *port de voix appuyé* is more graceful ascending than descending, but one should bear in mind that it must be preceded by a quarter note and that it is only beautiful in slow pieces.

    No *maître* uses the *port de voix* when the preceding note is two degrees lower, for this would lack grace. The mordent is much better in this context, especially the ornament that Mr. d'Anglebert calls *chutte & pincé,* composed of a *port de voix* and a mordent.

According to St.-Lambert the note preceding the *port de voix* is never on the same degree as the main note. When that occurs, he labels the *port de voix* an *aspiration.* It has a plaintive quality and can be played above or below the main note (see Ex. 27).[39] The *port de voix* is slurred to the main note, while the *aspiration* is slurred to the preceding note. D'Anglebert does not employ St.-Lambert's caret for the *aspiration,* but uses the old familiar hook symbol. The performer must judge whether to play the one-note grace above or below the main note. Since D'Anglebert occasionally uses this ornament in a rapid tempo, it seems more appropriate to slur the grace to the main note (as in Rousseau's *cheutes,* C of Ex. 21).

St.-Lambert, writing eleven years after D'Anglebert's death, seemingly disapproves of the on-beat *port de voix* in keyboard music. The *maître* appears not to have discussed this matter with D'Anglebert personally, but simply to have worked from D'Anglebert's ornament table, taking it at face value, as we have. We might draw the conclu-

Ex. 26. Ascending *port de voix,* St.-Lambert.
Courtesy of Éditions Minkoff.

E x e m p l e.   E x p r e s s i o n.

Port de Voix. fimple. Port de Voix appuyé. Por de Voix fimple. Port de Voix app.

Ex. 27. *Aspiration*, St.-Lambert. Courtesy of
Éditions Minkoff.

sion that D'Anglebert was one of the first to incorporate into keyboard music the vocal practice of performing some one-note graces on the beat. St.-Lambert implies that even by 1702 on-beat performance is not common in keyboard music. Nevertheless, Jacques Boyvin's table of *agréments* (c.1690) includes *ports de voix* that are designed to take their time from the main note.[40]

St.-Lambert's point is well taken with regard to the performance of D'Anglebert's *port de voix*, for instances abound where only a grace before the beat yields a musically satisfactory result. D'Anglebert, like Nivers, Lebègue, and others, wrote out the pre-beat one-note grace a number of times. Some of these ornaments, indicated by symbol in his autograph manuscript, are realized in his edition, and include both pre-beat and on-beat forms (see p. 62). The thicket of embellishment in Ex. 28 is simplified and clarified by

Ex. 28. D'Anglebert, Gaillarde in A minor,
mm.4–6.

Ex. 29. D'Anglebert, Sarabande in D minor,
m.6.

making most of the one-note graces fall before the note with the
symbol. It is necessary to play the bass voice grace in m.5 before the
beat so that the arpeggiated chord can strike against the proper
harmony note. I have realized the grace at the end of m.5 as a *port de
voix appuyé*. These pre-beat graces contrast with the expressive one
in the soprano voice (m.6), which forms a 4–3 suspension with the
bass when played on the beat.

Performing the one-note graces in Ex. 29 on the beat would only
serve to obscure the harmony, rhythm, and melodic line—the very
opposite of the grace intended by ornaments (in the following examples, the middle staff shows the realization). A *port de voix* on the
beat in Ex. 30 would negate the intended dissonance of the G as an
accented passing tone, making this beat merely part of a dominant
seventh chord. The same can be said of Ex. 31, in which an E in the
soprano voice against a G in the tenor would be harmonically unin-

Ex. 30. D'Anglebert, Passacaille, m.3.

Ex. 31. D'Anglebert, Variations, m.40.

teresting (a consonance resolving to a dissonance) and also obliterate the rhythmic line.

Occasionally D'Anglebert employs the hook symbol for the one-note grace in a situation that seems to require playing the ornament either very short before the beat or simultaneously with the main note, with an immediate release. Ex. 32 provides such an instance, with the grace approached by a large leap from above. Rhythmic and melodic integrity can be maintained only by performing the grace very short. C. P. E. Bach says that this grace is "played so rapidly that the following note loses scarcely any of its length" and gives numerous examples of contexts in which it is used.[41] This very short, or "crushed," performance for the one-note grace, usually associated with a later, eighteenth-century style, may be required several times in D'Anglebert's works.

D'Anglebert frequently combines a *port de voix* with a downward arpeggio, and it makes good musical sense to play the one-note grace before the beat. Ex. 33 also contains a one-note grace in the alto voice that simply provides a consonant interval of a sixth with the bass when played on the beat (the D before the C♯ in the soprano voice is indicated by a *cheute* symbol in D'Anglebert's manuscript).

Ex. 32. D'Anglebert, Gaillarde in A minor, mm.21–22.

Ex. 33. D'Anglebert, Variations, mm.192–193.

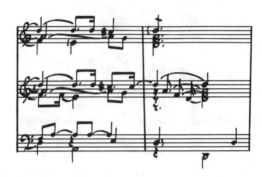

Ex. 34. D'Anglebert, Second Courante in D major, mm.3–4.

Ex. 34 calls for a *port de voix* before the beat in order to accommodate the mordent in the bass together with the arpeggio above. The simple act of playing graces before the beat in contexts such as this one does wonders for unlocking a seeming maze of ornament sym-

Ex. 35. D'Anglebert, Allemande in D major, m.15.

Ex. 36. D'Anglebert, Variations, mm.345–346.

bols. An on-beat performance of the *port de voix* in Ex. 35 would obscure the rhythmic interest of the subject in the bass voice.

An exception to the normal figured arpeggio may occur occasionally in D'Anglebert's works when its performance would be difficult. The last variation of the *Folies d'Espagne* contains several chords preceded by the symbol for the figured arpeggio (see p. 81). A performance like that of Ex. 18 is awkward because of the movement in the bass register, so perhaps only a one-note grace before the beat is intended, as in Ex. 36.

Why did D'Anglebert omit from his ornament table any mention of the one-note grace that falls before the main note? St.-Lambert, Chambonnières, Nivers, Raison, Chaumont, and Dandrieu indicate that the pre-beat form was customary in French keyboard music at this time. D'Anglebert may have forgotten it or may have taken its performance for granted, never for an instant suspecting that musicians three hundred years in the future would puzzle over a matter that was perfectly clear to him. His interest lay in promoting an expressive form of the one-note grace—one that creates a dissonance with the bass on a beat and then gracefully resolves. Such a usage in clavecin music probably appears for the first time in D'Anglebert's table, and it was widely copied. The downbeat form of the one-note grace originated later in the seventeenth century—a harbinger of the *style galant*.

Eighteenth-century writers observe that the pre-beat one-note grace was common in French music. According to Johann Joachim Quantz (1752), the little notes in

> Tab. XXII, Figs. 36 and 37 [see Ex. 37] must not be held, especially in a slow tempo; otherwise they will sound as if they are expressed with regular notes, as is to be seen in Figs. 38 and 39. This, however,

Ex. 37. Quantz, demonstration of how *not*
to play one-note graces. Courtesy of Eda
Kuhn Loeb Music Library, Harvard University.

would be contrary not only to the intention of the composer, but to
the French style of playing, to which these appoggiaturas owe their
origin. The little notes belong in the time of the notes preceding
them, and hence must not, as in the second example, fall in the time
of those that follow them.[42]

As late as 1768, Jean Jacques Rousseau depicted the *coulé* (written
with a grace note) as falling before the beat.[43]

Separate one-note graces, undifferentiated by either symbol or
name, create a perplexing situation. Moreover, the several symbols
(+, /, (, ∧, and the *pettite* note) for the one-note grace add to the
general confusion. The works of most clavecin composers after
D'Anglebert require analysis of the one-note graces to determine
whether they are best performed on or before the beat. By way of
contrast, J. S. Bach may have differentiated in the Aria from the
Goldberg Variations between the downbeat grace and the one that
falls before the principal note by using grace notes with one flag for
the former and two flags for the latter.

D'Anglebert's little hook symbol therefore seems to have multiple
meanings. In the majority of cases, the one-note grace is to be
played before the main note. Sometimes, when it enriches the harmony, it is to be played on the beat. Occasionally, it is played very
short before the beat or crushed with the main note and immediately released. In a few other cases, it may be played as an *aspiration*
and slurred to the preceding note.

But should the first note of the *chutte et pincé* (one-note grace and
mordent combination) also be performed before the beat in some
cases, despite the clear on-beat realization in D'Anglebert's table?
J.-F. Dandrieu's table depicts this ornament with the one-note grace

Ex. 38. Lully/D'Anglebert, *Ouverture de la Mascarade*, mm.7–8.

falling before the beat (see Ex. 6), a common usage in vocal music too, as Neumann points out.[44] Instances in D'Anglebert's composition of a simultaneous mordent with the *chutte et pincé* seem to indicate that the grace should come before the beat, thereby permitting the two mordents to sound together in parallel motion, as in Ex. 38.

Several times D'Anglebert approaches this ornament by leap, so an anticipated grace note adds fluency to the melodic line (see Ex. 39). In other cases, playing the grace note of the *chutte et pincé* on the beat draws attention away from the main note by placing an accent on an uninteresting note (*Variations*, m.208). Thus one could conclude that the first note of this ornament is to be anticipated in some contexts.

In the performance of D'Anglebert's one-note graces, gray areas subject to *bon goût* still exist. Nevertheless, these examples, together with those from F. Couperin cited by Neumann, lend authority to the belief that the performance of the one-note grace was governed by its context.

Ex. 39. Lully/D'Anglebert, *Air d'Apollon du Triomphe de l'Amour*, m.4.

Turns

The five-note turn, labeled *Double cadence* in the tables of Chambonnières and D'Anglebert, starts on the main note, descends a third, and returns to the main note. Usually found in cadential formulas, it appears in the Courante *La toute belle* (mm.9–10) by Chambonnières, whom St.-Lambert credits with its invention. Although this form of the turn is not found in subsequent ornament tables in France, it does emerge in the tables from Dieupart and the Möllersche Manuscript (see chapter 4), both of which appear to be modeled on D'Anglebert's. St.-Lambert says that the five-note turn is practiced by "everyone" and is appropriate when the turn is followed by some form of trill—a combination termed *double cadence* (see Ex. 40).[45]

When the turn is not followed by a trill, however, the four-note turn, corresponding to our modern turn and said to have been invented by D'Anglebert, is preferable (St.-Lambert incorrectly gives D'Anglebert's *Expression de la Tierce,* a variant of the four-note turn). Perhaps one reason for preferring a five note turn before a trill is that the upper auxiliary in the four-note turn would dilute the effect of the upper auxiliary in the trill since the turn is often found on the same pitch as the trill. In other instances, a five-note turn permits a more fluent melodic line.

D'Anglebert's manuscript furnishes several examples of written-out turns in both the five-note and four-note forms. In Ex. 41, all five notes are compressed into one beat in m.1, while the last note of the turn is allowed to fall on the following beat in m.4 (the edition uses a turn symbol in both cases). M.4 contains a rare occurrence of a five-note turn not followed by a trill, so one might wonder if D'Anglebert later intended it to be played as a four-note turn. He appears to use

Ex. 40. St.-Lambert's *double cadence.* Courtesy of Éditions Minkoff.

Ex. 41. D'Anglebert, Gaillarde in G major,
mm.1, 4; a. MS; b. edition.

the five-note turn and trill combination more frequently than do other composers, although it is common in Chambonnières's works. Louis Couperin's manuscript pieces contain relatively few ornaments (it is apparent that they can be added by the player), but there are similar constructions in which a five-note turn could be added advantageously before a cadential trill, as in his Sarabande in A minor, which employs a turn symbol before a trill (m.15).[46]

Although the turn–trill combination is encountered less often in the eighteenth century, Dagincour's *Pièces de clavecin* (1733) contains several examples (see mm.23–24 of the Sarabande from the first *ordre*). Rameau uses the turn–trill combination in a piece from his 1728 collection (see Ex. 42). A five-note turn does not lessen the effect of the dissonant upper-auxiliary D in the subsequent trill, as would a conventional four-note turn also beginning on D.

A written-out five-note turn in a cadential formula immediately preceding a note requiring a trill is found in a Praeludium in J. S. Bach's *Clavier-Büchlein* for Wilhelm Friedemann (see p. 59). His copy of D'Anglebert's ornament table indicates that he was aware of this turn and perhaps intended its use in selected locations in his own works. For example, the five-note turn avoids an awkward upward

Ex. 42. Rameau, Allemande, m.5.

leap of a seventh in the Courante from the third French Suite (BWV 814, m.27, copy from the Bach circle).

The fact that the five-note turn found its way into tables in Holland (Dieupart) and Germany (Bach and the Möllersche Manuscript) indicates its rather wide acceptance, although it is not found extensively. Its use can be considered whenever the combination of a turn and trill exists, particularly in seventeenth- and early eighteenth-century music.

Détaché

St.-Lambert credits D'Anglebert with defining the *détaché*, a detaching of the note before an ornament, and explains its importance:

> The practice of this *Détaché* is very necessary in certain pieces of lively movement, particularly when the note that precedes the trill is a degree higher, and that which precedes the mordent is a degree lower. It is not undesirable in other locations either, but good taste will determine where its use is necessary.[47]

Discussion

In concluding his chapter on ornamentation, St.-Lambert says that performers "can add ornaments even in places where they are not marked, omit those that are there if they do not enhance the piece, and add others to one's liking."[48]

François Couperin, however, did not grant players such freedom:

> I am always astonished, after the pains I have taken to indicate the appropriate ornaments for my pieces (of which I have given a fairly intelligible explanation under separate cover in a special Method, known as *L'Art de toucher le Clavecin*), to hear persons who have learnt them without heeding my instructions. Such negligence is unpardonable, the more so as it is no arbitrary matter to put in any ornament one wishes. I therefore declare that my pieces must be performed just as I have written them, and that they will never make much of an impression upon persons of real taste, as long as all that I have marked is not observed to the letter, without adding or taking away anything.[49]

It is likely that D'Anglebert too would have demurred, in view of the great care he lavished on his ornamentation. St.-Lambert may have been thinking of composers such as Lebègue, whose embellishment is much simpler, or of manuscript copies rather than a composer's carefully executed edition. When D'Anglebert wrote out the repeat of a phrase or section, he rarely changed the ornamentation (e.g., the Sarabande and Menuet in G major or the Gavotte and Menuet in D minor), although he occasionally varied the melodic line slightly. For this reason, a conservative approach of changing little or no ornamentation when sections are repeated would be appropriate. Why should we hesitate to play a beautiful piece of music the same way twice?

Modern-day performers should take care when adding ornamentation to French keyboard pieces. Rousseau cautions that

> a confusion of ornaments in airs and pieces only serves to diminish the beauty. This is why, as in architecture where one distributes ornaments with order and rules, it is necessary to practice ornaments in airs and pieces with order and rules . . . ornaments are a melodic salt that seasons the music and gives it flavor, without which it would be flat and insipid. As salt must be used prudently so that there is not too much nor too little (some meats require more and others less), so must the use of ornaments be applied with moderation. One must know how to discern where more are necessary and where fewer.[50]

Rousseau here is discussing instrumental music, in which *agréments* are not indicated as often or as carefully as in most clavecin music. However, his remarks temper St.-Lambert's advice about changing ornamentation in pieces. While it may be appropriate to add some *agréments* to pieces that are not already highly ornamented, one should resist the temptation to improve upon the composer's style by the addition of *coulades,* improvisatory flourishes, and doubling of voices. These elements of another period are foreign to this style. Although clavecin music of the seventeenth century is often technically simple, it offers its own pleasure and satisfaction. Michel-Pignolet de Montéclair (1736) describes these elaborate additions (*passages;* Ex. 43) somewhat reluctantly, for he seems bitterly opposed to the overly ornate Italian style they represent:

Ex. 43. Montéclair, illustration of *Passages*.
Courtesy of Éditions Minkoff.

> *Passages* are arbitrary, so one can use more or fewer, according to one's taste and bent. They are practiced less in vocal than in instrumental music. Especially at the present time, instrumentalists (in order to imitate the Italian taste) disfigure the nobility of simple melodies by some variations that are often ridiculous. The incomparable Lully, that great genius whose works will always be esteemed by true connoisseurs, preferred melody, beautiful modulation, pleasing harmony, appropriate expression, a natural and unaffected manner, and, in short, noble simplicity to the absurdity of some *Doubles* and musical eccentricities whose alleged merit only consists of wide stretches, roundabout modulations, harsh chords, din, and chaos. All of these fake diamonds reveal the composer's barren imagination, but ignorant people nevertheless continue to be impressed by them.[51]

This style seems to have become fashionable in France well after the seventeenth century had become history. Montéclair thus joins Foucquet and Ancelet in longing for the charm and simplicity of an earlier era. Born in 1667, Montéclair experienced the beauty of the *grand siècle* in his formative years. Despite the incursion of the Italian manner, the French continued to be known for notating their pieces with exactitude. According to C. P. E. Bach,

> there is a malicious prejudice against French keyboard pieces. These have always been good schooling, for this country is sharply distinguished from others by its flowing and correct style. All necessary embellishments are clearly indicated, the left hand is not neglected, nor is there any lack of held notes; and these are basic elements in the study of coherent performance.
>
> In justice to the French it must be said that they notate their ornaments with painstaking accuracy.[52]

Quantz notes that

pieces in the French style are for the most part *pièces caracterisées*, and are composed with appoggiaturas and shakes in such a fashion that almost nothing may be added to what the composer has already written. In music after the Italian style, however, much is left to the caprice, and to the ability, of the performer.

The [French style] requires a clean and sustained execution of the air, and embellishment with the essential graces, such as appoggiaturas, whole and half-shakes, mordents, turns, *battemens*, *flattemens*, &c., but no extensive passage-work or significant addition of extempore embellishments. . . . In the second manner, that is, the Italian, extensive artificial graces that accord with the harmony are introduced in the Adagio in addition to the little French embellishments. . . . French composers usually write the embellishments with the air, and the performer thus needs only to concern himself with executing them well. In the Italian style in former times no embellishments at all were set down, and everything was left to the caprice of the performer. . . . Thus it is undeniable that in Italian music just about as much depends upon the performer as upon the composer, while in French music far more depends upon the composer than upon the performer, if the piece is to be completely effective.[53]

Bach and Quantz thus provide compelling evidence for performing French music with discretion and according to the composer's indications.

St.-Lambert acknowledges that one cannot learn everything about ornamentation from written explanations because the *agréments* are performed in diverse ways according to the context. Since good taste must always prevail, it is preferable to hear them demonstrated by a master before attempting to play them. "According to the context" is a key phrase; for French ornamentation, especially the one-note grace and the trill, is open to a plethora of performance possibilities. Perhaps the only absolute in French ornamentation is *l'exception*. Since some contexts may permit more than one "correct" interpretation, the challenge to the modern player is both awesome and stimulating. Careful study will pay dividends, as one finds that the *agréments* begin to slip into place as effortlessly as they were intended.

French ornamentation still remains *un sujet très compliqué* because terminology and symbols for ornaments could vary greatly from one idiom to another, and even among composers of the same idiom. Montéclair indicates that they confused the French too, for even teachers "do not understand each other." The ornament tables cannot always be taken at face value. Apart from inaccuracies, e.g., Chambonnières's *port de voix*, it appears that many variant performance possibilities, particularly for the trill and the one-note grace, were simply omitted from the tables. Perhaps composers intended to give the commonest usages or, conversely, a new usage; perhaps they forgot the many *exceptions*, or perhaps the *agrément* could not be represented via notation. As early as 1636, Mersenne described an ornament resembling the grace that is played together with the main note and then released immediately (see Ex. 32):

> I am omitting several graces that the great *maistres* perform on the keyboard; for example, certain passages in which two adjacent tones are heard at the same time, while one finger holds one of the depressed keys so that the string which has been played retains its resonance.[54]

Since many ornaments were probably performed and taught by ear, it was no small matter to put them on paper accurately. Indeed, Montéclair complained that it was *presqu' impossible* to teach the *agréments* in writing.

Ornaments add brilliance and sparkle to rapid pieces and expressive elegance to leisurely ones. They adorn a melodic line and impart fluidity and grace. *Lent* pieces move with grandeur and profound beauty as the embellishment enchants the ear with inventive little twists and pungent dissonances. French music is the quintessence of refinement, the reflection of a society that valued the pursuit of the fine arts for the enjoyment of its privileged members. The French system of ornamentation became widely known in Europe by the first part of the eighteenth century. D'Anglebert was a leader in the codification of this system, and his table of ornaments attained international significance, influencing J. S. Bach, among others.

VI

TRANSCRIPTIONS, ARRANGEMENTS, AND VARIATIONS (*DOUBLES*)

To the modern reader, "transcription" may evoke an image of a luxuriant orchestral arrangement of J. S. Bach's organ Toccata and Fugue in D minor. Nevertheless, transcription was widely accepted and practiced in the Baroque period, and Bach himself artfully transcribed Vivaldi's violin concertos for harpsichord and organ. D'Anglebert, too, arranged lute and orchestral music for harpsichord so skillfully that, without the attributions, one might never suspect the origins of the pieces. The models he transcribed were probably among the most popular pieces at court. Modern readers should not overlook these works simply because they are transcriptions, for there are many treasures among them.

Although keyboard transcriptions are common in seventeenth-century French manuscripts, D'Anglebert provides the only examples in a harpsichord publication of the period. Bruce Gustafson's catalog lists 291 transcriptions of 189 pieces by Lully, most of which do not identify the arranger.[1] Music of the lutenists, particularly of Ennemond and Denis Gaultier, contributed a good share of the models for this repertory. D'Anglebert's transcriptions and *doubles* (variations) fall into three main categories (see Appendix 3 for a complete listing): lute pieces by Ennemond and Denis Gaultier, René Mesangeau, and Germain (or Pierre) Pinel; orchestral and other pieces by Lully; and *doubles* of keyboard pieces by Chambonnières, Louis Couperin, and Étienne Richard. The remaining pieces are *Sarabande.Marais* and four short arrangements from popular sources.

Transcriptions from Music of the Lutenists

D'Anglebert's fifteen transcriptions of lute pieces preserve music from the earlier part of the seventeenth century. They include twelve by Ennemond Gaultier *le vieux* (1575–1651) and one each by his cousin Denis Gaultier *le jeune* (1603–1672), René Mesangeau (d. 1638), and Germain Pinel (d. 1661), who probably wrote the sarabande attributed to Pinel.

Of the 119 sources for seventeenth-century French harpsichord music in Gustafson's catalog, only thirteen date from before 1650. Since these early manuscripts contain primarily lute transcriptions and popular music, rather than original pieces for the harpsichord, perhaps little was written for the instrument before the time of Chambonnières. The lute accumulated an impressive repertory because of its popularity in the first half of the seventeenth century, but as the century wore on the *épinette* and the clavecin began to come into their own. Since all three instruments have an evanescent tone, their compositional techniques (*style luthé* and free-voice texture) are similar.

D'Anglebert's transcriptions of lute pieces retain the broad melodic outline of the original piece (but have written-out embellishment and ornament symbols), add and subtract voices where needed, fill in

Ex. 1. Mesangeau, Sarabande, mm.1–4; a.
tablature transcription by A. Souris; b.
D'Anglebert's transcription.

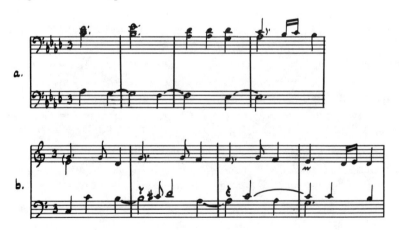

chords, and change the harmony occasionally. In his arrangement of Mesangeau's Sarabande (Ex. 1), D'Anglebert elaborates the static melodic line by means of dotted notes, additional pitches, and ornamentation, while maintaining a fluent accompaniment.

D'Anglebert's arrangements from the lute literature consist of an allemande, seven courantes, four sarabandes, two gigues, and one chaconne (no other source exists for several of E. Gaultier's pieces[2]). *Le vieux* Gaultier's Allemande in C major (*La Vestemponade*) is a fine classic example of this form—ceremonious and formal, with a well-constructed melody. His courantes are filled with intricate details, broken textures, and frequent syncopations, which are heard best at a slow tempo. Gaultier's gift for melody is shown advantageously in these courantes; particularly lovely are *Les Larmes* and *L'Immortelle*, which Titon du Tillet (1732) called one of Gaultier's best-known works. D'Anglebert's transcriptions of sarabandes from Pinel, Mesangeau, and the two Gaultiers are all attractive pieces. The beautiful *Sarabande du vieux Gautier* has the most-involved texture, with an accented second beat characteristic of many slow sarabandes.

E. Gaultier's two splendid duple-meter gigues present contrasting rhythmic devices (see p. 155 for examples and a discussion of duple- and triple-meter gigues). D'Anglebert arranged the gigue *La Poste* an octave higher, suggesting his desire to produce a work idiomatically suited to the harpsichord. Gaultier's Chaconne, written in 3/2 time rather than 3/4, is a striking piece with immediate appeal. A four-measure *Grand couplet* recurs at irregular intervals between intervening *couplets*, while an almost continuous procession of eighth notes permeates the intricate fabric.

These arrangements preserve the art of the famous French lutenists at its zenith in the mid-century. By 1732 lute music was seldom heard in Paris, for perhaps only three or four old players remained.[3] Titon du Tillet attributes this sad state of affairs to the difficulty of playing the instrument well and to the fact that it was seldom heard in concerts.

Transcriptions of Music by Lully

Lully's great popularity at the French court is reflected in D'Anglebert's many transcriptions for the royal patrons, who probably wished to hear their favorite pieces as often as possible. Further-more, since D'Anglebert spent a good portion of his time teaching the clavecin to the children of the royal family and of nobility, key-board arrangements of familiar melodies perhaps made useful teach-ing material.

According to Titon du Tillet, Lully's music had considerable im-pact on French taste. His pieces

> have a natural and graceful melody of a type totally different from those heard previously. . . . It is these pleasing licenses [dissonance treatment] that render Lully's works so beautiful, so brilliant, and so admirable, and that have saved our music from an often boring uni-formity and an insipid exactitude. . . . One finds in his *récits*, in his airs, in his choruses, and in all his instrumental works an appropriate and true character, a marvelous variety, a charming melody and harmony. His tunes are so natural and so ingratiating that even a person without an ear for music can remember them after four or five hearings. Both those of high rank and ordinary people sing most of the airs from his operas. The palace and the most beautiful apart-ments, as well as middle-class homes and the streets themselves, resound with them.[4]

With the complete support and encouragement of the king, Lully had an astoundingly successful career. He became known as "the incomparable Lully."

D'Anglebert's lavish praise of Lully's music in the Preface to *Pièces de clavecin* was not insincere. There can be no question that Lully possessed an extraordinary ear for melody and musical craftsman-ship. It is quite possible that the pieces D'Anglebert transcribed were the king's favorites, since he would have wanted to honor his employer's good taste.

He skillfully transcribed Lully's *Ouuerture* from *Cadmus et Hermi-one*, a five-part orchestral score. The most obvious alteration is the addition or subtraction of voices, a necessary part of writing for the harpsichord since nuances of shading are achieved in this manner.[5] D'Anglebert also arpeggiates the chords in the accompanying voices and adds an upbeat (see Ex. 2). Another visible change is the addi-tion of numerous ornamentation symbols, which are a trademark of D'Anglebert's writing. More subtle changes include reducing the wide spacing of the first chord and simplifying the inner voices. In adapting an orchestral bass line to the harpsichord, D'Anglebert

Ex. 2. a. Lully, *Ouuerture de Cadmus*, mm.1–
2; b. D'Anglebert's transcription.

achieves greater sonority by doubling octaves and repeating notes. He also changes fifths and octaves approached by parallel or similar motion, but one should note that Lully usually left the addition of the inner voices to assistants. Lully's whole note at the end of the first section of this overture is replaced with a pattern of two eighth notes followed by a half note (a common ending of D'Anglebert's dance settings), while the following upbeat is simplified to a single eighth note. As successive voices enter in the following fugue, other voices are dropped, so the texture is always manageable at a keyboard. Eighth notes are added to keep the motion flowing (e.g., in mm.16, 17, and 19); the texture is simplified; and parallel thirds, sixths, and tenths are omitted.

Exercising his artistic prerogative, D'Anglebert frequently changes the rhythmic values of Lully's outer voices. He imagines these works as a magnificent framework that can be effectively adorned with little rhythmic variations, turns of phrase, and ornamentation. They thereby reflect the transcriber's unique style and become eminently suited to the harpsichord.

Of D'Anglebert's twenty transcriptions from Lully, four are overtures (*Cadmus; Isis; Le Carnaval, Mascarade;* and *Proserpine*), while nine have a dance form included as part or all of the title:

Courante in G minor
Sarabande. *Dieu des Enfers*
Gigue in G minor
Menuet. *dans nos bois*
Menuet *la Jeune Iris*
Chaconne de Galatée
Chaconne de Phaéton
Passacaille d'Armide
Bourée. *Air de Ballet po* *Les Basques*

The remaining seven pieces are miscellaneous short airs or ballets:

Ritournelle des Feés de Rolland
Les Sourdines d'Armide
Les Songes agreables d'Atys
Air d'Apollon du Triomphe de l'Amour
Air de Ballet. Marche
Les Demons. Air de Ballet
2ᵉ Air des Demons

Thus the following stage works by Lully are represented in D'Anglebert's transcriptions:

Xerxés (1660) *Comédie en musique*	LWV	12
Ballet de la Naissance de Vénus (1665) *Ballet*		27
Le Carnaval, Mascarade (1668) *Mascarade*		36
Cadmus et Hermione (1673) *Tragédie en musique*		49
Thésée (1675) *Tragédie en musique*		51
Atys (1676) *Tragédie en musique*		53
Isis (1677) *Tragédie en musique*		54
Proserpine (1680) *Tragédie en musique*		58
Le Triomphe de l'Amour (1681) *Ballet*		59

D'Anglebert's arrangements make these imaginative pieces more accessible, for some of Lully's works have not been published in a modern edition and his stage works are seldom performed. The Gigue in G minor (for which no other source has been located) and the Courante in G minor may date from around 1660, since they have more in common with the courantes and gigues of Chambonnières and L. Couperin than with those of D'Anglebert. The Courante contains fine detailing of the lower voices; while the Gigue, which shifts between 3/2 and 6/4 time, reflects the fascinating rhythms of the French gigue from this period. These pieces make an excellent set with the *Sarabande Dieu des Enfers* ("God of the Underworld," from the ballet *La Naissance de Vénus*), in which the solemn melody moves majestically with a solid underpinning.

Lully's two menuets were written for the king's elaborate *coucher* (bedtime) ceremony (see chapter 1). Although the normal menuet tempo was rapid at this time, D'Anglebert marks his transcriptions *Lentement*, which is appropriate for their tranquil mood. An unobtrusive, fluent harmony accompanies the lovely melodies, perhaps selected by the king himself.

The two contrasting chaconnes, sets of variations constructed on a ground bass, complement each other. *Chaconne de Galatée* (marked *Lentement*) moves gracefully through ten variations of four measures each; but the lengthy and more energetic *Chaconne de Phaeton*—written for troops of Egyptian, Ethiopian, and Indian dancers—is designed to move in the customary, brisker tempo of the French chaconne. Jacques Hotteterre (1719) gives this particular chaconne as an example of a *mouvement* that is *gai* and the *Passacaille d'Armide* as one that is *grave*.[6]

The most monumental of these transcriptions, the *Passacaille d'Armide*, is also a large set of variations on a ground bass. It and *Chaconne de Phaeton* exemplify Sébastien de Brossard's definitions of these two forms, in which the passacaille is described as slower, more serious, and in the minor mode (see p. 164). The abundant ornamentation of *Passacaille d'Armide* furnishes further corroboration for a slow tempo. This magnificent passacaille, scored for five-part strings with interspersed solo flutes, fills nearly all of scene 2, a *divertissement* from act 5 of *Armide*. The use of flutes may be significant, for Brossard's *Dictionaire* mentions that the style associated with them is sad and languishing.[7] Passacailles often convey an *Affekt* of tenderness or lament, which in this instance is suggested by the text's warning to enjoy a short-lived happiness, because love reigns no longer in the winter of our years. Lully conceived the *Passacaille* on a grand scale. The instrumental portion transcribed by D'Anglebert is followed by three *récits*, each with an answering chorus, which are separated by ritornellos for flutes. Lully's instructions are to repeat the first *Récit & Choeur*, return to the beginning of the Passacaille, and continue to the end of the first *Récit & Choeur*.

Lully's other overtures and small-scale miscellaneous airs and dances are also interesting. *Les Songes agreables d'Atys* has considerable grace and charm; *Les Sourdines d'Armide* [*sourdines* meaning muted strings] expresses a haunting beauty; and *Air de Ballet. Marche*, from *Isis*, conveys the vigor of the dance.

Other Transcriptions

Sarabande. Marais is probably a transcription of a piece by Marin Marais, the famous gambist. No original has been located. It may have been written when Marais was about twenty years old, since D'Anglebert's manuscript has a posterior date of the late 1670s. The sarabande is a *tendre* piece, with an elegant, beautifully ornamented melody.

Finally, D'Anglebert's *Pièces de clavecin* contains arrangements of four well-known melodies of unknown origin: Two are slow gavottes marked *Air ancien* ("Ou estes vous allé" and "Le beau berger Tirsis"), and two are familiar melodies of a folklike nature called *Vaudevilles* ("La Bergere Anette" and "Menuet de Poitou"). D'Anglebert may have included them for their popular appeal, since he notes that they have a noble simplicity that is pleasing to everyone.

Not only did D'Anglebert consider his arrangements worthy of publication, but also he elevated transcription to an art form by means of his harmonic and rhythmic adjustments, use of *style luthé* and free-voice texture, simplification of orchestral textures, and added embellishment. He created idiomatic pieces for the harpsichord that can stand beside his own.

Doubles of Other Composers' Pieces

Keyboard *doubles* are in the tradition of the lutenists, who sometimes gave each part of an air twice, the repetition being an embellished version of the first rendition. D'Anglebert perhaps wrote the *doubles* based on other keyboard composers' pieces to honor his teacher, Chambonnières, and his colleagues Louis Couperin and Étienne Richard. He composed *doubles* for four of Chambonnières's courantes, two of his sarabandes, and one of his gigues; for the Allemande in G major by Louis Couperin; and for the sarabandes by Pinel and Richard. These *doubles* all appear in D'Anglebert's manuscript after the respective composer's original piece. Except for some added ornamentation, Richard's Sarabande is not altered, but D'Anglebert does make numerous small revisions in the given originals of Chambonnières's works that contribute to a fluent line. Most of D'Anglebert's *doubles* elaborate primarily the melodic line, but his attractive *double* for Louis Couperin's Allemande in G major subtly varies all the voices of this pseudopolyphonic piece. Composers well into the eighteenth century continued to vary their own pieces by means of *doubles*, but relatively few took D'Anglebert's route of embellishing other composers' works.

VII

THE ORGAN WORKS

Most clavecinistes of the period also played the organ, a profession that was highly regarded, according to Mr Ancelet, a forthright observer of the eighteenth-century musical scene:

> Let us now speak of wind instruments. I will begin with the organ, which is the father of harmony. For perfection it only lacks the ability to swell and diminish the sound. With the advantage of a continuous tone, no instrument can compare with it, for the organ forms by itself a concert of which the ensemble is perfect. What wonderful sounds, what variety in its different stops, what a career this majestic instrument provides to the musician who has some intellect and talent.[1]

D'Anglebert, who began his career as an organist, was employed by the Jacobins in 1660, when the organ was rebuilt. In the Preface to his *Pièces de clavecin*, he says that he is including five fugues (all on the same subject) and a *quatuor* in order to provide a sample of what he had previously written for the organ.[2] After being appointed *Ordinaire de la musique de la chambre du roy pour le clavecin* in 1662, he probably shifted his attention to the harpsichord because of the demands of his new position. The six organ selections in *Pièces de clavecin* are D'Anglebert's only organ works. They may have been written in the early 1660s, making them roughly contemporaneous with François Roberday's *Fugues et caprices* (1660) for organ or instruments.[3] Roberday (1624-1680) purchased an important title as one of the Queen's *Valets de chambre* in 1659. He had personal as well as professional ties with D'Anglebert, for the latter married Roberday's sister-in-law; and Roberday's wife, Charlotte Champagne, was godmother to D'Anglebert's son Nicolas.

Before Guillaume-Gabriel Nivers's first organ book in 1665, organ music in France was predominantly imitative. The definition of fugue in seventeenth-century France refers only to imitative tech-

118

nique and not to the structure generally associated with the term: "The simple fugue is a pure and simple imitation of the subject in which the parts enter after each other in similar motion."[4] The French *fugue grave* has the reserved character of a ricercar or fantasia, while the *fugue de mouvement* conveys the livelier movement of a canzona.

Very little French organ music has survived between the polyphonic organ works of Jean Titelouze (c.1562-1633), the noted Rouen organist, and the compositions of Roberday. Charles Racquet (organist of Notre Dame in Paris from 1618 to 1643) wrote twelve *Versets de Psaumes en duo sur les 12 modes* and a lengthy *Fantasie* in which the subject is transformed in four continuous contrapuntal, contrasting sections.[5] The Oldham Manuscript, dating from the 1650s, contains organ works by Louis Couperin: 33 fugues (some entitled *Fantasie*), two preludes, six *basses de trompette,* two duos, and 27 plainsong settings.[6]

The organ works of D'Anglebert and Roberday reflect the influence of the Frescobaldi school, transmitted via Johann Jakob Froberger, who was acclaimed during his visit to Paris in 1652. Despite the great turmoil and civil strife of the *Fronde* uprising against Mazarin, a concert with some 80 voices and as many instruments was given in Froberger's honor at the chapel of the Jacobins. A sarcastic account of the magnificence of this event appeared in *La Muse historique.* . . . . "Lettre du 29 septembre 1652":

> . . . Ayant en ce lieu réunies
> Mille charmantes harmonies,
> Mille et mille accents délicats,
> Dont même Orphée eût fait grand cas
> Enchantèrent de leurs merveilles
> Plus de douze cent trente oreilles. . . . [7]

Jean Loret, the author of this poem, found it "ridiculous" that all this splendor was not intended for the gods, or even for kings and queens, but for a certain German *piffre* ("stout person"). This *très médiocre personnage*, who was the Emperor's organist, can only be Froberger. His work was well known in Paris, for he and Chambonnières knew and respected each other.

Froberger's monothematic fugal works employ the transformation of the subject in a succession of short sections in varied time signatures.[8] A ricercar may contain from three to five sections; its countersubjects are usually more animated than its subjects; and cadences are found at the ends of sections. Froberger's technique involves continual entries of the subject and answer (but rarely transposition of the subject), great variety in the harmonization, and little emphasis on episodes. His canzonas and capriccios have lively subjects and slow harmonic rhythm, are mostly in fugal variation form, and usually include a section in triple meter or gigue rhythm.

The *Advertissement* to Roberday's *Fugues et caprices* states that three of the pieces are by Frescobaldi, Ebner, and Froberger, and that Roberday's subjects come from de la Barre, Coupperin [*sic*], Cambert, D'Anglebert, Froberger, Betalli, and Cavalli. Froberger's Ricercar I from the 1656 collection forms the basis of the fifth fugue in Roberday's edition, with a third section added, but the pieces by Frescobaldi and Ebner have not been identified. The chief difference between Roberday's fugues and caprices is rhythmic; and his pieces exhibit Froberger's traits of sectional construction and thematic transformation. Both Roberday and Froberger follow the Italian fugal practice of writing in *partitura,* or open-score notation, which makes it possible to perform the pieces with instruments.

D'Anglebert's five fugues also resemble Froberger's "Italian" style but are written in keyboard score. D'Anglebert expands and divides the form, however, making each section a complete fugue containing 30, 40, 38, 33, and 53 measures respectively, as compared with the 20, 25, 23, and 17 measures in the sections in Roberday's sixth Fugue and Caprice. D'Anglebert uses the first subject as the basis for the remaining fugues (see Ex. 1).

Fugue graue pour l'orgue, marked *fort lentement* and written in common time with doubled note values, conveys the sombre mood of a ricercar. The second fugue is in a slow compound duple meter with doubled note values (the time signature of 3 indicated triple movement in a variety of contexts), while the third fugue, in standard common time, employs a dotted rhythm. The conjunct motion, undotted rhythm, and 12/8 time of the fourth fugue resemble an Italian giga, in contrast to the dotted rhythms and compound duple meter of the last fugue. These compositions present an interesting study of French time signatures that affect tempo (see chapter 3). This usage appears to have been intentional on D'Anglebert's part, for the Preface to his edition refers to these fugues as being varied in different

Ex. 1. D'Anglebert's five fugue subjects.

mouvements. The first and third fugues are both in common time, but the larger note values of the first indicate a slower tempo. Likewise, the second and fifth fugues are in compound duple meter, but the 6/4 time and smaller note values of the fifth specify a faster tempo. The fourth fugue's 12/8 signature (Italian in origin) implies the quickest tempo of all. Thus the first fugue is the most majestic and *grave* (also because it is marked *fort lentement*), the second is very slow, the third resembles the slow tempo of a conventional seventeenth-century French allemande, the fourth is lively, and the fifth is probably moderate.

D'Anglebert's four-voice fugues do not modulate, and they use internal cadences only occasionally. The fugues are constructed of entries of the subject and its (usually) tonal answer in a pseudo-counterpoint in which successive entries are made without regard to maintaining the identity of the individual voices (in contrast to the voice leading of *partitura* notation). In general, D'Anglebert's fugues follow the seventeenth-century French practice of being imitative but not overly contrapuntal; i.e., fugal entries are often harmonized rather than being involved in the interplay of independent melodic lines. Although countersubjects and other fugal devices are infrequent or nonexistent, stretto is often found. According to Nivers, the common order of fugal entries is from top to bottom, but D'Anglebert follows his own formulas: TASB, TABS, BTAS, BTAS, and BTAS respectively. The second fugue is unusual for a French fugue, having an entry order of subject, answer, answer, subject. Occasionally D'Anglebert takes a fragment from the subject and tosses it among the voices in quick succession, as in mm. 33-36 of the second fugue and mm. 29-31 of the third.

D'Anglebert's fugues succeed in large part because of their rhythmic vitality (including cross-rhythms and hemiolas) and their varied harmonic and dissonance treatment. Harmonic restlessness, the propelling force of D'Anglebert's style, is created by his use of suspensions and other nonharmonic tones, seventh chords, 6/4 sonorities, false relations, oscillations between major and minor forms of the same triad, and avoidance of root-position triads. His fugue subject uses both the lowered and the raised sixth degree of the scale to produce a typical seventeenth-century harmonic ambiguity. In the course of the fugues, the other modal scale degrees (3, 4, and 7), also found in both forms as a result of the linear movement, are often responsible for creating false relations and other dissonances. D'Anglebert's second fugue includes cross-rhythm between the top voice and the lower voices (m.29), stretto (m.26), a dissonant passing tone (or an augmented mediant triad, beat 2 of m.28) emphasized with a trill, and a cross-relation (m.29), as shown in Ex. 2.

Ex. 2. D'Anglebert, Fugue 2, mm.26–30.

The chromaticism of these fugues, a trait borrowed from the Italians, is found only occasionally in D'Anglebert's harpsichord works. Also confined primarily to the organ pieces is the frequent use of the 6/4 sonority (which is used cadentially in the harpsichord pieces). D'Anglebert resolves one dissonance to another principally in his organ works and in his gaillardes, sarabandes, and the passacaille. His first four fugues close with pedal points—the first two fugues on the dominant only, the third and fourth on the dominant followed by the tonic.

A trademark of D'Anglebert's writing is the large number of ornamentation symbols, so it is not surprising to see as many in the fugues as in the harpsichord pieces. It has been suggested that Roberday's works should be similarly ornamented, but no satisfactory answer can be given to this question at present. Roberday says that three of the works in his volume are by Italian or German composers (it may be significant that D'Anglebert's *Quatuor*, written in a polyphonic Italian style, has no ornamentation whatever). Moreover, approximately 30 years separate Roberday's *Fugues et caprices* and D'Anglebert's *Pièces de clavecin*. Although the latter's fugues were probably written around 1660, it is possible that the ornamentation was added later.

D'Anglebert's only other known organ piece is a *quatuor* (piece in four parts) based on the Kyrie of Gregorian Mass IV, *Cunctipotens Genitor Deus*. Directions in the Preface of his *Pièces de clavecin* specify three different keyboards plus the pedalboard, with stops of equal weight and different timbre in order to distinguish the different voices. The *Quatuor* appears to be the earliest composition in French literature requiring this manner of performance, and D'Anglebert's explicit instructions seem to indicate that it is unusual. Each voice of this *stile antico* jewel presents the three subjects, given only partially in a few instances, in a different order. The first subject employs the first six notes of the first phrase of the Kyrie (but with a raised leading tone); the second subject consists of the second phrase; and the third subject includes the first four notes of the third phrase. The polyphony of the *Quatuor* is austere, without the chromaticism of the fugues. Beautiful suspensions, following one after another, produce a sublime effect quite unlike that of the fugues. The skillful treatment of the three subjects, which continually overlap, resembles that of Frescobaldi's fantasias. It is unusual writing for the period, for, as noted above, the French tended to harmonize subjects rather than work them out contrapuntally. The *quatuor* for four keyboards did not achieve great popularity, for only a few isolated examples are found after D'Anglebert; e.g., in J. A. Guilain, *Pièces d'orgue* (1706) and Louis Marchand, *Livre d'orgue* (c.1732).

Organ Registration

D'Anglebert held the position of organist to the Jacobins in 1660, when Estienne Énoc, one of the leading builders of the time, was instructed to enlarge the organ and revoice the reeds, tierces, and mixtures.[9] Énoc was to add an echo division containing a five-rank Cornet, but a little later he was asked to enlarge the *Grande orgue*, making it truly an instrument of magnificent proportions (an asterisk marks the new stops):

Montre	8'*	Bourdon	16'*	Trompette	8'
Prestant	4'*	Bourdon	8'	Clairon	4'
Doublette	2'	Grosse Tierce	3-1/5'*	Cromorne	8'*
Fourniture	IV	Flûte	4'	Voix Humaine	8'
Cymbale	III	Nasard	2-2/3'	Tierce	1-3/5'
		Quarte de Nasard	2'*		
		Larigot	1-1/3'*		
		Flageolet	1'*		

The remainder of the organ consisted of a Cornet on the *Récit;* a 37-note Cornet and Voix Humaine on the *Écho;* and a Montre 4', Flûte 4', Nasard, Tierce, and Fourniture II on the *Positif.* In view of the size of this instrument, it is unusual that there is neither a pedal division nor an 8' stop on the *Positif.* Perhaps stops that did not need repair were omitted from the contract, or maybe the case for the *Positif* was old and small, for the contract calls for replacing a Régal (probably 8') by a Fourniture II.

D'Anglebert gives no suggestions for registration, but from instructions in editions by Nivers, Lebègue, Boyvin, and others of the period, we can infer that fugal works use reed stops or the *Jeu de Tierce* combination:

Nivers (1665) says that fugues *graves* can be played with the *gros Jeu de Tierce* (consisting of the Bourdon, Prestant, Tierce, and Quinte on the *Grand orgue;* and possibly the Doublette and stops of 8' or 16' pitch) with tremulant, or the Trompette without tremulant.[10] One ordinarily uses only the Bourdon with reed stops; and the Cromhorne can even be played alone. Nevertheless, with the Trompette one may add the Bourdon, Prestant, Clairon, and sometimes even the Cornet. With the *Voix humaine* one can add the Bourdon, Flûte, and the tremulant with slow wind. Other fugues can be played on a *Jeu médiocre* or the *petit Jeu de Tierce* on the *Positif* (the same pitches as the *gros Jeu de Tierce,* but on the *Positif*).

Lebègue (1676) specifies the Bourdon, Prestant, Trompette, and Clairon of the *Grand orgue* for a *fugue grave,*[11] as does Antoine Furetière (1685).[12]

For a fugue *grave,* Jacques Boyvin (c.1690) prescribes the Trompette, Bourdon, and Prestant, with the Cromhorne coupled from the *Positif,* and adds that fugues can also be played on the *Positif* with the "Cromhorne, bourdon [8'] and a 4' foundation stop."[13]

Lambert Chaumont (1695) distinguishes between a *fugue gaye,* which is played on a bright combination of the *petite tierce*—Bourdon, Montre, Nasard, etc. (probably on the *Positif*), and a *fugue grave* employing the Trompette, Clairon, and Nasard (on small organs, the Cromhorne and Bourdon 4').[14]

Three of Louis Couperin's fugal works in the Oldham Manuscript are designated for the Cromhorne (Nos. 20, 57, and 65) and four are to be played on the *tierce du Grand Clavier avec le tremblant lent* (Nos. 29, 58, and 63, while No.64 has no reference to the tremulant).[15]

Given these prescriptions for registration from the late seventeenth century, performers might best choose their own for D'Anglebert's fugues. His fourth fugue, in an Italian giga style, however, would probably be more effective on the Cromhorne combination or on Chaumont's *petite tierce.*

A much later instruction for the registration of the four-keyboard *quatuor* was furnished in 1770 by Dom Bédos de Celles, who specifies:

Soprano voice: Trompette of the *Récit,* or two 8' stops (if they are separate)
Alto voice: small *Jeu de Tierce* of the *Grand orgue*

Tenor voice: Cromorne and Prestant of the *Positif*
Bass voice: *Pédale de Flûte,* or *Jeu de Tierce*

Alternatively:

Soprano voice: Cornet of the *Récit*
Alto voice: Trompette and Prestant of the *Grand orgue*
Tenor voice: *Jeu de Tierce* of the *Positif*
Bass voice: *Pédale de Flûte*

> This manner of playing a Quatuor is difficult to perform since one is
> scarcely able to play the two upper parts because of being obliged to
> use only the right hand on two different manuals, or one must use
> only the left hand to play the middle parts on two separate manuals.
> But one can also play the *quatuor* on three keyboards.[16]

The performance of D'Anglebert's *Quatuor* would be easier on a
French organ of the period, since the manuals are closer together. It
is possible to use a modern instrument if one plays the tenor voice
on the top manual, the alto voice on the middle manual, and the
soprano voice on the bottom manual.

D'Anglebert's organ works, which represent a high point in
French keyboard polyphony, were probably written just before
Nivers's *Premier livre d'orgue* (1665) inaugurated a new direction for
French organ writing. In the next period numerous short pieces in
widely varying styles, grouped together by key or mode, were intended to alternate with portions of the Mass. These groups often
included a short fugue, but the remaining movements (generally
homophonic) were designed to take advantage of the French organ's
coloristic possibilities. This new style was to dominate French organ
writing for many years.

VIII

CLASSICAL SUITE ORDER IN FRANCE

During the seventeenth century, French composers increasingly tended to group dances by key in a predetermined order, commonly an allemande–courante–sarabande (A–C–S) pattern, which is also found in lute collections. Scholarly opinion has held that the French keyboard dance suite never achieved the standard order of allemande–courante–sarabande–gigue (A–C–S–G). Both D'Anglebert and Elisabeth-Claude Jacquet de La Guerre, however, made significant contributions to the stabilization of the keyboard suite by their consistent use of the A–C–S–G order.

An important manuscript source for keyboard music, the Bauyn Manuscript (post 1676), contains numerous A–C–S groupings in various keys.[1] Isolated examples of classical suite order are seen in a set by (?) Jacques Hardel (A–3C–S–G) and another by Louis Couperin in C minor (A–C–S–G). The Parville Manuscript (c.1689) is also organized by key groups: prelude, A–C–S, and other dances.

Chambonnières's two editions of 1670 contain eleven key groupings, most of which follow the A–C–S order. A pavanne sometimes substitutes for the allemande, while some *ordres* (suites) have no gigue. In two instances a gigue is placed as the second dance of a set. Two suites in Chambonnières's engraved collections are in reality disguised A–C–S–G order.[2] The suite in D minor from the first book contains a gigue entitled only *Les Barricades* (misnamed a "courante" in the Bauyn Manuscript); and in the second book, the gaillarde from the suite in C major is entitled *Sarabande grave* in the Bauyn Manuscript (with different barring).

Nicolas-Antoine Lebègue's first book (1677) contains dances in five key groupings, each headed by a prelude. The first two sets contain pieces in a minor key followed by others in the parallel major key. Although one grouping utilizes the A–C–S–G pattern, little standardization of dance order is found, since not even the A–C–S order is used consistently. Lebègue's *Second livre de clavessin* (1687) includes six key groupings that are called *Suittes* (possibly the first use of this term in clavecin literature), of which two are ordered A–C–S–G.

La Guerre's recently discovered *Pièces de clauessin* (c.1687) represents the first known consistent A–C–S–G grouping in French harpsichord editions. Each' of the four suites is preceded by an unmeasured prelude (called *Tocade* in the fourth suite), and each of the gigues is followed by one or more miscellaneous dances. La Guerre's 1707 book contains two suites also in this order (they are rearranged in the modern edition). The one in D minor opens with an allemande and *double* (called *La Flamande*), followed by a courante and *double,* sarabande, gigue and *double* in 6/4 time, gigue in 6/8 time, two rigaudons, and a chaconne. The suite in G major is composed of an allemande, courante, sarabande, gigue, menuet, and rondeau.

The order of the four key groupings in D'Anglebert's *Pièces de clavecin* is given in Table 1 of Appendix 1. Three of the four groups begin with a prelude, followed by the classical suite order A–C–S–G. Some dances occur in multiples, but the order remains unchanged. The second gigue, which appears at the end of the long set in G major, bears a notation indicating that it is to be played between the first gigue and the gaillarde. The set in G minor has a courante, a sarabande, and a gigue from Lully that are inserted immediately following D'Anglebert's dances of the same names. Apparently D'Anglebert did not wish to alter the A–C–S–G order by placing these dances by Lully at the end of the key grouping with the other transcriptions. Each of D'Anglebert's gigues is followed by a gaillarde (called *Tombeau* in one instance) and miscellaneous dances.

Earlier (c.1660s–1670s), D'Anglebert's autograph manuscript presents evidence of his intent to group dances in an A–C–S–G order, since the C major and G major pieces are placed in this order (see Appendix 1). The other key groupings are incomplete. Numerous leaves were left blank, to be filled in at a later date. The middle of the manuscript reads as follows (only D'Anglebert's pieces are in his own hand):

No.18	Chaconne du Vieux Gautier in C major (transcription by D'Anglebert)
No.19	Three pages with the *Air de M. Lambert* (for voice and figured bass)
	One blank ruled page
	Three pages giving the letter names of notes on the treble staff and figured bass exercises
	One blank ruled page
No.19a	One page with a fugue fragment for keyboard
	One leaf cut out
	Four blank ruled pages
No.19b,c,d	Three pages, each with a melodic line that uses only a part of the page
No.19e	Two pages with an untitled keyboard piece
No.20	D'Anglebert's Gaillarde in A minor
No.20a	Three pages with a gigue-like keyboard piece
	One blank ruled page
No.20b	One page with a melodic fragment
	Seven blank ruled pages
No.21	Variations in D minor by D'Anglebert
No.22	*O beau jardin*
No.22a	*Double* by D'Anglebert
No. 23	Prelude in D minor by D'Anglebert
	Two blank ruled pages, but with "Allemande." inscribed at the beginning by D'Anglebert, indicating that he intended to fill these pages.
No.23a	Four pages with a melodic line in rough draft with numerous cross-outs. The last part of the title, "Courante" (in D'Anglebert's hand) is written over "Concerto" (?).
No.24	Sarabande in D minor by D'Anglebert
No.23a	Two pages with a continuation of No.23a, marked "presto"
	Five leaves cut out between the above two pages
No.25	*Courante du Vieux Gautier* in D minor (transcription by D'Anglebert)

Thus the blank pages and missing leaves occur as follows: 20 pages between Nos.18 and 20, twelve pages between Nos.20 and 21, six pages between Nos.23 and 24, and twelve pages between Nos.24 and 25. The blank pages and miscellaneous pieces and fragments in other hands appear in the middle, while there are substantial uninterrupted sections of D'Anglebert's work at both the beginning and the end of the manuscript. When his normal practice was to write a whole set of pieces in one key, why is there but one piece in A minor? Perhaps D'Anglebert planned to have his pieces appear in classical suite order. Since a gaillarde normally followed a gigue, he left sufficient blank leaves before the Gaillarde in A minor to accommodate a prelude, allemande, courante, sarabande, and gigue (as well as *doubles* and additional courantes) in the same key. The leaves following the Gaillarde could have been intended for yet other pieces in A minor.

A similar situation exists at No.23, where it appears that D'Anglebert is beginning a suite in D minor. The Prelude is followed by two blank pages with the heading of "Allemande." in his hand (the title of "Courante" at No.23a—which is partially written over—is also in his hand). He then left space in order to accommodate a courante and its *double*, or perhaps a second courante (these four pages, in another hand, were added later). After his Sarabande at No.24, he again left several leaves for a gigue and perhaps other dances. Thus it is entirely possible that D'Anglebert's plan for this manuscript included four complete prelude–allemande–courante–sarabande–gigue suites: the existing ones in the keys of C major and G major, plus two that are incomplete in A minor and D minor. D'Anglebert's placing the miscellaneous transcriptions in G minor from Lully at the end of the manuscript, following his own Prelude, suggests that his desire to include them superseded his original plan for his own pieces, since he was running out of space.

Three previously unknown pieces by D'Anglebert (alluded to in the Preface to his edition) have recently been discovered in an English household manuscript bearing the title "Mary Rooper her Booke" ("Elizabeth Roper: her Booke 1691" is written at the end): Courante, Sarabande (with *double*), and Gigue in A minor. Blank leaves before the Courante suggest that an allemande was planned. Since D'Anglebert's autograph manuscript contains only one piece in A minor (the Gaillarde), preceded by many blank leaves, it seems likely that these dances in the Roper Manuscript were designed to accompany it. Thus the existence of the dances in A minor gives weight to the view that D'Anglebert planned his manuscript to contain four A–C–S–G suites and that he was the first claveciniste to use this order consistently.

After D'Anglebert, French keyboard music shows little observance of this standard suite order. Louis Marchand's two suites (1702-1703) follow it, but Gaspard Le Roux's works (1705) continue a general adherence to an A–C–S pattern, with no consistency as to the use and location of the gigue. L.-N. Clérambault's *1er Livre de pièces de clavecin* (1704) provides an example of classical suite order by afterthought. Notations on pp.15 and 16 with the *Augmentation de la Suite en C. sol ut b.mol* state that this piece is a "Prelude that must be played before the Allemande" and "The Courante and the Sarabande must be played before the Gigue, immediately after the Allemande." Charles (François?) Dieupart, who emigrated to London, used the following order in his c.1705 Amsterdam edition of the *Six suittes de clavessin:* overture, allemande, courante, sarabande, gavotte, menuet or passepied, and gigue. Rameau did not use the A-C-S-G order in his books, and François Couperin employed it only in his fifth *ordre*.

The classical suite order favored by D'Anglebert, La Guerre, and Marchand was short-lived in French keyboard music, for the new century brought a decline in the use of the traditional dance forms and an increased popularity of character pieces with descriptive titles.

IX

THE UNMEASURED PRELUDES

The unmeasured prelude (*prélude non mesuré*), one of the most fascinating areas of music interpretation since 1600, is found in several French harpsichord editions and manuscripts from the late seventeenth and early eighteenth centuries. Unbarred in the conventional sense, it is sometimes notated with whole notes only, sometimes with mixed note values, and other times with interspersed sections of measured notation. The clavecin prelude is related to the improvisatory lute prelude, which developed before the mid-century as a means of testing the tuning and of introducing the following pieces. Ex. 1 shows the tablature for an unmeasured prelude by Denis Gaultier.[1]

Although the English continued to use measured notation, Thomas Mace (1676) provided a colorful description of the lute prelude:

> The *Praelude* is commonly a *Piece of Confused-wild-shapeless-kind of Intricate-Play*, (as most use It) in which no perfect *Form*, *Shape*, or *Uniformity* can be perceived; but a *Random-Business*, *Pottering*, and *Groop-ing*, up and down, from one *Stop*, or *Key*, to another; And generally, so performed, to make *Tryal*, whether the *Instrument* be *well in Tune*, or not. . . .[2]

Ex. 1. Gaultier, Prelude. Sys. 1, courtesy of Éditions Minkoff; and my transcription.

The fourteen preludes by Louis Couperin in the Bauyn Manuscript constitute the earliest known unmeasured preludes for harpsichord and the largest number by a single composer. Ten of these, as well as an additional two (and two more of questionable authorship), are contained in the Parville Manuscript.[3] Couperin's preludes, often large structures occupying as much as seven pages in the Bauyn Manuscript, are written completely in whole notes; slurs define harmonic notes to be sustained and passages of melodic or ornamental interest. Slurs connecting two notes probably have an articulation function; e.g., a pattern identical to the *port de voix* (see p.85) occurs many times. Other two-note slurs sometimes have the form of the descending *cheute* or the *aspiration*. Four of Couperin's preludes contain measured sections, a device used in La Guerre's and Rameau's editions. Couperin's preludes are carefully constructed, but the scribe has not always aligned the treble and bass notes properly. His writing is marked by many long melodic and scale passages, occasional chromaticism, frequently shifting key centers, and a number of sequential patterns; e.g., the Prelude in C major contains a sequence at the end of the first system (see Ex. 2). Couperin's preludes are outstanding examples of this genre; they

Ex. 2. L. Couperin, Prelude in C, Bauyn MS
facsimile. Courtesy of Éditions Minkoff.

Ex. 3. St.-Lambert's slur in disjunct motion.
Courtesy of Éditions Minkoff.

are freely improvisatory, harmonically interesting, and feature an inventive melodic line shifting between the treble and bass registers.

The seventeenth-century French composers use the slur imaginatively in their unmeasured preludes to indicate notes to be sustained. St.-Lambert writes that "the slur is employed particularly in preludes and sometimes also in pieces, but more rarely," and advises holding the following disjunct notes because of the slurs (see Ex. 3).[4]

When slurred notes move in conjunct motion, however, one holds only the first and last notes covered by the slur (see Ex. 4). The location of the slur in disjunct movement indicates whether to hold the notes. If the ends of the slur are close to the noteheads (A), hold only the first and last notes; but if the slur is turned in the opposite direction, so that it includes all the notes (B), hold them all (see Ex. 5). The application of this principle may not have been widespread, so one would be wise to work only with primary sources, not modern editions.

Some confusion, rather than elucidation, about the function of the slur is provided by a letter from Lebègue to an Englishman who had asked for advice in performing his preludes. Lebègue wrote that one plays the notes in the exact sequence in which they appear, and that "the thin curved line beginning at the low note and continuing to that above means that it is necessary to hold all the notes this line encircles, without releasing any after striking, in order to preserve

Ex. 4. St.-Lambert's slur in conjunct motion. Courtesy of Éditions Minkoff.

Ex. 5. St.-Lambert's moveable slur. Courtesy of Éditions Minkoff.

the harmony."[5] Gustafson, however, cites examples of notational inconsistency in Lebègue's Prelude in F major, suggesting that the dissonant E is held at the beginning of the first system but not at the beginning of the second system because the tie marks before the chord in the second instance imply that only the F major chord is sustained (see Ex. 6). St.-Lambert's instructions and examples above indicate that Lebègue's remarks on the usage of the slur are incomplete—a not uncommon fault. Thus the dissonant E in Ex. 6 would

Ex. 6. Lebègue, Prelude in F major. By permission of the Houghton Library, Harvard University.

not be sustained in either instance because one does not hold notes
that move in conjunct motion.

Composers who included preludes in their editions generally
thought it necessary to devise a clearer form of notation when their
works were to reach a wider audience, so they experimented with
differing styles. Notation for the *prélude non mesuré* was problemati-
cal in the seventeenth century, as can be seen from Lebègue's Preface to his first book:

> I have endeavored to notate the preludes with as much clarity as
> possible, as much for consistency of performance as for the playing
> style of the harpsichord, in which one separates the notes of chords
> and strikes them one after the other very quickly, rather than striking
> them together as on the organ. If one encounters something a little
> difficult and obscure, I hope the clever person will attempt to remedy
> it, in view of the great difficulty in rendering this method of prelud-
> ing intelligible to everyone.[6]

Ex. 7. D'Anglebert, Prelude in D minor. a.
MS, courtesy of the Département de la musique, Bibliothèque nationale, Paris; b. edition, reprinted by arrangement with Broude
Brothers Limited *(facing page)*.

"Rendering this method of preluding intelligible to everyone" was indeed a challenge that few composers sought—and at which even fewer succeeded.

D'Anglebert's Preludes

Three of the four suites of D'Anglebert's *Pièces de clavecin* open with unmeasured preludes in a unique notational style. The music is written in a mixture of whole and eighth notes with occasional ornamental sixteenth notes and is barred sporadically. D'Anglebert is the only composer from whom we have unmeasured preludes in both autograph and printed forms. Those in the manuscript (1660s-1670s), in semibreve notation, conform closely to the preludes in the *Pièces de clavecin*. However, some ornaments that are written out in the manuscript are indicated by symbol in the edition; the slurring is more precise in the edition; and occasional bar lines are added, usually to indicate the end of a phrase or section. Ex. 7 contains facsimiles of the Prelude in D minor from the manuscript and the *Pièces de clavecin*.[7]

Ex. 8. D'Anglebert, Prelude in G major, sys. 3.

In his edition, D'Anglebert customarily employs slurred whole notes for the harmonic structure and eighth notes for nonharmonic tones and melodic passages (with a few ornamental sixteenth notes). Slurred eighth notes are sometimes used to bolster the harmonic structure, and nonharmonic and melodic tones are occasionally notated in semibreves. Occasionally, the slur appears to have an articulation function, as in the two *port de voix* figures in the second bar of Ex. 7b. It seems that eighth notes have a more uniform rhythmic value, while whole notes can be played freely—sometimes like a rolled chord and other times deliberately and slowly. In Ex. 8, from the Prelude in G major, whole notes play a melodic role, while the single eighth notes have an anacrusic quality.

D'Anglebert's notational practice assists the performer, for one can immediately identify the slurred structural notes, as opposed to those with a nonharmonic or melodic function. The vertical alignment is more accurate and more easily grasped than that in Louis Couperin's preludes. D'Anglebert's unique slurring is the clearest in this genre, since slurs seem to be employed exclusively to mark notes to be sustained. A slur has application to one note only, and ties are not used or needed since the slur indicates the duration of the note. In Ex. 9, the first D in the bass register, suspended over a

Ex. 9. D'Anglebert, Prelude in D minor, sys. 3–4.

Ex. 10. D'Anglebert, Prelude in G minor,
sys. 3–4.

long pedal point on the dominant, resolves to C♯ , and is followed
by another suspension in the treble register.

In D'Anglebert's preludes, a continuous, expressive melodic line
constantly shifts between the treble and bass registers. Unlike Louis
Couperin, D'Anglebert tends to avoid repeated motives and sequences, but he is partial to irregular groupings. The beginning of a
slur often indicates a rhythmic stress (but not when used with notes
in the middle of rolled chords), while single eighth notes occurring
before a slur may be interpreted as upbeats. The melody sometimes
grows out of the harmonic texture, rather than being superimposed
on the harmony, and sustained notes of the melody then help to
constitute the harmonic structure. Melodic notes in Ex. 10 are
marked with an *x,* and a pattern beginning with an eighth note
occurs twice.

In the manuscript preludes, D'Anglebert wrote out the more-
involved ornaments and rarely used symbols other than those for
the simple trill and the mordent. In the edition he mostly indicated
ornaments with symbols (see Ex. 11). It is interesting that he often
substituted the trill *appuyé* symbol for the simple trill, particularly in
contexts for which Rousseau would prescribe a main-note trill.

The Prelude in G minor contains two instances of a common

Ex. 11. D'Anglebert, Prelude in G major,
sys. 11–12; a. MS; b. edition.

Ex. 12. D'Anglebert, a. Prelude in G minor,
sys. 5; b. Allemande in G minor, m.21.

D'Anglebert cadence trademark, which in his dances is sometimes
notated with an arpeggio symbol (see p.80). The notation in Ex. 12a
suggests that the arpeggio is not to be played quickly, but evenly, as
D'Anglebert's ornament table illustrates. Therefore, the passages in
Exx. 12a and 12b would be played identically, except that one would
restrike the D in the upper voice at the end of Ex. 12a and the G in
the bass register at the end of Ex. 12b (as noted above, there are no
ties in D'Anglebert's preludes).

D'Anglebert's manuscript contains an additional attractive short
prelude in C major, notated completely in semibreves. It does not
present many difficulties, for it has relatively little melodic movement and consists almost entirely of harmonic texture in which the
melody is embedded. Its brevity suggests that it may have been
intended as a teaching piece.

D'Anglebert's unmeasured preludes, with their many seventh and
ninth chords, suspensions and other dissonances, are filled with
rich sonorities, which produce expressive preludes of profound
beauty. The avoidance of sequential patterns and any semblance of
rhythmic pulse makes the form one of totally convincing improvisation, while the precise slurring indicates clearly which notes are to
be sustained and their rhythmic placement. Surely no better form of
notation could be devised, for D'Anglebert clarifies the structure for
the performer without sacrificing the improvisatory element. His
notation was not adopted by later composers, for interest in the
prélude non mesuré was waning by the end of the century. Thereafter,
it is found in editions only occasionally, rather than as the rule. The
pirated Amsterdam edition of D'Anglebert's works (1704-1705) omits
the preludes, giving weight to the belief that the unmeasured prelude was not popular outside France.

Three anonymous unmeasured preludes in the Parville Manuscript are thought by some to be in D'Anglebert's style, but Kenneth Gilbert declined to include them in his edition of D'Anglebert's works. All three are short, roughly comparable in length to the Prelude in C major from D'Anglebert's manuscript, with opening gestures resembling his. The tritone with leading tone is prominent in the beginning of the Preludes in C major and F major, and the sixth and seventh degrees of the scale are emphasized in the Prelude in G major. The final cadence of the Prelude in F major is the only cadence that is similar to D'Anglebert's. The harmonic treatment of the preludes is in keeping with D'Anglebert's style, but the scale passages of the Prelude in C major are not typical of his work, nor is the slurring style or the symbol for the mordent (although these elements of style could be attributed to the scribe's preference).

While it seems unlikely that these pieces are by another known composer of unmeasured preludes, it is possible that they were written by someone who left no signed unmeasured preludes, e.g., François Couperin. Whatever the case, these fine examples of the *prélude non mesuré* deserve to be better known. Their brevity makes them suitable for those who wish to become acquainted with this style, and their structure is easily grasped.

Preludes by Other Clavecin Composers

The unmeasured preludes by D'Anglebert and Louis Couperin furnish the most outstanding examples of this genre. Other French composers experimented with differing forms of notation, but none achieved D'Anglebert's notational clarity or his harmonic richness and melodic beauty. It is interesting to observe how they grappled with the thorny problem of notation for the unmeasured prelude. Chambonnières, the only major seventeenth-century claveciniste from whom we have no preludes, may have considered the notational difficulties insurmountable.

Lebègue included five unmeasured preludes in his first book (1677) (see Ex. 6), the first published attempt to convey the movement of the unmeasured prelude, but none in his second book. Lebègue's note values vary from breves to 32nd notes, with many passages written in measured, but unbarred, notation. Quarter notes as well as half notes are used for free arpeggiation, but the vertical alignment is occasionally inaccurate or unclear. Diagonal bar lines, found in all but the first prelude, have an obscure meaning; in some instances they may be intended to set off harmonic changes or to indicate pauses. Slurs indicate notes to be sustained, although they also are used to tie notes. Despite his good intentions, Lebègue's notation is sometimes mystifying (see the passage quoted on p.136 above, giving the performer license to correct faults in the notation).

All but one of the four preludes in Elisabeth-Claude Jacquet de La Guerre's first book of clavecin pieces follow Louis Couperin's precedent for a measured section in the middle and a brief unmeasured close.[8] The fourth suite opens with a *Tocade* (reflecting Italian influence) in which a short unmeasured introductory section launches into brilliant passage-work. La Guerre's notation is the most similar to D'Anglebert's, for it uses whole notes primarily to indicate harmonic structure and eighth or quarter notes to designate melodic or nonharmonic tones. The third prelude opens with an extended sixteenth-note run in the treble register that is echoed by the bass, but thereafter the sixteenth notes recur sporadically. Unike D'Anglebert, La Guerre places slurs over or to the right of notes (or groups of notes) to indicate that they are to be sustained. Occasionally, she employs an oblique line in the same contexts, the significance of which is not clear. La Guerre's edition might have included instructions for the performance of these preludes, for some of the prefatory pages in the only extant copy in Venice have been cut out. Her preludes, which often include sequences, tend to fall into recognizable patterns (see Ex. 13). La Guerre's notation seems experimental, but her directions are somewhat more precise than Lebègue's. It only remained for D'Anglebert to add his refinements; though simple, they clarify the composer's intentions.

Louis Marchand's first book (1702) contains an early instance of a French prelude written in conventional notation. Most of the notation of the prelude in his second book (1703) is measured but unbarred, with whole notes indicating free arpeggiated passages and quarter notes the nonharmonic tones. One finds a distinct rhythmic pulse in Marchand's prelude, together with three- and four-voice part writing.

Two preludes from Louis-Nicolas Clérambault's *Pièces de clavecin*

Ex. 13. La Guerre, Prelude in G minor.
Courtesy of the Conservatorio di Musica
Benedetto Marcello, Venice.

Prelude

(1704) also consist primarily of measured notation, with whole notes used only for free arpeggiated passages. The Prelude in C major contains numerous scale passages, sequences, and imitative writing, suggesting a dramatic, rapid performance and indicating a change of character for the prelude. In contrast, the chromatic Prelude in C minor, marked *Fort tendrement*, uses small motivic cells to construct melodic lines and relies heavily on sequence.

The four short preludes of Gaspard Le Roux in his *Pièces de clavessin* (1705) are the only known published unmeasured preludes notated in semibreves, in the style of Louis Couperin. They may have been written much earlier than their publication date, although it is also possible that Le Roux considered this notation adequate for his purpose—it is less cryptic than Lebègue's, for example. Two of the preludes contain a few figured bass numbers. Stylistically, Le Roux's

Ex. 14. Le Roux, Prelude in G minor. Courtesy of Éditions Minkoff.

Prelude

preludes have much in common with those of Louis Couperin and
D'Anglebert; e.g., their nonrhythmic quality and their melodic line,
which is exchanged between the treble and bass registers (see
Ex. 14).

A youthful work by Jean-François Dandrieu, *Pièces de clavecin courtes
et faciles de quatre tons differents* (early 1700s), contains four short,
simple unmeasured preludes in semibreve notation that fall into
easily recognizable rhythmic patterns. Dandrieu gives performance
directions (see also his ornament table, p.73): "The slur requires one
to hold the note with which it commences to that with which it ends,
although there may be others between the two notes."[9]

Jean-Philippe Rameau's *Premier livre de pièces de clavecin* (1706)
opens with a prelude consisting of a short unmeasured section followed by a measured portion in 12/8 time. Measured three- and
four-part writing is found intermixed in the opening section, with
only the few whole-note arpeggios left to the performer's discretion.
The unmeasured portion of the prelude seems to present a declama-
tory, recitative-like introduction to the measured section.

Descendants and mutants of the *prélude non mesuré* made occasional appearances through the eighteenth century. Nicolas Siret's *Second livre de pièces de clavecin* (1719) includes both a measured prelude and an unbarred prelude containing measured notation with a few free whole-note arpeggiated chords interspersed. Durocher's unbarred prelude (*Pièces de clavecin*, 1733) employs an unusual notational style with alternating whole and half notes in a type of triple movement; black note heads are found in chordal form with many ledger lines. Michel Corrette's *Premier livre de pièces de clavecin* (1734) includes two barred preludes containing measures with whole- or half-note chords marked *Arpeggio*. His ornament table realizes the arpeggio as a broken chord moving in sixteenth notes (like an Alberti bass). Balbastre's Prelude (1777), consisting of unbarred broken chords and runs in measured note values and regular patterns, implies a virtuoso performance.

François Couperin's eight preludes in his *L'Art de toucher le clavecin* (1716) are written in measured notation for "the ease with which one can teach or learn them." Thus Couperin believed it was better to write in a measured style than to have his intentions misinterpreted. These preludes, intended to serve as introductory pieces to the *ordres* of his first and second books, are to be played freely, unless marked *mesuré*:

> A prelude is a free composition in which the imagination is allowed free expression. It is, however, extremely rare to find talented persons capable of producing them instantly. Those who use these non-improvised preludes should play them in a relaxed manner without being concerned about strict rhythm, unless I have expressly indicated it by the word *Mesuré*. Thus, one may venture to say that in many ways music (like poetry) has its prose and its verse.[10]

Although the prelude was customarily improvised, few players were skilled at this art, and Couperin preferred that his metrical preludes be used as introductions to the respective *ordres* of his pieces.

The Unmeasured Prelude as Toccata or *Tombeau*

The unmeasured prelude has been compared to the harpsichord toccata and *tombeau*.[11] Froberger's toccatas (like some of Frescobaldi's) open with a whole-note chord that Frescobaldi earlier indicated was to be arpeggiated.[12] The openings of some unmeasured preludes might be related to this practice; e.g., the *Prelude . . . a l'imitation de M Froberger* by Louis Couperin, which has been compared to Froberger's first toccata for organ,[13] as well as his *Plainte faite à Londres*.[14] D'Anglebert likewise arpeggiates the tonic chord at the beginning of the Prelude in D minor (Ex. 7), and follows it with other sonorities over the tonic pedal.

After the opening chord, Froberger's toccatas have passage-work in mixed note values, alternating between upper and lower registers, followed by a fugal middle section and sometimes a return of the fantasia style. Louis Couperin may have modeled his four preludes with internal measured sections after this pattern. The comparison with toccata style is perhaps more relevant to Couperin's preludes than to D'Anglebert's, for the latter's lack the sweeping scale passages characteristic of the toccata.

The *tombeau*—a piece in memory of a deceased teacher or acquaintance—is also thought to have influenced the unmeasured prelude. Froberger's *Tombeau fait à Paris sur la mort de Monsieur Blancheroche* carries instructions to play "very slowly with discretion and without observing any metrical pulse," while his Lamentation for Ferdinand III is marked *lentement avec discretion*. From other contexts, it seems that *discretion* means to play with rhythmical freedom.

Although there are elements of the toccata and of the *tombeau* present in some unmeasured preludes, the *prélude non mesuré* is still a unique form having a connection with the lute prelude in its style of notation and in its improvisatory quality. Both the clavecin prelude and the lute prelude were intended to open a program. François Couperin says, "Not only do the preludes provide a pleasant announcement of the key of the pieces to follow, but they also serve to limber the fingers and to let the performer try out an unfamiliar instrument."[15] This description implies that the prelude was not considered a virtuoso piece. Couperin also speaks of students knowing only the little prelude with which they began study. D'Anglebert's preludes are most effective at a relaxed tempo that allows the luxuriant harmonies and lovely melodies to flow effortlessly.

Another slant on the function of the prelude is provided by Pierre Richelet (1680) and Jacques Ozanam (1691), who define the prelude as the first piece "played on some musical instrument for the purpose of establishing a rapport with the audience."[16]

That the prelude was a carefully thought-out improvisation is suggested by the similarity between D'Anglebert's preludes in his manuscript and in his *Pièces de clavecin*. Only a few composers dared to tackle the problem of conveying an improvisational style via notation. It is remarkable that Louis Couperin and D'Anglebert were able to do so. D'Anglebert's notational refinements simplify the performer's task, make these lovely pieces more accessible, and provide insights into the interpretation of Couperin's semibreve preludes.

X

THE KEYBOARD DANCES

Allemande

By D'Anglebert's time, the allemande had found its way into the repertory intended for a seated audience. Michel de Pure speaks of "some allemandes, sarabandes, and other dances that have more the majesty of vocal music than the vigor of the dance . . . the complex harmonies, while pleasing to the ear, only inhibit the feet."[1] These pieces are meant for instruments such as lute or theorbo, on which they can be played "for the quiet and serious entertainment of a seated audience." In a letter to Henri Du Mont in 1655, Constantijn Huygens refers to his allemandes, saying: "I have written some pieces less lively than the sarabandes or gigues."[2]

The allemande in the seventeenth-century French keyboard suite resembles that of the French lutenists. It is marked by a pseudopolyphonic texture with points of imitation, irregular phrases, ambiguous phrase structure, and broken chords (*style luthé*). With a few exceptions, the allemande is ceremonious and formal. Some were intended to be played even more slowly than usual; e.g., Denis Gaultier's tribute to a deceased acquaintance, which is identified in one source as *Allemande grave* and in another as *Tombeau.*[3] Louis Couperin instructed the performer of his Allemande in D major that "it is necessary to play this piece very slowly." The disjunct movement and syncopation of his *Allemande grave* in F major contrast with the smoothly flowing lines of most allemandes. Chambonnières prescribed *Lentement* for his *Allemande dit[e] L'Affligée;* the music itself does not require a slower tempo, but its title ("The Afflicted") describes its *Affekt.*

On the other hand, Lebègue and D'Anglebert have allemandes marked *gaye* and *gayement* respectively. In both instances, the texture is thinner than the average allemande, and a faster tempo is desirable. These pieces may reflect English influence, for Thomas Mace (1676) describes *Allmaines* as "very *Ayrey,* and *Lively;* and Generally of Two *Strains,* of the *Common,* or *Plain-Time."*[4] While the Italian *allemanda* could have widely varying tempi (Arcangelo Corelli's *Sonata da camera* of 1685 includes allemandes marked *Largo, Adagio, Allegro,* and *Presto*), most of the French composers continued to conceive this dance in a stately style. Sébastien de Brossard (1705) describes the *Allemanda* as a "*Symphonie grave,* ordinarily with two beats, often with four" [*symphonie* referred to any instrumental piece]; and Jacques Ozanam (1691) states that the allemande has four slow beats.[5] Conventional French keyboard allemandes of this period are written in common time (with the quarter note equivalent to the half note of 3/2 time), indicating a leisurely pace. The faster allemande became more common in the eighteenth century, so in 1768 Jean Jacques Rousseau speaks of two types: one is *gravement,* but the other, patterned after a popular dance in Switzerland and Germany, is performed with a great deal of gaiety.[6] D'Anglebert's traditional allemandes are serious pieces that convey the image of a "content spirit enjoying good order and calm," as Johann Mattheson described this dance form.[7]

D'Anglebert's four allemandes from the *Pièces de clavecin* are only slightly longer than previous examples, but the almost continuous sixteenth-note motion gives the impression of even greater length. The phrase structure of the allemandes in G major, G minor, and D minor (like that of earlier allemandes) is irregular and ambiguous, with a constant interplay of motives. For example, all the voices of the Allemande in G major have important roles in producing an intricate fabric (see Ex. 8).

In contrast, D'Anglebert's spirited Allemande in D major (marked *Gayement*) is constructed of an accompanied melody skipping about from one voice to another. The light, buoyant texture results from the accompanying voices having longer notes than the voice with the melody. His Allemande in C major, with a thin homophonic texture, features a continuous melody in the soprano voice. Since its structure resembles that of Lebègue's *Allemande gaye* in G minor, D'Anglebert probably would have marked the piece *gayement* if he had published it.

The allemandes of D'Anglebert's successors also demonstrate this

newer style and tempo. While Louis Marchand's first allemande in
Pièces de clavecin, 1702, is traditional, the one in the 1703 suite employs the faster 2 time signature and the melody in the soprano
voice throughout. Two allemandes in Gaspard Le Roux's *Pièces de
clavessin* (1705) are marked *gaye* (C time) and another two *grave* (2
time). Curiously, his time signatures for fast and slow movement
seem reversed. Rameau wrote magnificent allemandes in both the
older, pseudopolyphonic form (C time) and in the simpler style (2
time). François Dagincour, in *Pièces de clavecin*, 1733, opened his first
ordre with a fast allemande in 4/8 time, followed by one in the traditional manner in C time. Old and new elements are intertwined in
the superb allemandes of François Couperin. While in many instances he retains the *style luthé* and pseudopolyphony of the earlier
common-time allemande (e.g., the beautiful *L'Exquise* from his
fourth book, 1730), Couperin ventures into the sphere of the faster
allemande with *L'Ausoniéne* (*Ordre* 8), to be played *Légérement et
marqué* (4/8 time), and *Le point du jour* (*Ordre* 22), to be played *D'une
legereté modérée* (2/4 time).

Courante

The courante was a favorite dance at the court of Louis XIV. Long
afterward people fondly remembered the time when the Sun King
"danced the courante better than anyone at court, giving it an infinite grace."[8]

Seventeenth-century French keyboard courantes shift frequently
between 3/2 and 6/4 time, but most employ a time signature of 3
with six quarter notes per measure. Courante rhythmic patterns may
be combined in various ways to produce phrases of varying lengths
that follow no prearranged sequence or form, so it is rare to find two
successive measures of identical rhythm.[9] The rhythmic ambiguity,
blurred contours, and irregular phrase lengths of the courante make
it a distinctive dance of the period.

Although it was originally identified with a fast tempo, Curt Sachs
notes that the "lively *courante* had become a *danse très-grave*" by the
mid-seventeenth century in France; and Pierre Rameau (1725) mentions that "the Courante was formerly very fashionable; it is a most
solemn dance that suggests a nobler style than the others. . . . "[10]

Jacques Bonnet (1723) refers several times to "the gravity and nobility of serious dances . . . among others . . . , the courantes of
France." Describing the balls of the court, Bonnet says that only
danses graves & sérieuses, where the beautiful grace and nobility of the
dance appeared in all its glory, were played while the king was in
attendance. After the wedding of the Duc de Bourgogne (1697), one
could see the noble and serious dances (like the Bocanne, the Canaries, the Passepied, and the Duchesse) being discarded year by year:
"They have scarcely kept the Branle, the Courante and the Menuet."[11] This passage implies that the canaries, passepied, and menuet, dances all identified with a more rapid tempo at this time, were
also performed as slow dances at the height of the "old court." In
the play *Le Grondeur* by Brueys and Palaprat (1691), after fast dances
including the menuet, gavotte, and rigaudon, the character Lolive
suggests a slow dance to his victim, M. Grichard:

> LOLIVE: Vous voulez peut-être une danse grave et sérieuse?
> M. GRICHARD: Oui, sérieuse, s'il en est, mais bien sérieuse.
> LOLIVE: Eh bien, la courante, la bocane, la sarabande?[12]

The French courante spread its influence to Germany, where Johann Gottfried Walther (1732) substantiates the slow tempo: "The
tempo . . . that courantes . . . require is the most solemn of all."[13]
Johann Mattheson (1739) calls the courante the "lutenist's master-
piece, especially in France . . . on which his effort and art can be
employed advantageously."[14] D'Anglebert transcribed several splendid lute courantes by Ennemond Gaultier, whose pseudopolyphonic
texture resembles that of some clavecin courantes.

With Lebègue's first book (1677), a distinction is made between a
courante grave and the piece that follows, a *courante gaye.* Aside from
another *courante grave,* the remainder of Lebègue's courantes are
unmarked. D'Anglebert does not indicate a tempo for his numerous
courantes and *doubles,* all of which are written in a uniform, more
homophonic style. The fine, newly discovered Courante in A minor
(see Appendix 2) employs the same stylistic elements found in all
his other courantes. The beauty of D'Anglebert's melodic lines is
enhanced by a slow tempo and well-defined rhythm.

Subsequently, the clavecin courante tended to decline in popularity. Rameau's courantes sometimes use sequences and other regular
groupings (in contrast to the earlier courante's continual change of

rhythmic pattern), as do some courantes of Couperin *le grand*. The latter's courantes encompass a marvelous variety, such as the one from *Ordre* 1, which offers an alternate melodic line even more highly embellished than the original. The superb courante from Rameau's 1728 collection exemplifies particularly well an old form in more modern dress.

The courante continued to be identified as a slow dance in France; e.g., Montéclair's *Principes de musique* (1736) gives a *Courente à la maniere Françoise—Grave*. The contrast between the French and the Italian styles of this dance can be seen in the *Quatrième concert* from François Couperin's *Concerts royaux*, which includes both a *Courante Françoise* in 3/2 time (marked *Galamment*) and a *Courante a l'italiéne* in 3 time (marked *Gayement*). With rare exceptions, the courante seems to have enjoyed a more uniform character than most of the other dances in France.

Sarabande

The sarabande was transformed from the fiery Spanish *zarabanda*, which was brought to France near the beginning of the seventeenth century, to a slow dance favored in the French musical scene by the end of the century.[15] In 1630 Voiture writes of violins playing a sarabande so fast and gay that "everyone rose up joyfully, and, by skipping, dancing, flying about, pirouetting, and leaping, arrived home."[16] Daniel Devoto remarks that the sarabandes of Denis Gaultier and Chambonnières "still do not possess the solemnity of the later sarabandes, although they are not as undisciplined and noisy as those of the preceding period."[17]

Although it is uncertain when the slow French sarabande, with its more complex rhythmic devices, began to develop, Mersenne gives examples of two types of sarabande in *Harmonie universelle* (1636).[18] In 1657 Henry Du Mont marked an instrumental sarabande *Gayement* (*Meslanges*, II), but in 1668 de Pure referred to the "majesty" of allemandes and sarabandes (see p.148, above). Pierre Richelet (1680) defines the sarabande as "a type of *danse grave*," but gives another side of the dance when demonstrating the use of the word in a sentence: "The violins will play a very lively sarabande."[19] Furetière (1690) describes the sarabande as having *un mouvement gay &*

amoureux,[20] and in England, Thomas Mace (1676) says that it has "the *Shortest Triple-Time . . .* more *Toyish,* and *Light,* than *Corantoes.*"[21]

In 1703, Brossard compares and contrasts the sarabande and menuet: "One can best understand the sarabande as a kind of menuet whose movement is *grave, lent, sérieux & c.*"[22] Similarities exist among the forms of sarabande, menuet, and chaconne (e.g., uniform phrase structure), but one distinguishing characteristic is tempo. According to Michel L'Affilard (1705),

> When [3/4 time] is played *gravement,* as in the sarabande and the passacaille, one beats slowly in three equal quarter notes. The chaconne is beat in the same manner, but more quickly. Menuets have two unequal beats [half note and quarter note] because of their liveliness.[23]

At the turn of the century, then, the sarabande seems to be identified primarily with a slow tempo, although both types continued to be used. In 1736, Montéclair's *Principes de musique* gives two contrasting sarabandes: one marked *Grave* and the other *Sarabande legere—Mouvement de Chacone—Gay.*

The thin, transparent texture of many early clavecin sarabandes suggests a tempo that is perhaps *Moderato* to *Allegretto.* Sarabande texture is normally homophonic, so Louis Couperin's attractive *Sarabande en canon* represents an exception. Also of interest are the rhythmic stresses: those of the trailing voice fall on a different beat from those of the leading voice.

On the other hand, some of Couperin's sarabandes represent a contrasting style with a more complex texture, including dotted eighth notes, smaller note values, more figuration, and an accented second beat. A striking resemblance exists between some dotted-note motives in his Sarabande in A minor (Curtis edition, p.13) and D'Anglebert's sumptuous *Sarabande grave.* The melody of this sarabande reappears in G. F. Handel's Saraband in D minor (Suite 4, *Suites de pièces pour le clavecin,* 1733).

Couperin's works (found only in manuscript) date from a period before the common use of tempo marks, but stylistic evidence suggests that several of his sarabandes require a slow tempo. Chambonnières's *Sarabande grave* from the Bauyn Manuscript (reworked as a gaillarde in his edition of 1670, No.34) also exemplifies the slow sarabande. The stereotypical dotted-eighth and sixteenth-note pattern found in D'Anglebert's *Sarabande grave* is seen again, but before the downbeat in the manner of the slow gaillarde. Among Lebègue's sarabandes, one is marked *fort grave,* six are marked *grave,* and the four unmarked sarabandes suggest a faster tempo. Although the four expressive sarabandes in La Guerre's c.1687 book contain no tempo marks, they appear to have characteristics of the slow sarabande.

All D'Anglebert's sarabandes are marked *Lentement,* with the exception of the Sarabande in D major. (The manuscript sarabandes in A minor and C major lack tempo marks.) Since both Lebègue and D'Anglebert were careful to mark unusual tempi, these marks may imply that the standard keyboard sarabande tempo was still assumed to be more rapid (although a slow tempo for sarabandes in general must have been well known by 1680, in view of Richelet's description above). Some of D'Anglebert's slow sarabandes are set in a low register and are constructed with a thick texture that at times consists of five- or six-note chords. On the other hand, his Sarabande in D major, utilizing a thinner texture and a higher register, moves comfortably at a tempo similar to that of the chaconne. The absence of a tempo mark may suggest a resemblance to the early, faster clavecin sarabande. The fact that probably all but one of D'Anglebert's sarabandes were intended to be marked *lentement* indicates that the keyboard sarabande was undergoing a change in tempo and character, one that culminated in the sarabandes of Bach and other eighteenth-century composers. With his richly figured sarabandes, D'Anglebert was a prime exponent of this form.

The newly discovered Sarabande in A minor, a lovely piece with a *tendre* character, includes a *double;* while the Sarabande in C major, attributed to D'Anglebert, has little in common with his other work and would appear to date from his youth.

The dual nature of the sarabande continued into the eighteenth century. The sarabande in Marchand's 1702 book, with dotted eighth notes, accented second beats, and abundant ornamentation, suggests a slower tempo than does the one in his 1703 book. Le Roux's edition (1705) also includes sarabandes of both types, some marked *grave,* some *gaye.* The two sarabandes in Rameau's *Premier livre* (1706) are light and transparent; but the majestic, richly ornamented sarabande in his 1728 book requires a slow tempo. Most of François Couperin's sarabandes are weighty pieces much in the

D'Anglebert tradition; e.g., *Les Vieux Seigneurs* (*Ordre* 24) is termed a *Sarabande grave* and marked to be played *Noblement*. On the other hand, *Les Sentimens* (*Ordre* 1) is marked *Tres tendrement*.

It appears that the seventeenth-century slow sarabandes were written in two styles, so that their character could be either *noble* or *tendre*. Players must resolve for themselves the manner of performance of the unmarked sarabandes. For example, my inclination is to regard D'Anglebert's sarabandes in G major and A minor (and possibly the second sarabande in D minor) as having an *Affekt* of *tendre*, but those in G minor and D minor (*grave*) one of *noble*.

Gigue

The gigue is found in many different styles and in both duple and triple meter. The lutenists cultivated a form resembling the allemande; e.g., a piece by Denis Gaultier is entitled *Gigue* in one source and *Allemande* in another.[24] This type of gigue is similar to the allemande in that it is in duple meter, often has a head motive, and employs the same type of motivic treatment. Two allemandes in common time, given again as gigues in ₵ time in S[r]. Perrine's *Pièces de luth en musique*, carry the instruction: "This piece is to be played again as a gigue."[25] The gigue versions are quite similar to the corresponding allemandes, but they include numerous dotted notes. D'Anglebert's manuscript contains his transcription of two duple-meter gigues by Ennemond Gaultier (Ex. 1): the Gigue in C major (₵ time) has a simpler texture and melodic line than the Gigue in D minor (C time) named *La Poste* (the same gigue appears in the Perrine edition). The regularly accented Gigue in C major moves easily at a faster tempo than that of the Gigue in D minor, which features skillfully shifting rhythmic accents.

As defined by Ozanam (1691), "The gigue, an *Air de Musique* in three beats, is played quickly; its measures often begin with a dotted note. The French gigue [*Gigue à la Françoise*] has two beats and begins with an upbeat."[26] Thomas Corneille (1694) substantiates Ozanam's description of these two forms of gigue and adds that Gilles Ménage believes the word *Gigue* comes from the Italian *Giga*, a fiddle spoken of by Dante.[27] The Bauyn Manuscript contains two keyboard allemandes by La Barre that are later repeated with the

Ex. 1. E. Gaultier/D'Anglebert: a. Gigue in
C major, mm.1–3; b. Gigue in D minor,
mm.3–5.

title "Gigue."[28] The two versions are identical except for minor variants. The clavecinistes chiefly used triple or compound meter in the
gigue, but an interesting exception by Chambonnières from the
Bauyn Manuscript contains an eight-measure section in duple meter
near the end of the second strain (Ex. 2).[29]

A similar change of meter occurs in a gigue by Étienne Richard,
who also wrote a gigue completely in duple meter.[30] Johann Jakob
Froberger too includes a change from compound to duple meter at
the close of the gigue from the fourth suite of his 1656 collection, an
autograph manuscript that includes four gigues in duple meter and

Ex. 2. *Gigue de Mr de Chambonnieres*, mm.17–
20 (Brunold-Tessier, p. 65).

two in compound meter. The Bauyn Manuscript contains many of his pieces, among them several gigues in both duple and triple meters (barred in 3/4 and in 6/4 time). The cross-fertilization between Froberger and the musicians of Paris (see chapter 7) suggests that Froberger may have played the compound-meter gigue from his 1649 autograph manuscript during his visit there in 1652. Its regular rhythmic accents and fugal entries conform to our expectations for gigue style.

Each of the four suites in La Guerre's c.1687 book contains a triple- or compound-meter gigue (either fugal or imitative), but the second suite contains an additional gigue in duple meter (see Ex. 3). Further evidence for contrasting English and French gigue forms is found in Marc-Antoine Charpentier's *Concert pour quatre parties de violes* (1680-1681), which contains both a *Gigue angloise* with dotted rhythms in 3 time (barred in 3/4) and a *Gigue françoise* in barred ₵ time.[31]

Meredith Ellis Little notes that "scholars are still debating the question of whether the many gigues notated with duple subdivisions of the beat . . . should be played in the uneven rhythms of a triple subdivision."[32] In seventeenth-century France, however, the term "gigue" encompassed dances in duple as well as triple (or compound) meter, while a few gigues used both meters in a single piece. Some say that duple-meter gigues should be played in a triple form because three gigues by Froberger are notated in different me-

Ex. 3. La Guerre, Gigue in G minor, mm. 7–10.

ters in separate sources. It may be more plausible that Froberger (or a scribe) was giving examples of the gigue as it would sound in both French and English styles, rather than expecting performers to juggle rhythmic values from duple to triple in gigues where there is no written-out triple version. The French duple-meter gigue appears to have originated with the lutenists and to have been adopted only occasionally in other idioms.

The triple- or compound-meter gigue in France may be derived from the English jig, an example of which is William Byrd's *A Gigg*, from the *Fitzwilliam Virginal Book* of 1619 (this volume also contains a duple-meter *Nobodyes Gigge* by Richard Farnaby). One link between England and France is the French lutenist John Mercure, who worked at the English court (fl. 1640-1650), and whose known gigues (three for lute and one for harpsichord) employ compound meter, a thin texture, and in one instance an imitative opening. One of Mercure's gigues is constructed with the shifting rhythmic accents typical of French mid-century keyboard gigues.

Lully's *Comédie, Xerxés* (1660), includes a gigue barred in 3/4 time with fugal entries, regular accents, and dotted rhythm. This type of gigue is related to the *canaries*, a fast dance that opens with a single voice in a distinctive dotted pattern:

Although D'Anglebert did not use this dance form, Louis Couperin, Chambonnières, and La Guerre furnish a few examples.

The gigues of Louis Couperin and Chambonnières reflect a diversity of styles despite the fact that they all use a time signature of 3, no matter whether the pulse falls into 6/4, 3/2, or 3/4 time. Most of their gigues utilize imitation and a more complicated rhythmic structure, which can include accents shifting between 6/4 and 3/2 time, syncopation, and cross-rhythms. Another type of gigue by Chambonnières, the *Gigue ou il y a un canon*, employs imitation, regular rhythmic stresses, and some use of dotted notes. D'Anglebert transcribed an exceptionally fine gigue by Lully that represents still another type: the homophonic texture supports the melody, and hemiola patterns abound (Ex. 4).

Ex. 4. Lully/D'Anglebert, Gigue, mm.1–4.

Imaginative rhythmic patterns are characteristic of French gigues from the mid-century, but they give way to the regular accents found in the English jig and the Italian giga. The gigues of La Guerre's c.1687 collection, with a signature of 3 and barred in either 6/4 or 3/4, generally exemplify this rhythm. The three fine gigues and one *double* of her 1707 book, which carry time signatures of 6/4 and 6/8 and are longer than the earlier gigues, reflect Italian fluidity and polish. Lebègue's gigues are characterized by regular rhythmic pulses, thin texture, and some fugal techniques. This style, superseding the intricate rhythms and texture of many of Chambonnières's and Louis Couperin's gigues, invites a faster tempo—Lebègue's *Gigue dangleterre* in G major is marked *Fort viste.* Gigues with a complex rhythmic or imitative structure require a slower tempo than those with thin texture and regular accents, but seventeenth-century French gigues are vigorous, an *air de danse fort gay*, as described by Gilles Ménage.[33]

D'Anglebert's use of compound 6/8 or 12/8 time is perhaps the first occurrence of these Italian signatures in the clavecin gigue. They reflect a stabilizing of the rhythmic pulse, in contrast to the rhythmic ambiguity of many early French gigues. D'Anglebert marked two gigues (in 6/4 and 3/4) *guayement*, perhaps to avoid confusion because the note values are larger than those of the 12/8 or 6/8 gigues. Another feature of his compound-meter gigues is greater length; e.g., the triple-meter gigue in D major has 36 beat units (= dotted half note), not including repeats, while the 12/8 gigue in G major has 76 beat units (= dotted quarter note).

By the latter part of the seventeenth century, clavecin gigues could have a time signature of 3, 6/4, 3/8, 6/8, or even 12/8 (which was very unusual in France). St.-Lambert observes:

But these signatures [12/4, 12/8, 9/4, and 9/8] are so rare in our music that I have never seen any compositions using them, except for three that are in 12/8: two gigues by M. d'Anglebert, and the beautiful Italian air of *Europe Galante*, "Ad un cuore" [André Campra, 1697].[34]

But St.-Lambert overlooked some gigue-like pieces in compound meter found in the organ music of François Roberday (*Fugues et caprices*, 1660, which includes works by Italian composers—see p.119), D'Anglebert's fourth organ fugue, and François Couperin's *Offertoire* from the *Messe pour les paroisses* (1690). The 12/8 signature was associated with the Italian giga, which developed in a different direction from the fugal entries and dotted rhythms of the French gigue.

The gigue has many personalities. As Johann Mattheson described it, the common gigue is English and is characterized by

a fiery and a fickle passion, like an anger that soon vanishes. The *Loures*, or slow and dotted ones, reveal on the other hand a proud, arrogant character; hence they are very beloved by the Spanish. *Canaries* reflect great eagerness and swiftness, but at the same time must convey a little innocence. The Italian *Gige*, which are not used for dancing but for fiddling (from which the name may also derive), force themselves as it were to the greatest speed or rapidity, though for the most part in a fluent and easy manner.[35]

In his six gigues, D'Anglebert combines elements of his predecessors with stylistic traits of his own. A dotted figure is customary in five of the gigues, but the fascinating rhythmic shifts between 6/4 and 3/2 of the earlier gigues are absent from all except the homophonic 6/4 Gigue in G major. The 12/8 gigues employ a pseudopolyphonic texture in which short motives are exchanged among the voices. The frequent syncopation adds rhythmic interest in the marvelously constructed Gigue in G minor (see Ex. 5).

Ex. 5. D'Anglebert, Gigue in G minor,
mm.7–8.

D'Anglebert's melodious triple-meter gigues in D major and A minor are composed of fugal entries in each strain, which then yield to a more homophonic structure. The construction of the newly discovered Gigue in A minor (see Appendix 2) is similar to that of the Gigue in D major. The fugal entries of the Gigue in D minor constitute the beginning of a monothematic composition (most unusual for this period in France) in which the subject and its fragments are skillfully woven in throughout.

Of François Couperin's few entitled gigues for the harpsichord, one is in the style of an Italian *giga* in 12/8 time (*Ordre* 1), and two use a dotted style with fugal entries in 6/4 time (*Ordres* 5 and 8). Rameau's 6/4 Gigue from his *Premier livre* employs fugal entries, some dotted rhythms, and a thin texture; while the two 6/8 gigues *en rondeau* from his 1724 collection are basically homophonic. By 1768, J. J. Rousseau could mention that the gigue was out of fashion and scarcely heard in France.[36]

Gaillarde

Although Thomas Morley described the galliard in 1597 as "a lighter and more stirring kind of dancing than the Pavan,"[37] Thomas Mace observed in 1676 that it is "perform'd in a *Slow, and Large Triple-Time;* and (commonly) *Grave, and Sober.*"[38] Across the Channel, Mersenne indicated that the French gaillarde was a fast, vigorous dance: "The gaillarde . . . derived its name from the liveliness of the dance, and from the freedom that permits going obliquely, across, and lengthwise all over the room, sometimes gliding and sometimes leaping. . . . "[39] But Mersenne's description may be appropriate only for a piece like Louis Couperin's Gaillarde in F major, which is barred in 3/4 time and characterized by thin texture, dotted notes, and disjunct melodic movement.

Another type of gaillarde, similar to the slow sarabande discussed above, is barred in 3/2 time. The Oldham Manuscript contains D'Anglebert's *Sarabande, façon de Gaillarde* (Gaillarde in G minor) and the Bauyn Manuscript his *Sarabande graue en forme de gaillarde*, apparently modeled after Chambonnières's Gaillarde in C major (also found as a *Sarabande grave* barred in 3/4 time). It appears again in D'Anglebert's manuscript with the title of Gaillarde, together with a

Ex. 6. D'Anglebert, Gaillarde in C major,
mm.1–4.

double (see Ex. 6). Louis Couperin's Gaillarde in G major furnishes another example of the 3/2 gaillarde, which uses a variety of note values in a distinctive rhythmic pattern typified by a recurrent anacrusic figure of a dotted quarter and eighth note, and the sustaining of the first note of the measure.

Information regarding tempo for the gaillarde is contradictory, since Mersenne considers it a lively dance, but Mace describes it as *"Grave, and Sober."* Some seventy years after Mersenne, Brossard lists *Gayement* and *Légèrement* as synonyms for *Gaillardement*.[40] Indeed, the meaning of the French word *gaillarde* is "fast and lively." The gaillardes in D'Anglebert's edition, however, are all marked *Lentement;* and the *Tombeau* (which is in the form of a gaillarde), *Fort lentement.* Since the danced French gaillarde retained its fast character into the eighteenth century, it is possible that the clavecinistes were influenced by the English version of the galliard. A stylistic resemblance exists between the slow French gaillarde and a "grave and sober" galliard for lute from Thomas Mace's *Musick's monument* (Ex. 7).[41] This varied evidence suggests that the gaillardes in 3/2 time require a slow tempo, while those in 3/4 can move more energetically.

One might wonder why D'Anglebert wrote so many gaillardes, for aside from Chambonnières and L. Couperin, no keyboard con-

Ex. 7. Thomas Mace, Galliard from the 4th
Sett, mm.1–4.

temporary or successor composed any, to our knowledge. Although the form of the gaillarde varies in Chambonnières's and Couperin's works, D'Anglebert is consistent in using only 3/2 time. He must have been intrigued with the gaillarde's possibilities, for he included one in each of his four suites, as well as two others in his manuscript. Although not entitled as such, the *Tombeau de M.* de Chambonnieres from the suite in D major is clearly a gaillarde and opens nearly identically to the Gaillarde in D minor.

The seventeenth-century French lutenists, among them Ennemond and Denis Gaultier, Charles Mouton, and Jacques Gallot, left numerous *tombeaux*. Froberger and Louis Couperin, as well as the lutenist Dufaut, wrote *tombeaux* in honor of Blancrocher, a lutenist who fell down stairs to his death in 1652. Froberger's *Tombeau* for Blancrocher carries the instruction to play very slowly and freely (*se joue fort lentement à la discretion sans observer aucune mesure*). The *tombeau* usually follows the form of the allemande, as in Denis Gaultier's *Allemande grave*, which is entitled *Tombeau* in another source.[42]

D'Anglebert's gaillardes all have distinctive rhythmic patterns and a similar structure, with regular phrase lengths. A *petite reprise* is included in every gaillarde except the one in C major; the *petite reprise* is written out with embellishment in the Gaillarde in G minor. The Gaillardes in D minor and D major open with a long upbeat pattern that fills most of a measure. These harmonically luxuriant pieces are largely homophonic, with an occasional use of a motive in other voices to enliven a sustained soprano note.

D'Anglebert's gift for melody is shown to greatest advantage in his six gaillardes, which are elegant, highly sophisticated, and perhaps a bit melancholy. The form of the gaillarde serves as a perfect vehicle in the *Tombeau* for Chambonnières, in contrast to those of other composers who cast their *tombeaux* as allemandes. These two dance forms furnish an interesting comparison. The dignified mid-seventeenth century French allemande acquired an additional faster form and continued to flourish as the first dance in harpsichord suites until the time of Bach and Handel. The danced gaillarde was rapid, but as a keyboard piece the gaillarde lost this identification in mid-seventeenth century France, perhaps because of English influence. After the few examples by Chambonnières, Louis Couperin, and D'Anglebert, the keyboard gaillarde virtually disappeared.

Chaconne and Passacaille

A good deal has been written about distinguishing between the chaconne and the passacaglia,[43] a task that is generally simpler in French music. Brossard defined them as follows:

> CHACONE. It is a melody composed over an obligatory bass of four measures, ordinarily in triple meter with quarter notes, that is repeated as many times as the Chacone has couplets or variations—that is, of different melodies over the notes of the bass. Often in this type of piece one passes from the major to the minor mode. Because of the constraints of this style, one accepts many things that would never normally be permitted in a freer composition.
> PASSACAILLE. It is really a Chacone. The major difference is that the movement is ordinarily slower than that of the Chacone, the melody more delicate, and the style less animated. For this reason, Passacailles are almost always in minor keys. . . .[44]

According to Thomas Corneille, *passacaille* comes from the Spanish *passar* (to go) and *calle* (street), for the Spanish were accustomed to playing this type of music with guitars while strolling in the streets at night.[45] Even as late as 1768, J. J. Rousseau defined the passacaille as a type of chaconne with a more tender melody and a slower tempo, and said that passacailles from *Armide* (Lully, transcribed for harpsichord by D'Anglebert) and *Issé* (André Cardinal Destouches?, 1697) were still celebrated in French opera.[46]

French chaconnes (and occasionally passacailles) customarily employ the rondeau form, in which a repeated refrain (*Grand couplet* of four or eight measures) alternates with three or four couplets of free design. A chordal texture, low register, and often considerable dissonance accompany the bass patterns of the *Grand couplet* (usually the scale degrees of 3–4–5–1 or 1–7–6–5). In the secondary couplets, the melody becomes dominant, the register is higher and often ascends with successive couplets, and note values can be smaller. Chaconnes and passacailles may use an alternate form, with a regularly recurring bass formula, that comprises repeated sections (usually four measures) strung together.

One of Denis Gaultier's lute pieces is identified as a *Chaconne* in one source and as a *Sarabande* in another,[47] while Jacques Ozanam's *Dictionaire* compares the chaconne to a sarabande.[48] The two forms have much in common—four-measure phrases, hemiola, and the patterns of ♩. ♪♩ and ♩ ♩. ♪, but chaconnes have more rhythmic variety and a structural bass. All three of D'Anglebert's chaconnes move easily at a tempo similar to that of the faster sarabande. Exceptions to the commonly accepted tempo are indicated by composers; e.g., Lebègue's two pieces entitled *Chaconne grave* and D'Anglebert's transcription of Lully's *Chaconne de Galatée,* marked *Lentement.* The title and denser texture of L. Couperin's *La Complaignante* suggest a slower tempo.

D'Anglebert's suites in G major and D major each contain a *Chaconne rondeau* constructed with a *Grand couplet* of eight measures (with a *double* written out for the repeat of the one in D major) and four or five couplets of sixteen measures each. The Chaconne in C major in D'Anglebert's manuscript employs an ostinato bass undergirding twelve repeated four-measure melodic variations. This delightful small-scale work must have achieved great popularity, for it is found in many manuscripts. The vitality of D'Anglebert's chaconnes is heightened by a moderate tempo and well-articulated rhythmic energy. Their texture is more uniform throughout than those of Louis Couperin, which become increasingly complex with succeeding *couplets.*

The clavecinistes excelled at the chaconne and wrote most of them in rondeau form; e.g., several by Louis Couperin that are justifiably famous, Chambonnières's fine Chaconne in F major (Brunold-Tessier, p.92), and La Guerre's imaginative, harmonically interesting, and more sombre chaconnes from her c.1687 collection, of which *L'Inconstante* has internal changes of mode. Her other chaconne is unusual for being set in the minor mode.

After D'Anglebert, the chaconne is encountered only occasionally. Marchand's rondeau Chaconne in D minor contains four couplets of increasing complexity, while Le Roux's Chaconne in F major utilizes continuous movement and some Italianate features. An exceptional example from François Couperin—a rondeau in duple meter—is entitled *La Favorite—Chaconne a deux tems* (*Ordre* 3) and is marked *Gravement, sans lenteur.*

D'Anglebert's only passacaille bears a superficial resemblance to his Chaconne in C major in that they both consist of repeated short sections on a ground bass. The Passacaille, with twenty repeated sections that vary the bass line, melody, rhythm, texture, and harmony, is clearly adapted and expanded from an anonymous Italian work in the *Codex Chigiano.*[49]

Magnificent dissonance permeates D'Anglebert's passacaille; e.g., m.3 almost conveys the impression of a D-major chord in the upper register against a C-minor chord in the lower register. It is impressionistic writing, designed to engage the listener in a wash of sound. These complicated dissonances can often be analyzed as simply tonic–dominant harmony with an advanced suspension technique. It is remarkable how much harmonic and melodic variety can be provided in a simple four-measure phrase that almost always ends with the same cadence. Although the bass pattern of the Passacaille is G–F–E♭–D–G, D'Anglebert ingeniously alters the rhythmic placement of these notes, adds other bass notes, and varies the harmonic structure. This work is almost hypnotic in its endless solemn movement toward a cadence. The form of the passacaille may have been associated with the operatic *Affekt* of pathos and languishing (see p.116). A very leisurely tempo enables D'Anglebert's sumptuous harmonies to distill and blend.

In this period the passacaille does not occur as often as the chaconne. The texture of Louis Couperin's superb Passacaille in C major (perhaps the only other example in 3/2 time) resembles that of D'Anglebert's passacaille, while his two passacailles in G minor are barred in 3/4 time. The fact that Couperin called one of the latter *Chaconne ou Passacaille* suggests that in the 1650s the passacaille had not yet solidified its distinctive slow and melancholy personality. Yet much later, François Couperin gave sectional movements from *Les Nations* (*La Françoise*) and *Pièces de violes* the title *Chaconne ou Passacaille*, so it seems that exceptions to conventional practice always exist. The monumental Passacaille in B minor for harpsichord (*Ordre* 8) by Couperin *le grand* is in rondeau form, while *L'Amphibie—Mouvement de Passacaille—Noblement* (*Ordre* 24), a unique work incorporating several tempo changes, is intended to open with the *mouvement* of a passacaille.

Menuet and Gavotte

At Versailles, the popular menuet became the concluding dance of a suite consisting of branle, courante, and gavotte. Lully composed nearly 100 titled menuets, many more than any other dance form. With its well-defined phrase structure, tonal clarity, and lovely melody, the menuet had great popular appeal. Brossard describes it as a very quick dance, usually in binary form (but sometimes in rondeau form):

> . . . a very lively dance that originated in Poitou. One owes to the imitation of the Italians the use of the signs 3/8 or 6/8 for marking the movement, which is always very lively and very fast. However, the practice of marking it with a simple 3, or three quarter notes, has remained. This dance ordinarily has two strains, each of which is played twice. The first has four, or at the most eight measures. . . .[50]

Jacques Ozanam describes the menuet as "an *Air de Musique* in three beats, or a fast sarabande."[51] Walther's *Lexikon* defines it as a French dance in triple meter that is beat almost as though it were in 3/8 time.[52] St.-Lambert too says that although menuets are written with a signature of 3, they are to be beat faster, as though written in 3/8 time (except for some clavecin menuets).[53]

The character of the menuet changed over the following half century. In 1768 J. J. Rousseau disagreed with Brossard's description: "On the contrary, the character of the menuet is one of an elegant and noble simplicity. The movement is more moderate than quick. One can say that the menuet is the least lively of all the dances used in our balls." He adds cryptically, "C'est autre chose sur le Théatre," suggesting that the fast menuet continued its life on the stage.[54]

Kenneth Gilbert marks two of D'Anglebert's menuets with a bracketed *Lentement*,[55] perhaps because the composer indicated that his two menuet transcriptions from Lully were to be played *Lentement*. The latter menuets, however, are from the *Trios pour le coucher du Roi* ("Trios for the King's Bedtime") and were probably intended to have a different character from the standard lively menuet. D'Anglebert appears to have used tempo indications only when his desired tempo deviated from the accepted norm. His transcriptions of Lully's menuets have a more complicated rhythmic structure, which flows better at a relaxed tempo.

In his charming menuets in G major and D minor, D'Anglebert follows the customary features of this dance. In both pieces, he writes out the repeat of the first strain, changing the last measure in the case of the G-major menuet, and lowering the register of the left hand an octave in the D-minor menuet.

The menuet presents perhaps the most standardized dance form of the entire period, for its simple texture and 3/4 time remained constant until François Couperin's 3/8 and 6/8 menuets, which feature running sixteenth notes. While Chambonnières and Louis Couperin each provided one or two menuets, Lebègue wrote around thirteen and La Guerre included one in each of the suites of her c.1687 book.

The French gavotte, characterized by C or ₵ time and rhythmically similar phrases that often begin in the middle of a measure, began its vogue in Lully's ballets and operas. Although Mersenne indicates in 1636 that it is slow (*Gauote . . . sa mesure est binaire assez graue . . .*),[56] Brossard in 1703 describes it as either fast or slow:

> This is a type of dance in which the melody has two strains, the first of four and the second ordinarily of eight measures in duple meter, sometimes fast and sometimes slow. Each strain is played twice. The first strain begins with an upbeat of a half note or two quarter notes, or an equivalent value. . . .[57]

The dual fast/slow nature of the gavotte is noted too by Walther: "sometimes quick, but also now and then performed slowly,"[58] and by J. J. Rousseau: "The movement of the *Gavotte* is ordinarily graceful, often lively, but sometimes also tender and slow."[59] Pierre Richelet (1680) defines the gavotte as a *danse gaie*.[60] By the end of the seventeenth century in France, the gavotte was perhaps more often associated with a lively tempo and an upbeat, although there are examples in the keyboard literature (notably by D'Anglebert) beginning on the downbeat.

D'Anglebert gave his Gavotte in G major a tempo of *Lentement*, which might have led Kenneth Gilbert, in his 1975 edition, to mark D'Anglebert's other Gavotte with a bracketed *Lentement*. D'Anglebert, however, wrote the former in common time, but the latter in 2 time. According to St.-Lambert, the 2 signature is even faster than ₵ time (see chapter 3). D'Anglebert transcribed two anonymous gavottes, marking them both *Lentement*. The fact that they are labeled *Air ancien* might account for the slow tempo, in view of Mersenne's description.

Among the relatively few examples of this dance form in the keyboard literature are Louis Couperin's gavotte and *doubles* on gavottes by Hardel and Lebègue. The latter's editions contain nine gavottes, two of which begin on the first beat of the measure. La Guerre's first book includes a gavotte in ¢ time that appears to have a character of *gaye*. François Couperin indicated that his gavotte from *Ordre* 8 be played *Tendrement* and added a highly embellished alternate melodic line to the Gavotte in G minor from *Ordre* 1. Rameau's famous Gavotte with *Doubles* exemplifies the Italian virtuoso style.

Variations on *Les folies d'Espagne*

Folias, from the Portuguese, means lunacy, and the folia originated as a noisy, very fast carnival dance of fertility. The later form of the folia in France and England (c.1672–1750) differs from the earlier Spanish and Italian form in certain details.[61] Its tempo became slower, and its lovely melody helped to make it tremendously popular throughout much of Europe.

The guitarist Francesco Corbetta, who had come to Paris around 1656, is given credit for playing "the key role finally in transmitting the fully developed earlier type of folia to France."[62] Michel Farinel too may have brought the folia melody from Portugal to Paris around 1672, when he wrote his variations (included in John Playford's *Division Violin*, London, 1685) for the noted violinist Guillaume Dumanoir.[63] Lully incorporated the folia in his *Air des hautbois* for four winds (LWV 48, 1672), and Jacques Gallot wrote lute variations on the theme at about the same time. Lully's work, commissioned by the king, may mark the earliest use of the later folia structure, which features melodic variation over fixed harmonies, in contrast to the rhythmic and harmonic variants of the earlier folia. The folia melody and bass, widely circulated in France and other parts of Europe, forms the basis of the well-known variations for violin by Corelli (1700) and for gamba by Marin Marais (1701).

In a letter dated 24 July 1689 Mme de Sévigné suggests that the *folies d'Espagne* was a popular dance in France:

> [the son of the Seneschal of Rennes] dances these beautiful chaconnes, the *folies d'Espagne*, and especially *passepieds* with his wife,

with a perfection, with a harmony, impossible to describe; no set steps, nothing but a true cadence, with the most whimsical figures, now in the *branle* like the others, now alone in couples as in the minuet, now very serenely, now scarcely touching their feet to the ground. . . .[64]

Feuillet's *Recueil de dances* gives the steps for the *folies d'Espagne,* while his *Chorégraphie* includes instructions for the use of castanets with this dance.[65]

    D'Anglebert follows the form of the later folia closely, but varies the final cadence by using submediant or subdominant harmonies. His 22 variations constitute an early instance of keyboard melodic variations. The form is defined as having a generally fixed harmonic scheme and constant formal proportions; the main notes of the melody are retained but may be embellished in any number of ways by the addition of nonharmonic tones and rhythmic variation. The melody of D'Anglebert's Variations undergoes continual alteration in the soprano voice, supported by the harmonic structure and fluent movement of the lower voices. Since D'Anglebert adheres to the constraints of the form, the harmonies are simple. Occasionally the rhythmic interest shifts to a lower voice or voices, or a distinctive rhythmic pattern may be tossed between the hands, as in Variation 16. In Variation 21 the melodic notes are trilled with alternating upper and lower auxiliaries, almost producing the effect of a continuous trill. The scale and arpeggio patterns in the bass of the last variation resemble the Italianate violin style.

    Although numerous settings of the folia melody occur in French manuscripts of the period, D'Anglebert's Variations are possibly the first published keyboard melodic variations on the folia, preceding those of Pasquini (in manuscript from the 1690s), Alessandro Scarlatti (1715), and C. P. E. Bach (1778). D'Anglebert's Variations had great popularity and longevity, for they are also found in a late eighteenth-century German manuscript. They reflect characteristics of the Italian school—notably those of Bernardo Pasquini:

> [Pasquini's] harpsichord variations take a middle position between the older contrapuntal techniques and the later, more homophonic variation type with fixed harmonies. The bass and harmony are usually fixed in his variations, and the ornamentation, often very rich, is embedded in a chordal framework. Indeed with Pasquini the history of variations "alla maniera Italiana" begins. . . .[66]

D'Anglebert's Variations also fall into this classification of melodic variations, with a homophonic texture and fixed harmonies, and they appear to antedate those of Pasquini. Whatever the case, D'Anglebert was probably influenced by the Italians, for traits such as violinistic gestures occur. His Variations, however, do not reflect the virtuoso style, sharp contrasts, and vivid imagination of those by Marais. One senses that Marais's variations were for the pleasure of a seated audience, while D'Anglebert's could have accompanied dancers and may have been included in his edition for their popular appeal. Although simply constructed, these variations succeed admirably within their strict harmonic and formal framework.

Characteristics of D'Anglebert's Clavecin Pieces

Unlike most other clavecin music of the seventeenth century, D'Anglebert's dances generally are characterized by a uniform texture throughout, a use of melodic sequences, greater harmonic stability, and a unity between the two strains.

D'Anglebert was perhaps the first French keyboard composer to unify binary dances to a substantive degree. He does so by means of rhythmic and melodic motives that recur in the second strain. Sometimes the imitation is exact, but it also might be slightly altered, as in the Allemande in D major (mm.9 and 21–22). This unification is found to some degree in all the binary dances, with the gaillardes having the least. The Menuet in D minor even includes an exact repetition in the second strain of a phrase from the first strain. The *Sarabande grave* in D minor opens with a two-measure pattern repeated in a modulating sequence, a pattern that is suggested in the second strain (mm.14 and 18).

Imitative features exist in all six gigues to a greater or lesser extent. The gigues in 12/8 are filled with motivic exchange among all the voices; the imitation often is not exact but is similar enough in shape and rhythmic form to convey an impression of thematic unity between the strains. The complex texture of the Gigue in G minor has many unifying small motives; e.g., a fragment of the tenor from m.2 is found in sequence in m.16. The Gigues in D minor and D major feature a unified monothematic structure in which both strains open with the same subject. The Gigue in A minor employs fugal entries throughout both sections, with the subject of the second strain based on material from mm.3 and 4.

D'Anglebert's harpsichord works, many of which modulate frequently, contrast and complement his nonmodulatory contrapuntal organ pieces. His first three suites contain numerous shifts of key center typical of the French school at this time, but they are usually well established by a dominant-seventh chord. The fourth suite in D major, however, replaces the frequent key shifts with a tonic–dominant polarity in which a substantial section in the tonic is set off against a section in the dominant (or on occasion in the subdominant). The tonic is established for the first 5 ½ measures of the Allemande in D major, while the second half of the strain alternates between the dominant and tonic:

| First strain | TDTD |
| Second strain | DTDT |

In contrast to many of D'Anglebert's harpsichord dances, his preludes establish the home key firmly at the beginning and modulate infrequently (except for the Prelude in G minor, which moves through the circle of fifths from D major downward to B♭ major). The long Prelude in D minor includes substantial sections in the home key, the relative major, and the minor dominant, as well as a sizeable coda that emphasizes the subdominant.

The use of harmony and dissonance in the harpsichord dances is rich and imaginative. D'Anglebert employs many secondary dominants, seventh chords on all scale degrees, and root movement generally by fifths. Cadences favor the dominant or dominant seventh to tonic, preceded by a chord of the subdominant (II or IV) or the tonic in second inversion. An interesting exception is the use of a Phrygian cadence to end some first strains of the D-minor dances. D'Anglebert employs the circle of fifths a number of times; e.g., the second strain of the Sarabande in G minor, in which the fifths ascend from B♭ to D and then descend. Many of D'Anglebert's harpsichord pieces demonstrate a constantly shifting tonal center that is often brought about by the linear use of the affective modal steps of 3, 4, 6, and 7. Occasionally there is no dominant after the opening chord of a piece, but an immediate chromatic shift toward another key center (e.g., in the Allemande in G minor). A passage in the Allemande in G major includes a cross-relation involving the third

Ex. 8. D'Anglebert, Allemande in G major,
mm.4–5.

degree of the scale, several seventh chords, and dissonance resolving to further dissonance (see Ex. 8).

An augmented chord on the third degree of the scale in minor is
an unusual, but not a rare, occurrence in French literature of the
period. D'Anglebert limits its use (normally functioning as a dominant) primarily to his sarabandes and gaillardes; e.g., the *Sarabande
grave* in D minor, m.21. The Sarabande in G minor, m.14, furnishes
an example of a sophisticated suspension technique, the superimpo-
sition of D minor on G minor (Ex. 9).

Some say that D'Anglebert wrote in a heavy five-voice style, and
that this thick texture precludes a fast tempo for gigues. Most of his
clavecin writing is actually in a free-voice texture of two to four
parts. The third and fourth voices are added or subtracted at will,
and occasionally a fifth or sixth voice is inserted into a chordal structure to achieve the illusion of dynamic variation. D'Anglebert's facile
writing style does permit a suitably brisk tempo for gigues and other
rapid pieces.

Ex. 9. D'Anglebert, Sarabande in G minor,
mm.13–16.

CONCLUSION

Jean-Henry D'Anglebert figured prominently in the *grand siècle* by virtue of his position at court from 1662 to 1691. His music is characterized by a flair for shaping a melodic phrase, a superb sense of rhythmic timing, a highly developed harmonic language, and a sophisticated suspension technique. It is crowned by luxuriant ornamentation that reflects the elegance of his time.

D'Anglebert published his only edition of keyboard works in 1689. It duplicates several of the pieces in his autograph manuscript, making possible some interesting comparisons, particularly with regard to ornamentation and the unmeasured prelude. The table of 29 ornaments, many of which D'Anglebert devised, greatly expanded the number of ornaments and symbols in use. His works also played a role in establishing the standard suite sequence of allemande, courante, sarabande, and gigue in French keyboard music. The dances in D'Anglebert's *oeuvre,* with the exception of the courante, present contrasting personalities among pieces in the same form; they invite us to a new consideration of tempo for Baroque dances.

D'Anglebert, whose music reflects the French ideal of a "stile naturel, coulant, tendre, & affectueux," emerges as the dominant figure of seventeenth-century clavecin literature. Had Louis Couperin had the good fortune to attain D'Anglebert's longevity, the conclusion might be different. As it is, Couperin's works—most of which were written 30 years before D'Anglebert's edition appeared—reflect remarkable creativity. Much of the credit for the achievements of these two men must go to Chambonnières, the master teacher who influenced the next generation immeasurably. While Lebègue was an innovative composer with regard to contemporary trends, his pieces depend more extensively on formulas. His music achieved great popularity abroad, possibly because its simple texture was easily grasped by foreigners who wished to learn about the "French style." La Guerre's music is of considerably more interest than Lebègue's, so it is surprising that only one copy of each of her harpsichord books seems to have survived, and few manuscript copies have been found. The forthcoming modern edition of her early works will be most welcome.

The French were fond of *l'exception*. While one may make some valid generalizations about the music of the seventeenth century, it would be risky to insist that anything always followed the same formula. One purpose of this book is to show the great diversity that existed. This is not to say that any interpretation will do. Rather, it places a greater responsibility on the performer to examine the various possibilities before arriving at a conclusion.

Willi Apel has called D'Anglebert

> the most outstanding among the numerous pupils of Chambonnières. . . . Although little known today, he represents the highest development of French harpsichord music, even more so than François Couperin, who is usually considered the most outstanding of the clavecinistes. In d'Anglebert the loftiness and grandeur of Baroque mentality found a most impressive realization. . . .[1]

APPENDIX 1

SOURCES AND EDITIONS

Sources

Some of the information in this section is derived from Bruce Gustafson's valuable *French Harpsichord Music of the 17th Century* (Ann Arbor: UMI Research Press, 1977). Table 1 gives the location of D'Anglebert's harpsichord pieces (numbered by Gustafson through 93) in the *Pièces de clavecin* and the autograph manuscript Rés. 89ter. The letters T and D preceding the Gustafson numbers indicate "transcription" and "double" respectively; those in parentheses following the names of the pieces refer to the keys—capital for major, lower case for minor.

Table 1

D'Anglebert's Harpsichord Pieces

Gustafson Number		Number in 1689 Edition	Number in Rés. 89ter MS
1	Prelude (G)	1	32
2	Allemande (G)	2	
3	Courante (G)	3	
3a	Double de la Courante (G)	3a	
4	2.ᵉ Courante (G)	4	
5	3.ᵉ Courante (G)	5	
6	Sarabande (G)	6	
7	Gigue (G)	7	
8	Gaillarde (G)	8	38
9	Chaconne Rondeau (G)	9	
10	Gavotte (G)	10	39
11	Menuet (G)	11	40
T12	Ouuerture de Cadmus (G)	12	
T13	Ritournelle des Feés de Rolland (G)	13	
T14	Menuet. dans nos bois (G)	14	
T15	Chaconne de Phaeton (G)	15	
16	2ᵉ Gigue (G)	16	37
17	Prelude (g)	17	42a
18	Allemande (g)	18	
19	Courante (g)	19	
20	2.ᵉ Courante (g)	20	
T21	Courante M.ʳ de Lully (g)	21	42d

Gustafson Number		Number in 1689 Edition	Number in Rés. 89ter MS
21a	Double de la Courante (g)	21a	42e
22	Sarabande (g)	22	
T23	Sarabande Dieu des Enfers (g)	23	
24	Gigue (g)	24	
T25	Gigue M.r de Lully (g)	25	
26	Gaillarde (g)	26	
27	Passacaille	27	44
T28	Menuet la Jeune Iris (g)	28	
29	Gavotte. Ou estes vous allé (g)	29	
30	Gavotte. le beau berger Tirsis (g)	30	
31	La Bergere Anette.Vaudeville (g)	31	
T32	Ouverture de la Mascarade (g)	32	42b
T33	Les Sourdines d'Armide (g)	33	
T34	Les Songes agreables d'Atys (g)	34	43
T35	Air d'Apollon du Triomphe de l'Amour	35	
36	Menuet de Poitou. Vaudeville (g)	36	
T37	Passacaille d'Armide (g)	37	
38	Prelude (d)	38	23
39	Allemande (d)	39	
40	Courante (d)	40	
40a	Double de la Courante (d)	40a	
41	2.e Courante (d)	41	
42	Sarabande grave (d)	42	
43	Sarabande (d)	43	24
44	Gigue (d)	44	
45	Gaillarde (d)	45	
46	Gavotte (d)	46	
47	Menuet (d)	47	
T48	Ouuerture de Proserpine (d)	48	
49	Variations sur les folies d'Espagne (d)	49	21
50	Allemande (D)	50	
51	Courante (D)	51	
52	2.e Courante (D)	52	
53	Sarabande (D)	53	
54	Gigue (D)	54	
T55	Chaconne de Galatée (D)	55	
56	Chaconne Rondeau (D)	56	
57	Tombeau de M.r de Chambonnieres (D)	57	
58	Prelude (C)		1
59	Allemande (C)		1a
D60	(Courante/Chambonnières) Double (C)		2a
D61	(Courante/Chambonnières) Double (C)		3a
T62	Sarabande. Pinel (C)		4
D62a	Double (C)		4a

Gustafson Number		Number in 1689 Edition	Number in Rés. 89ter MS
D63	(Gigue *La Verdinguette*/Chambonnières) Double (C)		5a
64	Gaillarde (C)		6
64a	Double (C)		6a
65	Chaconne (C)		7
T66	Boureé. Air de Ballet po.' Les Basques (C)		8
T67	Les Demons. Air de Ballet (C)		9
T68	2.ᵉ Air des Demons (C)		9a
T69	Air de Ballet. Marche (C)		10
T70	Gigue du Vieux Gautier (C)		11
T71	Courante du Vieux Gautier (C)		12
T72	Courante du Vieux Gautier (C)		13
T73	Sarabande. Mezengeot (C)		14
T74	Courante du Vieux Gautier (C)		15
T75	Allemande du Vieux Gautier (*La Vestemponade*) (C)		16
T76	Courante du Vieux Gautier (C)		17
T77	Chaconne du Vieux Gautier (C)		18
78	Gaillarde (a)		20
D79	(Sarabande O beau jardin/Chambonnières) Double (F)		22a
T80	Courante du Vieux Gautier (*Les Larmes*) (d)		25
T81	Courante du Vieux Gautier (*La petite bergère*) (d)		26
T82	Sarabande du Vieux Gautier (d)		27
T83	Gigue du Vieux Gautier (d)		28
T84	Courante du Vieux Gautier. L'Immortelle (d)		29
T85	Sarabande.Gautier le Jeune (d)		30
D86	(Allemande/Couperin) Double (G)		33a
D87	(Courante/Chambonnières) Double (G)		34a
D88	(Courante/Chambonnières) Double (G)		35a
D89	(Sarabande/Chambonnières, *Jeunes zéphirs*) Double (G)		36a
D90	(Sarabande/Richard) Double (G)		41a
T91	Sarabande. Marais (G)		42
T92	Ouuerture d'Isis (g)		42c
93	Courante (C), Oldham MS, #4		
94	Courante (a), Roper MS, #32		
95	Sarabande (a), Roper MS, #33		
95a	Double (a), Roper MS, #33a		
96	Gigue (a), Roper MS, #34		
97	Sarabande (C), Troyes MS		

D'Anglebert's known works (97 for harpsichord and six for organ) are contained in the following primary sources: two issues of the first edition of the *Pièces de clavecin* (1689), published by the composer; a second edition published by Christophe Ballard in 1703; a third edition, with the preludes omitted, pirated in Amsterdam by Estienne Roger in 1704–1705; and twelve manuscripts (eight French, two German, and two English), including one in the composer's hand. The 1703 Ballard edition uses the same watermark as the second issue of the first edition and, according to Gustafson (p.137), is identical except for the title page. Therefore, Ballard did not use the old plates to run a new issue, but used a new type-set title page on the remaining stock of the second 1689 issue.

The *Pièces de clavecin*, in oblong quarto format with a plate size of 19 × 21.5 cm., contains 128 pages with an additional seven pages of preliminary material (title page, dedication, portrait, preface, ornamentation table, and king's *privilège*). Gustafson lists the following distinguishing variants in the two 1689 issues:

		First issue	Second issue
p. a		"Ruë Ste. Anne"	"Rüe St. Honoré"
		"Au bout de la Rue du hazard"	No notation
p. 127		"Fin du premier Livre"	No notation
p. 128		No notation	"Fin du 1.er Livre /Reveu et corrigé"

Gustafson provides the locations of sixteen copies; in addition Harvard University owns a copy of the Ballard edition, and the Gemeente Museum, The Hague, has a copy of the Amsterdam edition. Marguerite Rosegen-Champion, in her edition of D'Anglebert's *Pièces de clavecin* (Paris: Publications de la Société française de musicologie, 1934), lists other copies at the Landes Bibliothek, Dresden; at the Städtische Bibliothek, Leipzig; and in Henry Prunières's and her personal collections.

The manuscript in D'Anglebert's hand, F-Pn Rés. 89ter (1660s–late 1670s), contains three preliminary leaves, 93 numbered leaves, and one unnumbered leaf at the end (oblong quarto format (17.7 × 23.2 cm.). According to Gustafson, there are actually 91 leaves, since Nos.59–60 are cut out. An additional three leaves, moreover, have been torn out at this location, and another leaf has been removed after the fugue fragment at No.19a. The manuscript is bound in gilt-tooled full red morocco leather with multicolored marbled pastedowns and end papers. A folded piece of paper from more modern times, glued in the front of the volume, gives information about the contents, but the writer errs in stating that only Đ'Anglebert's Variations are included from his edition. Since only the numbering of Nos.1 and 2 appears to be in D'Anglebert's hand, Table 2 follows Gustafson's numbering system.

Table 2

Contents of Rés. 89ter

		Gustafson No.
1	Prelude./D'Anglebert	58
1a	Allemande./D'Anglebert	59
2	Courante./Chambonnieres (*Iris*)	

		Gustafson *No.*
2a	Double	D60
3	2.e/Courante./Chambonnieres	
3a	Double	D61
4	Sarabande./Pinel	T62
4a	Double.	D62a
5	Gigue./La Verdinguette./Chambonnieres	
5a	Double.	D63
6	Gaillarde./D'Anglebert	64
6a	Double.	64a
7	Chaconne./D'Anglebert	65
8	Boureé./Air de Ballet po.^{r}/Les Basques. (Lully)	T66
9	Les Demons./Air de Ballet. (Lully)	T67
9a	2.e Air des Demons. (Lully)	T68
10	Air de Ballet./Marche.	T69
11	Gigue du Vieux/Gautier.	T70
12	Courante du/Vieux Gautier.	T71
13	Courante du Vieux/Gautier. (*La Superbe*)	T72
14	Sarabande./Mezangeot.	T73
15	Courante du/Vieux Gautier.	T74
16	Allemande/du Vieux Gautier. (*La Vestemponade*)	T75
17	Courante du/Vieux Gautier.	T76
18	Chaconne du/Vieux Gautier.	T77
19	Air/De M. Lambert (voice and figured bass), followed by miscellaneous anonymous fragments in another hand	
20	Gaillarde./D'Anglebert	78
20a	Anonymous untitled gigue, a blank page, a fragment in another hand, and seven blank pages	
21	Variations sur/les folies d'Espagne./D'Anglebert	49
22	O beau jardin/Sarabande. (Chambonnières)	
22a	Double	D79
23	Prelude./D'Anglebert.	38
23a	Two blank pages, followed by melodic line in another hand	
24	Sarabande./D'Anglebert.	43
24a	Melody marked "presto"	
25	Courante du/Vieux Gautier. (*Les Larmes*)	T80
26	Courante du/Vieux Gautier. (*La petite bergère*)	T81
27	Sarabande du/Vieux Gautier	T82
28	Gigue du Vieux/Gautier. (*La Poste*)	T83
29	Courante du/Vieux Gautier./L'Immortelle.	T84
30	Sarabande./Gautier le Jeune	T85
31	Anonymous air for voice and figured bass (*Non printemps*) in another hand	
32	Prelude./D'Anglebert.	1

		Gustafson No.
33	Allemande./Couperin.	
33a	Double	D86
34	Courante./Chambonnieres.	
34a	Double.	D87
35	Courante./Chambonnieres.	
35a	Double.	D88
36	Sarabande./Chambonnieres. (*Jeunes zéphirs*)	
36a	Double.	D89
37	Gigue./D'Anglebert	16
38	Gaillarde./D'Anglebert.	8
39	Gavotte./D'Anglebert.	10
40	Menuet./D'Anglebert.	11
41	Sarabande./Richard.	
41a	Double.	D90
42	Sarabande./Marais.	T91
42a	Prelude. D'Anglebert.	17
42b	Ouuertuor dela/Mascarade (Lully)	T32
42c	Ouuertuor/d'Isis. (Lully)	T92
42d	Courante. (Lully)	
42e	Double dela/Courante.	T21
43	Air de Ballet./les Songes agreables. (Lully)	T34
44	Passacagle./D'Anglebert	27

Pieces contained in both the autograph manuscript and the 1689 edition are remarkably similar except in details of ornamentation and the spacing of voices. Ornament symbols in the manuscript are generally confined to the simple trill, mordent, one-note grace, and slide, with occasional use of the arpeggio, *cadence, double cheute,* and trill-mordent combination. A simple trill in the manuscript is often replaced with a trill *appuyé* or a *cadence* in the edition. Turns are written out in the manuscript, rather than being designated by a symbol. One might speculate, therefore, that much of this manuscript might have been compiled in the 1660s, because Chambonnières's books of 1670 include the symbol for the five-note turn. In general, the edition employs more ornament symbols than does the manuscript, although it occasionally removes *agréments* found in the manuscript. Sometimes the edition sustains a note or notes (usually in the lower register), thereby creating an extra voice or voices and increasing the sonority. A summary of the major variants in the two sources follows:

Variations. In addition to many substitutions of a *cadence* or a trill *appuyé* for a simple trill, the edition adds arpeggios, *détachés,* and sometimes a one-note grace between two mordents. The manuscript Variations do not begin on the downbeat; the left hand starts on the second beat, the right hand on the second half of the first beat. The second couplet of the edition incorporates revised voice leading in the lower register for three bars—a change that recurs in numerous later couplets. The notation of the 21st couplet differs considerably (see p.61). Two mordents in the bass voice of the last couplet of the manuscript version are removed in the edition.

Sarabande in D minor. Trills *appuyé* and arpeggios are added in the edition, while a recurring ornamental figure of an eighth and two sixteenth notes in the manuscript is altered to a dotted eighth and two 32nd notes in the edition. The one-note graces of m.6 are added in the edition. M.24 of the edition contains a written-out one-note grace before the third beat of the soprano voice, while m.26 contains one written out on the beat. Mm.19 and 26 include examples of dotted eighth and sixteenth notes (left hand) that are written as equal eighth notes in the manuscript. Many small ornamentation changes occur in the *reprise*.

Gigue in G major. The time signature is 3 in the manuscript (barred in 3/4) but 6/4 in the edition. The two readings are close except for added *détachés* in the edition and the use of a symbol in the edition to indicate arpeggios written out in the manuscript (see p.80).

Gaillarde in G major. The time signature is 3 in the manuscript but 3/2 in the edition. Turns indicated by symbol in the edition are written out in the manuscript (mm.1 and 4, see p.102). Some one-note graces indicated by symbol in the manuscript are written out (both before and on the beat) in the edition (mm.5, 15, 18, 19, 20, and 22). Examples of pairs of equal notes in the manuscript that are dotted in the edition occur in mm.21 and 23. An arpeggio symbol is placed on the note stem in m.2 of the edition but between the staves in the manuscript; and a mordent on the first tenor note of this measure is removed in the edition. The melodic line of mm.3, 15, and 16 is slightly different in the two sources. The slide on the first beat of m.12 is between D♯ and F♯ in the manuscript (which may be a stronger reading), instead of between F♯ and A. The rhythm of the alto line in the first part of m.22 is altered in the edition. The edition adds many arpeggios and makes numerous small changes and additions of ornamentation.

Gavotte in G major. The time signature is ₵ in the manuscript but C in the edition with the instruction *Lentement* added. All dotted eighth- and sixteenth-note groupings in the edition are written as equal eighth notes in the manuscript. A *cheute* is written out in m.5, and many one-note graces are added in the edition. Small melodic changes occur in mm.2, 3, 10, and 11.

Passacaille. The manuscript includes only the first four couplets. M.2 of the edition contains a written-out one-note grace in the bass before the second beat and an added one on the last beat. The first two notes of the bass (m.3) are dotted in the print but equal in the manuscript. Ornamentation is added in the edition, and small changes in the left-hand voicing give increased sonority.

Préludes. Many *cadences* are written out in the manuscript. In the edition, a trill *appuyé* is often substituted for a simple trill, occasional bar lines are added, and the slurring is more precise. Three whole notes in the edition version of the Prelude in G major (system 5 of the Gilbert edition, A–D–A) omit the slurs (probably an oversight). In two instances, notes in the right hand are written as a chord in the manuscript but separated in the edition: Prelude in G minor, D–A–C (p.28 of the Gilbert edition, system 4) and the Prelude in D minor, A–F–C (p.48, system 1). The G before the final F♯ of the Prelude in G minor is not found in the manuscript.

Table 3

D'Anglebert's Pieces in Other Manuscripts

Gustafson No.	MS No.	p. or l.No.	
			FRENCH MANUSCRIPTS
			Bauyn
64	63	44r	Sarabande graue en forme ("de gaillarde" crossed out)
			Dart
65	39	25v	Chacone
			La Barre-11
T14		205	Dans nos bois de Mʳ de lully
T55		206–207	Chaconne de Galatée de Mʳ de lully
65		212–214	Chaconne de Mʳ D'anglebert
65		229–230	Chaconne D'Anglebert
			Menetou
T21	117	33Ar-v	Courante de Mʳ de lully
T34	114	30Av-31Ar	Les Songes agreables d'atis
			Oldham
93	4		Courante. D'anglebert
26	12		Sarabande, façon de Gaillarde. D'anglebert
			Parville
T80	17	34	Courante du Vieux gautier
T21	41	72	Courante de Mʳ Lully
21a	41a	73	Double De La courante Lully
65	65	124–125	Chaconne Danglebert
T14	109	211	Menuet dans nos bois. Mʳ de Lully
T23	141	256–257	Dieu des Enfers
31	142	257	La Bergere Anette
36	143	258	Menuet de poitou
			Troyes
		77v	Quatuor sur le Kyrie double, à 3 sujets tires du plein chant; de Mʳ d'Anglebert
65		82v-83r	Chaconne d'Anglebert
97		85r	Sarabande de Mʳ D'anglebert
		85v	Menuet (uncertain authorship)

ENGLISH MANUSCRIPTS

Babell

65	204	151	Chaconne

Roper

94	32	37v-38r	Courante
95	33	38v-39r	Sarabande
95a	33a	39r-v	Double
96	34	40v-41r	Gigue

GERMAN MANUSCRIPTS

Mus. Ms. Bach P 801

39-45	259-273	Suite in D minor

Mus. Ms. 30,206

49	40-44	Variations sur les Folies d'Espagne par J. Henry Anglebert

A few miscellaneous pieces and transcriptions by D'Anglebert are contained in eleven other manuscripts (see Table 3). The Bauyn Manuscript (F-Pn, Vm^7 674–675), the most significant single source of harpsichord music in seventeenth-century France, was compiled in three volumes by one unidentified professional scribe. The coat of arms of the Bauyn d'Angervilliers and Mathefelon families appears on the covers of the volumes. Bauyn-I contains works by Chambonnières only, Bauyn-II those of Louis Couperin; but Bauyn-III includes works by J. J. Froberger, G. Frescobaldi, H. Du Mont, E. Richard, and other composers of this period. Recent external evidence obtained by Gustafson indicates that this manuscript could not have been compiled earlier than 1676, despite its contents from an earlier period. Further information about the dating of this manuscript can be found in Bruce Gustafson and Peter Wolf, editors, *The Bauyn Manuscript* (New York: Broude Bros., forthcoming), Preface by Bruce Gustafson.

D'Anglebert is represented in the Bauyn Manuscript only by a *Sarabande graue en forme de gaillarde*, No.63 (G. 64), which corresponds to the Gaillarde in C major (Rés. 89ter, No.6). In general, the setting in the Bauyn Manuscript shows simpler ornamentation, thinner texture, wide spacing between the hands at cadences, and less rhythmic movement. A peculiarity of this manuscript is the careful crossing out with the letter *d* of many titles and even one complete piece; *de gaillarde* is crossed out in the title of D'Anglebert's piece.

The Oldham Manuscript, now in London and largely unpublished, bears dates from the 1650s on individual pieces. Its contents are described in Guy Oldham's article in *Recherches* I (1960): 51–59. The manuscript is an important source for the organ music of Louis Couperin. It also contains works by several other composers, including two by D'Anglebert, probably in his own hand (Gustafson, p.267): a Courante in C major, found in no other source, and a *Sarabande, façon de Gaillarde* in G minor (G. 26). These pieces employ a type of French letter notation closely related to lute tablature (Gutafson, p.94).

Gustafson, one of the few scholars to gain access to the Oldham Manuscript, observes that the reading of this gaillarde has less melodic figuration and a thinner left-hand texture than that in D'Anglebert's edition (personal communication). D'Anglebert's hand is also seen in a Courante by Monnard and a Sarabande by Richard, both also in the Bauyn Manuscript. The Oldham readings are close, but not identical, to those in Bauyn according to Gustafson, for there are small figurations in the melodic lines, and the voicing of chords is somewhat altered.

The Dart Manuscript, of French origin after 1687, contains miscellaneous harpsichord pieces and transcriptions. At the present time, it is in the estate of the late Thurston Dart, care of Kings College, London. D'Anglebert is represented only by the Chaconne in C major (G. 65), which is incomplete after m.28 since the next two leaves of the manuscript have been cut out.

The Parville Manuscript (US-BE, MS 778), a major seventeenth-century collection of keyboard music, served as the main source for Alan Curtis's edition of Louis Couperin's works. Although Couperin's pieces form the bulk of the manuscript, it also includes many works by Lully and Chambonnières, and fewer pieces by numerous other composers. Gustafson dates the manuscript post 1686 because of the inclusion of a transcription from Lully's *Acis et Galatée*. Parville contains D'Anglebert's Chaconne in C major (G. 65) and several of his transcriptions. The arrangements from his *Pièces de clavecin* (all but Nos.17 and 65) show only slight variants, which could be attributed to scribal error or preference. These pieces could therefore have been copied directly from the edition, thus dating this manuscript as post 1689. Because of the large number of variants, Nos.17 and 65 probably were copied from a source other than Rés. 89ter. Gustafson suggests that Nos.110 and 111 might be D'Anglebert transcriptions because of the ornamentation style, but the resemblance is mostly visual. The scribe begins all trills and mordents with a flourish that resembles D'Anglebert's *cadence*, but the context indicates a simple ornament. The hook before the note to designate a one-note grace is turned in the opposite direction (see St.-Lambert, p.93 above). The pieces also lack D'Anglebert's distinctive *style luthé* treatment.

The Menetou Manuscript (US-BE, MS 777, post c.1689), entitled *Airs de mademoiselle Menetou*, contains mostly transcriptions of Lully's works, including D'Anglebert's arrangement of his Courante in G minor (G. T21) and *Les Songes agreables* (G. T34, not noted by Gustafson). The errors in these pieces, probably copied from D'Anglebert's 1689 edition, indicate carelessness on the part of the scribe rather than variants.

Gustafson dates the La Barre-11 Manuscript "post 1724 with additions post 1753" (US-BE, MS 775). A mixture of keyboard and vocal scores, its 352 pages include keyboard works by D'Anglebert, François Couperin, Lully, and others. The D'Anglebert transcriptions from Lully (G. T14 and T55) are virtually exact copies of D'Anglebert's 1689 edition, except for simplified ornamentation. Curiously, this manuscript contains two versions of D'Anglebert's Chaconne in C major (G. 65), both by the same copyist, indicating that the scribe might have considered the variants significant enough to warrant making a second entry (this chaconne received wide circulation, appearing in six known manuscripts). Since the La Barre copies were probably made more than 30 years after D'Anglebert's death, their accuracy is questionable. The copyist did not know the meaning of D'Anglebert's *cheute* and *coulé* symbols, for they are often rendered as the wavy arpeggio symbol.

Of the foreign manuscripts, one from Weimar (D-ddr, Bds, Mus. Ms. Bach P 801, c.1712 to post 1731, named "Walther" by Gustafson), a large source for the music of J. S. Bach and various German and French composers, is of especial interest, for the scribes were from the Bach circle: J. G. Walther, J. T. Krebs, and J. L. Krebs. According to Gustafson (p.77), Walther is the scribe for D'Anglebert's suite in D minor, which appears to have been copied from the *Pièces de clavecin*, since it is identical except for a few errors and changes of ornamentation.

A much later German manuscript, Berlin 30,206 (D-ddr, Bds, Mus. Ms. 30,206, c.1750–1770), includes D'Anglebert's *Variations sur les folies d'Espagne*. D'Anglebert is the only Frenchman represented in this company of Galuppi, Hiller, and Wagenseil, and he is older than the others by a century. This manuscript too copies D'Anglebert's edition, but all the ornamentation is omitted except a *t* (trill) at the final cadence.

The Babell Manuscript (GB-Lbm, Add. 39569) was copied by Charles Babell, a London musician and francophile. This important 360-page collection of keyboard works originated in London (1702) and includes works by numerous French composers. D'Anglebert is represented by the Chaconne in C major (G. 65), but the variations are ordered differently. Since many pieces are unattributed, there may be others by D'Anglebert, particularly some transcriptions from Lully.

The newly discovered pieces by D'Anglebert from the Roper Manuscript (US-Cn, Case VM 2.3 E58r, c.1691), an English household manuscript also containing French and English keyboard pieces, are given in Appendix 2. While they have no attribution, the style and ornamentation clearly point to D'Anglebert as the composer.

A previously unknown Sarabande in C major by D'Anglebert appears in a manuscript from Troyes, France (F-T, MS 2682) of mostly organ works by Nivers, Raison, Lebègue, and Boyvin. Despite its attribution, the style of this sarabande lacks the polish of D'Anglebert's known works. The Menuet immediately following the Sarabande has no attribution but could be D'Anglebert's since it is grouped with his other pieces. The Troyes Manuscript also contains his Chaconne in C major (G. 65) and *Quatuor* for organ.

Modern Editions

Marguerite Roesgen-Champion's edition of D'Anglebert's *Pièces de clavecin* of 1934 was the first complete publication since those of 1689–1704. Kenneth Gilbert's performing edition of D'Anglebert's works was published in 1975 (Paris: Heugel) with brief biographical notes, information regarding the 1689 edition and the autograph manuscript, performance practice suggestions, editorial policy, the table of ornaments, facsimile pages, and a critical commentary listing editorial changes. Gilbert included all of D'Anglebert's known *oeuvre* in this volume, with the exception of the Courante in C major, found only in the inaccessible Oldham Manuscript, and the recently discovered pieces in the Roper and Troyes manuscripts. He rearranged the contents of the 1689 edition by placing the fifteen transcriptions from Lully and the four from anonymous sources together in two sections following

D'Anglebert's suites. Gilbert also changed the order of some lute pieces in the manuscript to produce the allemande–courante–sarabande–gigue suite order. He supplied repeat signs where they are lacking in the edition—almost exclusively in the small forms of gavotte, menuet, and *vaudeville*.

Only occasionally may Gilbert's editorial judgment be open to question. In some cases, he indicates an editorial preference by an accidental above the note, but at other times he makes such a change without notice and lists it in the Critical Commentary. Gilbert changes the barring of the *Courantes du Vieux Gautier* and the *Gigue La Verdinguette* from the 3/4 time of the manuscript to 6/4 (noted in the Commentary). A few variants in Gilbert's edition, located in a comparison with the 1689 edition (second issue) and the manuscript, are listed in Table 4. For pieces contained in both the 1689 edition and the autograph manuscript, only the print has been used for comparison.

Table 4

Gilbert Edition of D'Anglebert's Works
Variants in a comparison with the 1689 edition
(second issue) and the autograph manuscript

Key:
S A T B: soprano, alto, tenor, or bass voice
RH, LH: right hand or left hand
p.250, 5 S7: the seventh note in the soprano voice of
    m.5 on p.250 of the Gilbert edition.
The items marked with an asterisk are also included in Gilbert's Critical
    Commentary, but are given again because of their possible significance.

p.14, 8 RH chord, no sharp on *re**
p.30, 4 A4 *si*-flat
p.41, 45 LH3 no trill*
p.47, system 6 B last slur goes to *re* (p. 48)
p.48, system 1 B another *la* (semibreve) after fifth note*
p.53, 8 S1 no trill*
p.60, 1 B2 *cheute* before *do*-sharp
p.60, 14 S7 no flat on *si**
p.61, 21 RH1 no arpeggio*
p.83, 39 RH1 no arpeggio
p.94, 43 RH1 slide on right, not left
p.96, 14 B2 no flat on *mi**
p.98, 4 S1 trill under note as well as *cadence* above
p.107, 25 S4-5 eighth notes*
p.111, 104 S1 mordent
p.114, 16 S1 trill
p.121, 10 B arpeggio on 2, not 1 (although this location for the arpeggio
    seems dubious, placing it on the first chord does not appear to be the
    proper solution either)*

p.123, 8 S3 no mordent

p.125, 17 S7 *fa*-natural

p.127, 28 S5 *do*-natural

p.128, 8 RH3 *si*-natural

p.129, 24 RH2 *la* may be tied, not slurred

p.147, 13 LH last note is *sol**

p.148, 6 S2-4 sixteenth notes, D'Anglebert error?

p.150, 4 RH2 *port de voix*, not slide, before *do*

p.153, 12 S1-3 rhythm is dotted quarter and two sixteenth notes

p.154, barred in 3/4 time*

p.155, barred in 3/4 time*

p.157, 13 S5 pitch is *sol**

p.160, 15 LH1 no mordent

p.167, partially barred in 3/4 time

p.168, barred in 3/4 time*

p.169, barred in 3/4 time*

p.170, barred in 3/4 time*

p.170, 2 LH1 A middle voice begins on tenor *sol* also, and is barred
    together with the following *mi* as two eighth notes.

p.171, 23 T2 trill

p.176, 8 S1-2 eighth notes*

p.179, 11 B2 no mordent after trill

p.180, barred in 3/4 time*

p.181, barred in 3/4 time*

p.181, 10 B1-2 eighth notes

p.182, barred in 3/4 time*

p.183, 14 S5 no trill*

p.183, 14 T3 no flat*

p.185, 7 S8 mordent instead of *port de voix*

p.187, 12 RH last chord, *cheute* before *la* instead of slide

p.187, 18 A6 *cheute* before *do*

p.190, 8 S4 quarter note

p.193, 4 B4 stemmed separately

p.193, 17 S turn written as five 32nd notes with no slur

Principal Sources for Other Composers

Chambonnières:
Two editions of 1670: *Les Pièces de clauessin*
Manuscripts: principally Bauyn-I
                F-Psg, Gen. 2348/53
                Oldham
                Parville
                Miscellaneous pieces in sixteen other manuscripts

Louis Couperin:
Manuscripts: Bauyn-II
                Parville
                Miscellaneous pieces in twelve other manuscripts

Nicolas-Antoine Lebègue:
Editions: *Les Pièces de clauessin* (1677)
      Second liure de clavessin (1687)
Manuscripts: Miscellaneous pieces in numerous French and foreign manuscripts; all identified pieces by Lebègue appear to be in his two editions.

Elisabeth-Claude Jacquet de La Guerre:
Editions: *Les Pièces de clauessin . . . premier livre* (c.1687)
      Pièces de clauecin (1707)

APPENDIX 2
NEWLY DISCOVERED PIECES BY D'ANGLEBERT FROM THE ROPER MANUSCRIPT

Courante in A minor.
Courtesy of The Newberry Library, Chicago.

Sarabande in A minor.

Courtesy of The Newberry Library, Chicago.

Double, Sarabande in A minor.

Courtesy of The Newberry Library, Chicago.

Gigue in A minor.

Courtesy of The Newberry Library, Chicago.

[Fin]

APPENDIX 3

TRANSCRIPTIONS BY D'ANGLEBERT

No.	Composer	Pièces de Clavecin	LWV
12	Lully	Ouuerture de Cadmus	49/1
		(*Cadmus et Hermione*, 1673)	
13	Lully	Ritournelle des Feés de Rolland	65/78
		(*Roland*, 1685)	
14	Lully	Menuet. dans nos bois	35/4
		(*Trios pour le coucher du Roi*)	
		F-Pc Rés. 1397	
15	Lully	Chaconne de Phaeton	61/40
		(*Phaéton*, 1683)	
21	Lully	Courante M.ᵉ de Lully	75/24
		F-Pc, Rés. F 533	
21a		Double	
23	Lully	Sarabande Dieu des Enfers	27/41
		(*Ballet de la Naissance de Vénus*, 1665)	
25	Lully	Gigue (no other source)	75/52
28	Lully	Menuet la Jeune Iris	35/10
		(*Trios pour le coucher du Roi*)	
		F-Pc Rés. 1397	
29	Anonymous	Gavotte. Ou estes vous allé. Air ancien	
30	Anonymous	Gavotte. le beau berger Tirsis. Air ancien	
31	Anonymous	La Bergere Anette. Vaudeville	
32	Lully	Ouverture de la Mascarade	36/1
		(*Le Carnaval, Mascarade*, 1668)	
33	Lully	Les Sourdines d'Armide	71/39
		(*Armide*, 1686)	
34	Lully	Les Songes agreables d'Atys	53/58
		(*Atys*, 1676)	
35	Lully	Air d'Apollon du Triomphe de l'Amour	59/58
		(*Le Triomphe de l'Amour*, 1681)	
36	Anonymous	Menuet de Poitou. Vaudeville	
37	Lully	Passacaille d'Armide	71/61
		(*Armide*, 1686)	
48	Lully	Ouuerture de Proserpine	58/1
		(*Proserpine*, 1680)	
55	Lully	Chaconne de Galatée	73/32
		(*Acis et Galatée*, 1686)	

MS Rés. 89ter

No.	Composer		Page Number Modern Edition*	LWV
2	Chambonnières	Courante.	D'Anglebert 148 Chambonnières 7	
2a		Double.	D'Anglebert 149	
3	Chambonnières	2ᵉ Courante.	D'Anglebert 150 Chambonnières 8	
3a		Double.	D'Anglebert 151	
4	Pinel	Sarabande.	D'Anglebert 152 cf. Bauyn-III, No.90	
4a		Double.	D'Anglebert 153	
5	Chambonnières	Gigue. La Verdinguette.	D'Anglebert 154 Chambonnières 31	
5a		Double.	D'Anglebert 155	
8	Lully	Bouree. Air de Ballet poᵣ Les Basques. (*Xerxès*, 1660)	D'Anglebert 162	12/2
9	Lully	Les Demons. Air de Ballet. (*Thesée*, 1675)	D'Anglebert 164	51/53
9a	Lully	2ᵉ Air des Demons. (*Thesée*, 1675)	D'Anglebert	51/55
10	Lully	Air de Ballet. Marche. (*Isis*, 1677)	D'Anglebert 163	54/43
11	E. Gaultier	Gigue du Vieux Gautier.	D'Anglebert 172	
12	E. Gaultier	Courante du Vieux Gautier.	D'Anglebert 169	
13	E. Gaultier	Courante du Vieux Gautier.	D'Anglebert 167 E. Gaultier 48	
14	Mesangeau	Sarabande. Mezangeot.	D'Anglebert 171 Mesangeau 13	
15	E. Gaultier	Courante du Vieux Gautier.	D'Anglebert 168	
16	E. Gaultier	Allemande du Vieux Gautier. (La Vestemponade)	D'Anglebert 166	
17	E. Gaultier	Courante du Vieux Gautier.	D'Anglebert 170	
18	E. Gaultier	Chaconne du Vieux Gautier.	D'Anglebert 173	

*The modern editions are listed in the Bibliography. Chambonnières's works are cited from the Brunold-Tessier edition.

No.	Composer		Page Number Modern Edition*	LWV
22	Chambonnières	O beau jardin Sarabande.	D'Anglebert 178 Chambonnières 88	
22a		Double	D'Anglebert 179	
25	E. Gaultier	Courante du Vieux Gautier. (Les Larmes)	D'Anglebert 180 E. Gautier 64	
26	E. Gaultier	Courante du Vieux Gautier. (La petite bergère)	D'Anglebert 181 E. Gaultier 37	
27	E. Gaultier	Sarabande du Vieux Gautier.	D'Anglebert 183 E. Gaultier 54	
28	E. Gaultier	Gigue du Vieux Gautier. (La Poste)	D'Anglebert 185 E. Gaultier	
29	E. Gaultier	Courante du Vieux Gautier.L'Immortelle.	D'Anglebert 182 E. Gaultier 88	
30	D. Gaultier	Sarabande. Gautier le Jeune.	D'Anglebert 184 D. Gaultier 125	
33	L. Couperin	Allemande. Couperin.	D'Anglebert 186 Couperin 136	
33a		Double.	D'Anglebert 188	
34	Chambonnières	Courante.	D'Anglebert 190 Chambonnières 49	
34a		Double.	D'Anglebert 191	
35	Chambonnières	Courante.	D'Anglebert 192 Chambonnières 51	
35a		Double.	D'Anglebert 193	
36	Chambonnières	Sarabande. (Jeunes zéphirs)	D'Anglebert 194 Chambonnières 52	
36a		Double.	D'Anglebert 195	
41	Richard	Sarabande.	D'Anglebert 196 L'Orgue Parisien 14	
41a		Double.	D'Anglebert 197	
42	Marais	Sarabande.	D'Anglebert 198	
42b	Lully	Ouuertuor dela Mascarade. (Le Carnaval, Mascarade, 1668)	D'Anglebert 90	36/1
42c	Lully	Ouuertuor d'Isis. (Isis, 1677)	D'Anglebert 199	54/1
42d	Lully	Courante. F-Pc Rés.F 533	D'Anglebert 95	75/24
42e		Double dela Courante.	D'Anglebert 97	
43	Lully	Air de Ballet. les Songes agreables. (Atys, 1676)	D'Anglebert 116	53/58

APPENDIX 4

OTHER FIGURES OF THE SEVENTEENTH

AND EIGHTEENTH CENTURIES

Claude-Bénigne Balbastre (1727–1799). Paris organist at St. Roch, Notre Dame, and court. Published *Pièces de clavecin* (1759), *Recueil de Noëls* (1770), and *Sonates en quatuor* (1779).

Jacques Boyvin (c.1649–1706). Organist of Notre Dame Cathedral, Rouen. Published two books of organ music (1689–1690 and 1700) and a treatise on figured-bass accompaniment (1705).

Marc-Antoine Charpentier (c.1645/1650–1704). *Maître de musique* for the Duchesse de Guise, the Dauphin, the Jesuit church of St. Louis, and Sainte-Chapelle. Prolific composer of sacred and secular vocal and instrumental music, including operas and other stage works.

Lambert Chaumont (c.1630–1712). Priest and composer in southern Netherlands. Published *Pièces d'orgue sur les 8 tons* (1695), written in the French manner of the day.

Louis-Nicolas Clérambault (1676–1749). Paris organist (Grands Augustins, St. Sulpice, Jacobins, and court). Prolific composer of solo cantatas, sacred music, *Pièces de clavecin* (1704), and *Livre d'orgue* (c.1710).

François Couperin *le grand* (1668–1733). Active as a harpsichordist at court. Published four books of clavecin music (1713, 1716–1717, 1722, 1730), an instruction manual—*L'Art de toucher le clavecin* (1716), and *Pièces d'orgue* (1690). Also composed much chamber music and sacred and secular vocal music.

François Dagincour (1684–1758). Organist at Notre Dame Cathedral, Rouen, and the royal chapel. Composer of the *Pièces de clavecin* (1733) and organ music.

Jean-François Dandrieu (c.1682–1738). Paris organist at St. Merry, St. Barthélemy, and the royal chapel. Published several books for clavecin (three early books, c.1704–1720; and *Pièces de clavecin* of 1724, 1728, and 1734) and *Pièces d'orgue* (1739, posthumous).

Charles [?François] Dieupart (after 1667–c.1740). French harpsichordist and violinist who emigrated to London. Composer of *Six suittes de clavessin* (1701), songs, and instrumental music.

Henry Du Mont (1610–1684). Harpsichordist and Paris organist of St. Paul and the royal chapel. Composer of much sacred vocal music and a few keyboard pieces.

M. Durocher. Organist of St. Jean de Lus. Published *Pièces de clavecin* (1733).

Pierre-Claude Foucquet (c.1694–1772). Paris organist at St.-Honoré, Abbey of St. Victor, St. Eustache, Notre Dame, and the royal chapel. Published three books of clavecin music (1749, 1750–1751, 1751).

Johann Jakob Froberger (1616–1667). Worked at Viennese court. Composed large quantity of music for organ and harpsichord. Foremost German keyboard composer of the seventeenth century.

Denis Gaultier *le jeune* (1603–1672). Paris lutenist and composer of "La Rhétorique des dieux" (c.1652), *Pièces de luth* (1669), and *Livre de tablature* (c.1672).

Ennemond Gaultier *le vieux* (1575–1651). Lutenist at court, composer, and cousin of Denis Gaultier. Wrote numerous lute pieces in many printed collections of the seventeenth century, including those containing Denis Gaultier's works above.

?Jacques Hardel (d. late 1670s). Pupil of Chambonnières and composer of nine surviving pieces, mostly for harpsichord.

Jacques (-Martin) Hotteterre [*Le Romain*] (1674–1763). Instrumentalist at court and composer of numerous instrumental works, particularly for flute. Published *Principes de la flûte traversière . . .*(1707), *L'Art de préluder . . .* (1719), and *Méthode pour la musette . . .* (1737).

Joseph de La Barre (1633–c.1678). Organist for the royal chapel from 1656 and composer of vocal and keyboard music.

Michel-Richard de Lalande (1657–1726). Held several positions at court and succeeded Lully as *Surintendant de la musique de la chambre* (1689). Composer of sacred music (particularly *grands motets*), stage works, instrumental music, and airs.

Michel Lambert (1610–1696). *Maître de musique de la chambre du Roi* from 1661. Foremost French composer of airs in the mid-century.

Gaspard Le Roux (?–d.1705–1707). Noted Paris harpsichordist. Published *Pièces de clavessin* (1705).

Jean-Baptiste Lully (1632–1687). An Italian who came to Paris at age fourteen and rose to dominate French music. Appointed *Surintendant de la musique et compositeur de la musique de la chambre* in 1661 and *Maître de la musique de la famille royale* in 1662. Composed music for numerous ballets, *tragédies en musique*, and other stage works, as well as motets and instrumental music.

Marin Marais (1656–1728). Well-known composer and gambist at court from 1685. Published five books for the viol as well as chamber music.

Louis Marchand (1669–1732). Paris organist at St. Benoit, St. Honoré, and the royal chapel and for the Cordeliers. Published *Pièces de clavecin* (1702 and 1703) and *Livre d'orgue* (n.d.).

John Mercure (fl.1640–1650). French lutenist and composer at the court of Charles I in England.

Marin Mersenne (1588–1648). Philosopher, mathematician, music theorist, and author of numerous treatises, including *Harmonie universelle* (1636) and *Harmonicorum libri* (1635–1648).

René Mesangeau (d.1638). Noted lutenist at court and composer of numerous lute pieces.

Michel Pignolet de Montéclair (1667–1737). Parisian *maître* and prolific composer of airs, cantatas, stage works, sacred music, and instrumental music. Published five treatises between 1709 and 1736, including the *Principes de musique*.

Guillaume-Gabriel Nivers (c.1632–1714). Organist at St. Sulpice in Paris and the royal chapel, composer, and theorist. Published three books for organ (1665, 1667, and 1675), sacred vocal music, and treatises, including the *Traité de la composition de musique* (1667).

Germain Pinel (d.1661). Lutenist at court and composer of assorted lute pieces.

André Raison (before 1650–1719). Organist at Ste. Geneviève in Paris and later to the Jacobins de St. Jacques. Published *Livre d'orgue* (1688) and *Second livre d'orgue* (1714).

Jean-Philippe Rameau (1683–1764). Published three books of clavecin music (1706, 1724, and 1728), *Pièces de clavecin en concerts* (1741), numerous stage works, and important theoretical treatises.

François Roberday (1624–1680). Composer, organist, and *Valet de chambre* of the Queen. Published *Fugues et caprices, à quatre parties* (1660) for organ or instruments.

Jean Rousseau (1644–c.1700). *Maître* of the viol, composer, and noted author of two treatises: *Traité de la viole* (1687) and *Méthode claire, certaine et facile pour apprendre à chanter la musique* (six editions from 1678 to 1710).

Monsieur de Saint-Lambert. At present nothing is certain but that this Parisian *maître* published two important treatises: *Les principes du clavecin* (1702) and *Nouveau traité de l'accompagnement du clavecin, de l'orgue, et des autres instruments* (1707).

Nicholas Siret (1663–1754). Organist of the Cathedral and church of St. Jean in Troyes. Published *Pièces de clavecin* (c.1710 and 1719).

Jean Titelouze (c.1562–1633). Organist of Rouen Cathedral and the first important French composer of organ music. Published *Hymnes de l'église* (1623) and *Le Magnificat. . .* (1626) for organ in a contrapuntal style.

BIBLIOGRAPHY

Manuscripts

Berkeley, University of California, Music Library, MS 775, La Barre-ll. Mixture of keyboard and vocal works, post 1724 with additions post 1753.

———, MS 777, Menetou. Primarily transcriptions from Lully, post 1689.

———, MS 778, Parville. Primarily works by Louis Couperin, plus numerous works by many other keyboard composers, post 1689.

Berlin, Deutsche Staatsbibliothek, Musikabteilung, Mus. Ms. 30,206. Primarily keyboard works of early classic period, c.1750–1770.

———, Bach Mus. Ms. P 801. Large collection of keyboard works by J. S. Bach and other German and French composers, c.1712–post 1731.

Berlin, Staatsbibliothek Preussischer Kulturbesitz, Mus. Ms. 40,644, Möllersche. Works by J. S. Bach, G. Böhm, and others, and an ornament table patterned after D'Anglebert's.

Chicago, Newberry Library, Special Collections, Case MS VM 2.3 E58r, Roper. Household manuscript containing keyboard works by French and English composers, c.1691.

Frankfurt/Main, Stadt- und Universitätsbibliothek, Mus. Hs. 1538. Copy in J. S. Bach's hand of Nicolas de Grigny's *Livre d'orgue* and D'Anglebert's ornament table.

London, British Library, Reference Division, Add. 39569, Babell. Large collection of French keyboard works by many composers, copied by Charles Babell, c.1702.

London, private collection from estate of Thurston Dart, on permanent loan to the Faculty of Music, King's College; No.2 on "Handlist of Manuscripts from the Dart Collection. . . ." Miscellaneous keyboard works of French origin, post 1687.

London, private collection of Guy Oldham. Primarily autograph of Louis Couperin, plus additional miscellaneous keyboard pieces, c.1650s.

Paris, Bibliothèque nationale, Vm⁷ 674–675. Published in facsimile with Introduction by François Lesure as *Manuscrit Bauyn. Pièces de clavecin c. 1660.* Geneva: Minkoff, 1977. Large manuscript of works by Chambonnières, Louis Couperin, and many other keyboard composers, post 1676.

———. Rés. 89ter (*olim* Conservatoire de musique 18223). Primarily D'Anglebert autograph with some later additions, c.1660s–1670s.

Paris, Bibliothèque Sainte-Geneviève, MS 2348 and MS 2353. Organ and harpsichord works, primarily by Chambonnières, post 1658?

Troyes, Bibliothèque municipale, MS 2682. Organ and harpsichord works by Nivers, Boyvin, Lebègue, D'Anglebert, Raison, and Siret.

Original Editions or Facsimiles

Bach, J. S. *Clavier-Büchlein vor Wilhelm Friedemann Bach*. Facsimile of 1720 manuscript. Preface by Ralph Kirkpatrick. New Haven: Yale University Press, 1959.

Chambonnières, Jacques Champion de. *Les Pièces de clauessin*. Facsimile of 1670 Paris editions. New York: Broude Bros., 1967.

Clérambault, Louis-Nicolas. *Premier livre de pièces de clavecin*. Facsimile of 1704 Paris edition. Geneva: Minkoff, 1982.

Corrette, Michel. *Premier livre de pièces de clavecin*. Facsimile of 1734 Paris edition. Geneva: Minkoff, 1982.

Couperin, François. *Pièces de clavecin I–IV*. Facsimile of 1713, 1716–1717, 1722, and 1730 Paris editions. New York: Broude Bros., 1973.

———. *L'Art de toucher le clavecin*. Paris: Author and Boyvin, 1716.

Dandrieu, Jean-François. *Pièces de clavecin courtes et faciles de quatre tons differents*. Paris: Author, Foucault, n.d.

D'Anglebert, Jean-Henry. *Pièces de clavecin*. Facsimile of 1689 Paris edition. New York: Broude Bros., 1965.

Dieupart, Monsieur. *Six suittes de clavessin*. Amsterdam: E. Roger, n.d. [c.1702].

Durocher. *Pièces de clavecin*. Facsimile of 1733 Paris edition. Geneva: Minkoff, 1982.

Foucquet, Pierre-Claude. *Pièces de clavecin*, Books I and II. Facsimile of 1751 Paris editions. Geneva: Minkoff, 1982.

Gaultier, Denis. *La Rhétorique des dieux et autres pièces de luth*. Facsimile of manuscript and c.1670 Paris edition. Publications de la Société française de musicologie, Vol. 6. Paris: Droz, 1932–1933. (Vol. 7 includes a transcription by André Tessier of the lute tablature.)

Gaultier, Denis and Ennemond. *Pièces de luth . . . sur trois différens modes nouveaux*. Facsimile of c.1670 Paris edition. Geneva: Minkoff, 1975.

La Guerre, Elisabeth-Claude Jacquet de. *Les Pièces de clauessin . . . premier livre*. Paris: Author and Sr de Baussen, c.1687. Only extant copy at Biblioteca del Conservatorio Benedetto Marcello, Venice.

———. *Pièces de clauecin qui peuvent se jouer sur le viollon*. Paris: Author, Foucault, Ribou, and Ballard, 1707.

Lebègue, Nicolas-Antoine. *Les Pièces de clauessin*. Paris: Author, 1677.

———. *Second liure de clavessin*. Paris: Lesclop, 1687.

Le Roux, Gaspard. *Pièces de clavessin*. Facsimile of 1705 Paris edition. Geneva: Minkoff, 1982.

Lully, Jean Baptiste de. *Armide*. Paris: Ballard, 1686.

Marchand, Louis. *Pièces de clavecin . . . premier livre* and *. . . second livre*. Facsimiles of 1702 and 1703 Paris editions. Geneva: Minkoff, 1982.

Nivers, Guillaume-Gabriel. *Livre d'orgue contenant cent pièces de tous les tons de l'église*. Paris: Author and Ballard, 1665.

Perrine. *Pièces de luth en musique auec des règles pour les toucher parfaitem^t sur le luth, et sur le claussin*. Facsimile of 1680 Paris edition. Geneva: Minkoff, 1982.

Raison, André. *Livre d'orgue*. Paris: Author, 1688.

Rameau, Jean-Philippe. *Premier livre de pièces de clavecin*. Paris: Author, 1706.

————. *Pièces de clavessin.* Facsimile of 1724 Paris edition. New York: Broude Bros., 1967.

————. *Nouvelles suites de pièces de clavecin.* Facsimile of c.1728 Paris edition. New York: Broude Bros., 1967.

Siret, Nicolas. *Pièces de clavecin.* Facsimile of c.1710 and 1719 editions. Geneva: Minkoff, 1982.

Modern Editions

Bach, Johann Sebastian. *Clavier-Büchlein vor Wilhelm Friedemann Bach* in *Neue Ausgabe sämtlicher Werke,* V/5, and *Kritischer Bericht.* Edited by Wolfgang Plath. Kassel: Bärenreiter, 1962.

————. *Die sechs Französische Suiten.* Edited by Alfred Dürr. Kassel: Bärenreiter, 1984.

————. *Goldberg Variations.* Edited by Christoph Wolff. Kassel and Basel: Bärenreiter, 1977.

Balbastre, Claude-Bénigne. *Pièces de clavecin, d'orgue et de forte piano.* Edited by Alan Curtis. Le Pupitre 52. Paris: Heugel, 1974.

Boyvin, Jacques. *Oeuvres complètes d'orgue.* Edited by Alexandre Guilmant. In Archives des maîtres de l'orgue. Paris: Durand, 1905.

————. *Premier livre d'orgue.* Edited by Jean Bonfils. Paris: Les Éditions ouvrières, 1969.

Chambonnières, Jacques Champion. *Oeuvres complètes.* Edited by Paul Brunold and André Tessier. Publications de la Société française de musicologie. Reprint of 1925 Paris edition. New York: Broude Bros., 1967.

————. *Les deux livres de clavecin.* Edited by Thurston Dart. Monaco: L'Oiseau-Lyre, 1969.

Chaumont, Lambert. *Pièces d'orgue sur les 8 tons.* Edited by Jean Ferrard. Le Pupitre 25. Paris: Heugel, 1970.

Clérambault, Louis-Nicolas. *Pièces de clavecin.* Edited by Paul Brunold, revised by Thurston Dart. Monaco: L'Oiseau-Lyre, 1964.

Couperin, François. *Pièces de clavecin,* I–IV. Edited by Kenneth Gilbert. Le Pupitre 21–24. Paris: Heugel, 1969–1972.

Couperin, Louis. *Pièces de clavecin.* Edited by Alan Curtis. Le Pupitre 18. Paris: Heugel, 1970.

————. *Pièces de clavecin.* Edited by Paul Brunold, revised by Thurston Dart. Monaco: L'Oiseau-Lyre, 1959.

Dagincour, François. *Pièces de clavecin.* Edited by Howard Ferguson. Le Pupitre 12. Paris: Heugel, 1969.

Dandrieu, Jean-François. *Trois livres de clavecin de jeunesse.* Edited by Brigitte François-Sappey. Publications de la Société française de musicologie 1:21. Paris: Heugel, 1975.

D'Anglebert, Jean-Henry. *Pièces de clavecin.* Edited by Kenneth Gilbert. Le Pupitre 54. Paris: Heugel, 1975.

————. *Pièces de clavecin.* Edited by Marguerite Roesgen-Champion. Paris: Publications de la Société française de musicologie, 1934.

Dieupart. *Six suites pour clavecin.* Edited by Paul Brunold, revised by Kenneth Gilbert. Paris: L'Oiseau-Lyre, 1979.

The Fitzwilliam Virginal Book. Edited by J. A. Fuller Maitland and W. Barclay

Squire. Reprint of 1899 Breitkopf & Härtel edition. New York: Dover, 1963.

Froberger, Johann Jakob. *Oeuvres complètes: Livres de 1649, 1656 & 1658.* Edited by Howard Schott. Le Pupitre 57. Paris: Heugel, 1979.

Gaultier, Ennemond. *Oeuvres du vieux Gautier.* Edited by André Souris. Paris: Centre national de la recherche scientifique, 1966.

La Guerre, Elisabeth-Claude Jacquet de. *Pièces de clavecin* (1707). Edited by Paul Brunold, revised by Thurston Dart. Monaco: L'Oiseau-Lyre, 1965.

Lebègue, Nicolas-Antoine. *Oeuvres de clavecin.* Edited by Norbert Dufourcq. Monaco: L'Oiseau-Lyre, 1956.

———. *Oeuvres complètes d'orgue.* Edited by Alexandre Guilmant. In Archives des maîtres de l'orgue. Paris: Durand, 1909.

Le Roux, Gaspard. *Pièces de clavecin.* Edited by Albert Fuller. New York: Alpeg, 1959.

Lully, Jean-Baptiste. *Nine seventeenth-century organ transcriptions from the operas of Lully.* Edited with an Introduction by Almonte C. Howell, Jr. Lexington: The University of Kentucky Press, 1963.

———. *Oeuvres complètes.* Edited by Henry Prunières. Reprint of 1930–1939 Paris editions. New York: Broude Bros., 1966.

Marchand, Louis. *Pièces de clavecin.* Edited by Thurston Dart. Monaco: L'Oiseau-Lyre, 1960.

Mercure, John. *Oeuvres des Mercure.* Edited by Monique Rollin and Jean-Michel Vaccaro. Paris: Centre national de la recherche scientifique, 1977.

Mesangeau, René. *Oeuvres.* Edited by André Souris. Paris: Centre national de la recherche scientifique, 1971.

Nivers, Guillaume-Gabriel. *Premier livre d'orgue.* Edited by Norbert Dufourcq. Paris: Bornemann, 1963.

L'Orgue parisien sous le règne de Louis XIV. Edited by Norbert Dufourcq. Copenhagen: Hansen, 1956.

Rameau, Jean-Philippe. *Pièces de clavecin.* Edited by Kenneth Gilbert. Le Pupitre 59. Paris: Heugel, 1979.

———. *Pièces de clavecin.* Edited by Erwin R. Jacobi. Kassel: Bärenreiter, 1972.

Roberday, François. *Fugues et caprices.* Edited by Jean Ferrard. Le Pupitre 44. Paris: Heugel, 1972.

Seventeenth-Century Keyboard Music in the Chigi Manuscripts of the Vatican Library. Edited by Harry B. Lincoln. Corpus of Early Keyboard Music, No. 32, vol. 3. N.p.: American Institute of Musicology, 1968.

Titelouze, Jean. *Hymnes de l'église pour toucher sur l'orgue avec les fugues et recherches sur leur plain-chant.* Edited by Norbert Dufourcq. Paris: Bornemann, 1965.

General

Ancelet, M! *Observations sur la musique, les musiciens, et les instrumens.* Facsimile of 1757 Amsterdam edition. Geneva: Minkoff, 1984.

Anthony, James R. *French Baroque Music from Beaujoyeulx to Rameau.* New York: Norton, 1974, rev. 1981.

Apel, Willi. *The History of Keyboard Music to 1700*. Translated and revised by Hans Tischler. Bloomington: Indiana University Press, 1972.
———. *Masters of the Keyboard*. Cambridge: Harvard University Press, 1947.
Arbeau, Thoinot. *Orchésographie* (1589). Translated by Mary S. Evans. New York: Dover, 1967.
Bach, Carl Philipp Emanuel. *Essay on the True Art of Playing Keyboard Instruments* (1753). Translated and edited by William J. Mitchell. New York: Norton, 1949.
Bacilly, Bénigne de. *L'Art de bien chanter* (1668). Facsimile of 1679 Paris second edition. Geneva: Minkoff, 1971.
———. *A Commentary upon The Art of Proper Singing*. Translated and edited by Austin B. Caswell. Brooklyn, N.Y.: Institute of Mediaeval Music, 1968.
Bédos de Celles, Dom François. *L'Art du facteur d'orgues*. Facsimile of 1770 Paris edition, edited by Christhard Mahrenholz. Kassel: Bärenreiter, 1963–1966.
Benoit, Marcelle. *Musiques de cour, chapelle, chambre, écurie: recueil de documents 1661–1733*. Paris: Picard, 1971.
———. *Versailles et les musiciens du roi 1661–1773; étude institutionnelle et sociale*. Paris: Picard, 1971.
Bérard, M. *L'Art du chant dedié à Madame de Pompadour*. Facsimile of 1755 Paris edition. Geneva: Minkoff, 1972.
Boalch, Donald H. *Makers of the Harpsichord and Clavichord 1440–1840*. Oxford: Clarendon, 1974.
Bonnet, Jacques. *Histoire de la musique*. Facsimile of 1715 Paris edition. Geneva: Slatkine, 1969.
———. *Histoire générale de la danse sacrée et prophane*. Facsimile of 1723 Paris edition. Geneva: Slatkine, 1969.
Borrel, Eugene. *L'Interprétation de la musique française*. Reprint of 1934 Paris edition. Introduction by Erich Schwandt. New York: AMS Press, 1978.
Borren, Charles van den. "Esquisse d'une histoire des 'tombeaux' musicaux," *Studien zur Musikwissenschaft* XXV (1962):56–67.
———. *The Sources of Keyboard Music in England*. Translation of 1914 edition by J. E. Matthew. Westport, Conn.: Greenwood Press, 1970.
Borroff, Edith. *An Introduction to Elisabeth-Claude Jacquet de la Guerre*. Brooklyn, N.Y.: Institute of Mediaeval Music, 1966.
Boulay, Laurence. "Réflexions sur François Couperin," in *Mélanges François Couperin*. Paris: Picard, 1968. Pp.119–120.
———. "Du Goût dans l'interprétation de la musique française au temps de Couperin et Rameau." In *L'interprétation de la musique française aux XVIIe et XVIIIe siècles*. Paris: Éditions du Central national de la recherche scientifique, 1974. Pp.59–65.
Bouquet, Marie-Thérèse. "Quelques relations musicales Franco-Piémontoises au XVIIe et XVIIIe siècles," *Recherches* X (1970):5–18.
Bouvet, Charles. *Les Couperins, une dynastie de musiciens français: organistes de l'église Saint-Gervais*. Paris: Delagrave, 1919.
———. "Les deux d'Angleberts," *Revue de musicologie* IX (1928): 86–92.
Brenet, Michel (Bobillier, Marie). *Les Concerts en France sous l'ancien régime*. Paris: Fischbacher, 1900. Reprint, New York: Da Capo, 1970.

_____. "La Librairie musicale en France de 1653 à 1790, d'après les registres de privilèges," *Sammelbände der Internationalen Musikgesellschaft* VIII (April–June, 1907):401–466.

Brossard, Sébastien de. *Dictionaire de musique*. Facsimile of 1705 Paris second edition. Hilversum: Frits Knuf, 1965.

_____. *Dictionary of Music*. Translation of 1703 Paris edition by Albion Gruber. Henryville: Institute of Mediaeval Music, Ltd., 1982.

Brossard, Yolande de. "Musique et bourgeoisie au dix-septième siècle d'après les Gazettes de Loret et de Robinet," *Recherches* I (1960):47–49.

_____. *Musiciens de Paris 1535–1792; actes d'état civil d'après le fichier Laborde de la Bibliothèque nationale*. Paris: Picard, 1965.

_____. "La Vie musicale en France d'après Loret et ses continuateurs 1650–1688," *Recherches* X (1970):117–193.

Brunold, Paul. *Traité des signes et agréments employés par les clavecinistes français des XVIIe et XVIIIe siècles*. Nice: G. Delrieu, 1965.

Bukofzer, Manfred. *Music in the Baroque Era*. New York: Norton, 1947.

Cantagrel, Gilles, and Harry Halbreich. *Le Livre d'or de l'orgue français*. N.p.: Calliope-Marval, 1976.

Caswell, Judith. "Rhythmic Inequality and Tempo in French Music between 1650 and 1740." Ph.D. diss., University of Minnesota, 1973.

Citron, Pierre. "Autour des folies françaises," *La Revue musicale*, numero special No.226 (1955):89–96.

Cohen, Albert. "Symposium on Seventeenth-Century Music Theory: France," *Journal of Music Theory* XVI (1972):16–35.

Collins, Michael. "The Performance of Triplets in the 17th and 18th Centuries," *Journal of the American Musicological Society* XIX (1966):281–328.

_____. "In Defense of the French Trill," *Journal of the American Musicological Society* XXVI (1973):405–439.

Corneille, Thomas. *Dictionnaire des arts et des sciences*. Paris: 1694.

Couperin, François. *L'Art de toucher le clavecin*. Facsimile of 1717 Paris second edition. New York: Broude Brothers Ltd., 1969. *L'Art de toucher le clavecin*. Edited by Anna Linde with translations. Wiesbaden: Breitkopf & Härtel, 1933.

Curtis, Alan. "Musique classique française à Berkeley; pièces inédites de Louis Couperin, Lebègue, La Barre, etc.," *Revue de musicologie* LVI (1970):123–164.

_____. "Unmeasured Preludes in French Baroque Instrumental Music." Master's thesis, University of Illinois, 1956.

Dadelsen, Georg von. *Beiträge zur Chronologie der Werke Johann Sebastian Bachs*. Trössingen: Höhner-Verlag, 1958.

Danckert, Werner. *Geschichte der Gigue*. Leipzig: Kistner & Siegel, 1924.

Demoz de la Salle. *Méthode de musique selon un nouveau système*. Paris: Pierre Simon, 1728.

Denis, Jean. *Traité de l'accord de l'espinette*. Facsimile of 1650 Paris edition. Introduction by Alan Curtis. New York: Da Capo, 1969.

Devoto, Daniel. "La folle sarabande," *Revue de musicologie* XLV (July 1960): 3–43; XLVI (December 1960):145–180.

_____. "De la zarabanda à la sarabande," *Recherches* VI (1966): 27–72.

Dodge, Janet. "Ornamentation as indicated by Signs in Lute Tablature,"

Sammelbände der Internationalen Musikgesellschaft IX (1907–1908): 318–335.

Donington, Robert. *The Interpretation of Early Music.* New York: St. Martin's Press, 1974.

———. "Ornamentation." In *The New Grove Dictionary of Music and Musicians,* 6th ed. Edited by Stanley Sadie. London: Macmillan, 1980. Vol. XIII, p.851.

———. *Baroque Music: Style and Performance.* London: Faber and Faber, 1982.

Douglass, Fenner. *The Language of the French Classical Organ.* New Haven: Yale University Press, 1969.

Dufourcq, Norbert. *Le Livre de l'orgue français 1589–1789.* 5 vols. Paris: Picard, 1972.

———. "Recent Researches into French Organ Building from the Fifteenth to the Seventeenth Century," *The Galpin Society Journal* X (May 1957):66–81.

———. *La Vie musicale en France au siècle de Louis XIV: Nicolas Lebègue.* Paris: Picard, 1954.

———. "Die klassiche französische Musik, Deutschland und die deutsche Musikwissenschaft," *Archiv für Musikwissenschaft* XXII (1965):194–207.

———. *La Musique d'orgue française de Jehan Titelouze à Jehan Alain.* Paris: Floury, 1941.

Dupont, Auguste, ed. *École de piano,* vol. III. Leipzig: Breitkopf & Härtel, 1884.

Écorcheville, Jules. *Vingt suites d'orchestre du XVIIe siècle français.* Paris: Marcel Fortin, 1906.

Eitner, Robert. *Biographisch-bibliographisches Quellen-lexikon.* Leipzig: Breitkopf & Härtel, 1900.

Ellis, Meredith. "Inventory of the Dances of Jean-Baptiste Lully," *Recherches* IX (1969):21–29.

Epstein, Ernesto. *Der französische Einfluss auf die deutsche Klaviersuite im 17. Jahrhundert.* Würzburg: K. Triltsch, 1940.

L'État de la France. Paris editions of 1665, 1686, and 1687.

Farrenc, L., ed. *Le Trésor des pianistes.* Paris: C. Philipp, 1871.

Fétis, François Joseph. *Biographie universelle des musiciens et bibliographie générale de la musique.* Facsimile of 1873 Paris edition. Brussels: Culture et civilisation, 1972.

Feuillet, Raoul Auger. *Chorégraphie* and *Recueil de dances.* Facsimile of 1700 Paris editions. New York: Broude Bros., 1968.

Fuller, David. "Eighteenth-century French Harpsichord Music." Ph.D. diss., Harvard University, 1965.

———. "French harpsichord playing in the 17th century—after Le Gallois," *Early Music* IV (January 1976):22–26.

———. "Suite." In *The New Grove Dictionary of Music and Musicians,* 6th ed. Edited by Stanley Sadie. London: Macmillan, 1980. Vol. XVIII, pp.333–350.

———. "An unknown French ornament table from 1699," *Early Music* IX (1981):55–61.

———. Review of *French Baroque Music from Beaujoyeulx to Rameau* by James Anthony. *Journal of the American Musicological Society* XXVIII (1975): 374–384.

Furetière, Antoine. *Essais d'un dictionaire universel.* Amsterdam: Desbordes, 1685.

Gaussen, Françoise. "Actes d'état-civil de musiciens français 1651–1681," *Recherches* I (1960):153–203.

Gerber, Ernst Ludwig. *Historisch-biographisches Lexikon der Tonkünstler.* Edition by Othmar Wesseley. Facsimile of 1790–1792 edition. Graz, Austria: Akademische Druck-u. Verlagsanstalt, 1977.

Goldmann, Helmut. *Das Menuett in der deutschen Musikgeschichte des 17- und 18-Jahrhunderts.* Nürnberg: Helmut Goldmann, 1956.

Grassineau, James. *A Musical Dictionary.* Facsimile of 1740 London edition. New York: Broude Bros., 1966.

Gruber, Albion. "Evolving tonal theory in seventeenth-century France." Ph.D. diss., University of Rochester, 1969.

Gustafson, Bruce. *French Harpsichord Music of the 17th Century.* 3 vols. Ann Arbor: UMI Research Press, 1977.

———. "A Letter from Mr Lebègue Concerning His Preludes," *Recherches* XVII (1977):7–14.

———. "A Performer's Guide to the Music of Louis Couperin," *The Diapason* LXVI:7 (1975):7–8.

Hardouin, Pierre. "François Roberday," *Revue de musicologie* XLV (1960):44–62.

———. "Naissance et élaboration de l'orgue français classique d'après sa composition," *La Revue musicale* 295–296 (1977): 7–34.

Harley, John. "Ornaments in English keyboard Music of the seventeenth and early eighteenth Centuries," *The Music Review* XXXI (August 1970):177–200.

Herrmann-Bengen, Irmgard. *Tempobezeichnungen.* Tutzing: Hans Schneider, 1959.

Higginbottom, Edward. "D'Anglebert." In *The New Grove Dictionary of Music and Musicians,* 6th ed. Edited by Stanley Sadie. London: Macmillan, 1980. Vol. V, p.223.

Hitchcock, H. W. *Les Oeuvres de Marc-Antoine Charpentier.* Catalogue raisonné. Paris: Picard, 1982.

Hofman, Shlomo. *L'Oeuvre de clavecin de François Couperin le grand.* Paris: Picard, 1961.

Hotteterre, Jacques. *L'Art de préluder sur la flûte traversière, sur la flûte à bec, sur le hautbois et autres instrumens de dessus.* Facsimile of 1719 Paris edition. Geneva: Minkoff, 1978.

Hubbard, Frank. *Three Centuries of Harpsichord Making.* Cambridge: Harvard University Press, 1965.

Hudson, Richard. "Folia." In *The New Grove Dictionary of Music and Musicians,* 6th ed. Edited by Stanley Sadie. London: Macmillan, 1980. Vol. VI, pp.690–692.

———. *The Folia, the Saraband, the Passacaglia, and the Chaconne.* 4 vols. American Institute of Musicology. Neuhausen-Stuttgart: Hänssler, 1982.

Isherwood, Robert M. *Music in the Service of the King.* Ithaca: Cornell University Press, 1973.

Jal, Auguste. *Dictionnaire critique de biographie et d'histoire.* Facsimile of 1872 Paris edition. Geneva: Slatkine, 1970.

Jonckbloet, W.J.A., and J.P.N. Land, eds. *Musique et musiciens au XVIIe siècle. Correspondance et oeuvre musicales de Constantin Huygens.* Leyden: E. J. Brill, 1882.

Jurgens, Madeleine. *Documents du Minutier central concernant l'histoire de la musique (1600–1650).* 2 vols. Paris: SEVPEN, La Documentation française, 1967–1974.

Krebs, Carl. "J. J. Froberger in Paris," *Vierteljahrschrift für Musikwissenschaft* X (1894):223–234.

Kroll, Maria, trans. and ed. *Letters from Liselotte.* New York: McCall, 1971.

Laborde, Jean-Benjamin de. *Essai sur la musique ancienne et moderne.* Facsimile of 1780 Paris edition. N.p.: American Musicological Society, 1978.

L'Affilard, Michel. *Principes très faciles pour bien apprendre la musique.* Facsimile of 1705 Paris edition. Geneva: Minkoff, 1971.

La Laurencie, Lionel de. *Le goût musical en France.* Facsimile of 1905 Paris edition. Geneva: Slatkine, 1970.

La Rousselière, Jean-Baptiste-Charles de. *Traitté des languettes impérialles pour la perfection du clavecin.* Facsimile of 1679 Paris edition. Geneva: Minkoff, 1972.

La Voye, Mignot de. *Traité de musique.* Facsimile of 1666 Paris edition. Geneva: Minkoff, 1972.

Le Cerf de La Viéville. *Comparaison de la musique italienne et de la musique française.* Facsimile of 1705–1706 Brussels edition. Geneva: Minkoff, 1972.

Le Gallois, Jean. *Lettre . . . à Mademoiselle Regnault de Solier touchant la musique.* Facsimile of 1680 Paris edition. Geneva: Minkoff, 1984.

Le Moël, Michel. "Les dernières années de Champion de Chambonnières, 1655–1672," *Recherches* I (1960):31–46.

Leonhardt, Gustav. "Johann Jakob Froberger and his Music," *L'Organo* VI (January–June 1968):15–38.

Léris, Antoine de. *Dictionnaire portatif des théâtres.* Paris: Jombert, 1754.

Lesure, François. "Chambonnières, organisateur de concerts (1641)," *Revue belge de musicologie* III (1949):140–144.

————. "Une querelle sur le jeu de la viole en 1688: J. Rousseau contre Demachy," *Revue de musicologie* XLVI (1960):181–199.

————. "Réflexions sur les origines du concert parisien," *Polyphonie* V (November 1949): 47–51.

Lewis, Warren Hamilton. *The Splendid Century.* Garden City, N.Y.: Doubleday, 1957.

Lincoln, Harry B. "I Manoscritti Chigiani di musica organo-cembalistica della Biblioteca Apostolica Vaticana," *L'Organo* V (1967):63–82.

Lindley, Mark. "Mersenne on Keyboard Tuning," *Journal of Music Theory* XXIV, No.2 (1980):167–203.

Little, Meredith Ellis. "Dance under Louis XIV and XV," *Early Music* III (1975): 331–340.

————. "Gigue." In *The New Grove Dictionary of Music and Musicians*, 6th ed. Edited by Stanley Sadie. London: Macmillan, 1980. Vol. VII, pp. 368–371.

Lough, John. *An Introduction to Seventeenth Century France.* London: Longmans, Green & Co., 1954.

Loulié, Étienne. *Elements or Principles of Music.* Translated and edited by
Albert Cohen. Brooklyn: Institute of Mediaeval Music, Ltd., 1965.
————. *Éléments ou principes de la musique.* Facsimile of 1696 Paris edition.
Geneva: Minkoff, 1971.
Mace, Thomas. *Musick's monument.* Vol. I, facsimile of 1676 London edition.
Vol. II, commentary by Jean Jacquot and transcriptions by André
Souris. Paris: Éditions du Centre national de la recherche scientifique,
1966.
Machabey, A. "Les origines de la chaconne et de la passacaille," *Revue de
musicologie* XXVIII (1946):1–21.
Massip, Catherine. *La vie des musiciens de Paris au temps de Mazarin (1643–
1661).* Paris: Picard, 1976.
Masson, Charles. *Nouveau traité des règles pour la composition de la musique.*
Facsimile of 1699 Paris edition. Introduction by Imogene Horsley.
New York: Da Capo, 1967.
Mattheson, Johann. *Der vollkommene Capellmeister.* Facsimile of 1739 Ham-
burg edition. Kassel: Bärenreiter, 1954.
Mellers, Wilfrid. *François Couperin and the French Classical Tradition.* Reprint
of 1950 London edition. New York: Dover, 1968.
————. "d'Anglebert." In *Grove's Dictionary of Music and Musicians,* 5th ed.
Edited by Eric Blom. London: Macmillan, 1954. Vol. I, p.158.
Ménage, Gilles. *Dictionaire étymologique.* Paris, 1694.
Menestrier, Claude François. *Des Représentations en musique anciennes et mo-
dernes.* Facsimile of 1681 Paris edition. Geneva: Minkoff, 1972.
Mersenne, Marin. *Harmonie universelle.* Facsimile of 1636 Paris edition. 3
vols. Introduction by François Lesure. Paris: Éditions du Centre na-
tional de la recherche scientifique, 1965.
————. *Harmonicorum Libri XII.* Facsimile of 1648 Paris edition. Geneva:
Minkoff, 1972.
Mirimonde, A. P. *L'Iconographie musicale sous les rois Bourbons.* Paris: Picard,
1975.
Mitford, Nancy. *The Sun King.* London: H. Hamilton, 1966.
Mohr, Ernst. *Die Allemande in der deutschen Klaviersuite.* Zurich: Buchdrucke-
rei Berichthaus, 1931.
Montéclair, Michel-Pignolet de. *Principes de musique.* Facsimile of 1736 Paris
edition. Geneva: Minkoff, 1972.
Morley, Thomas. *A Plain and Easy Introduction to Practical Music* (1597).
Edited by R. Alec Harman. Reprint of 1952 edition. New York: W. W.
Norton, 1973.
Moroney, Davitt. "The performance of unmeasured harpsichord preludes,"
Early Music IV (1976):143–151.
————. "Prélude non mesuré." In *The New Grove Dictionary of Music and
Musicians,* 6th ed. Edited by Stanley Sadie. London: Macmillan, 1980.
Vol. XV, pp.212–214.
Moser, Andreas. "Zur Genesis der Folies d'Espagne," *Archiv fur Musikwis-
senschaft* I (1918–1919):358–371.
Mossiker, Frances. *Madame de Sévigné.* New York: Alfred A. Knopf, 1983.
Neumann, Frederick. *Ornamentation in Baroque and Post-Baroque Music.* Prince-
ton: Princeton University Press, 1978.

————. "Misconceptions about the French Trill in the 17th and 18th Centuries," *Musical Quarterly* L (1964):188–206.

————. *Essays in Performance Practice*. Ann Arbor: UMI Research Press, 1982.

Nivers, Guillaume-Gabriel. *Traité de la composition de musique*. Paris: Ballard, 1667.

————. *Treatise on the Composition of Music*. Translated and edited by Albert Cohen. Brooklyn: Institute of Mediaeval Music, 1961.

Norlind, Tobias. "Zur Geschichte der Suite," *Sammelbände der Internationalen Musikgesellschaft* VII (1905–1906):172–303.

Oldham, Guy. "Louis Couperin: A New Source of French Keyboard Music of the Mid 17th Century," *Recherches* I (1960):51–59.

Ozanam, Jacques. *Dictionaire mathématique*. Amsterdam: Huguetan, 1691.

Paris: Archives nationales, Minutier central. Documents Z472,f.207; LIII,104; XVI,657; LIII,225; LIII,266; LIII,319; XLV,213; CXV,183; O¹80,f.168; O¹18,f.29v°.

Pécour, Louis. *Recueil de danses* and *La nouvelle gaillarde*. Facsimile of 1700 Paris editions. N.p.: Gregg International Publishers, Ltd., 1970.

Perrault, Charles. *Les Hommes illustres qui ont paru en France pendant ce siècle*. Paris: A. Dezallier, 1696.

Pirro, André. *J. S. Bach*. Paris: Alcan, 1907.

————. *Les Clavecinistes*. Paris: H. Laurens, 1924.

————. "Louis Couperin à Paris," *La Revue musicale* II (February 1921):129–150.

Pont, Graham. "Handel's overtures for harpsichord or organ," *Early Music* XI (1983):309–322.

Powell, Newman. "Rhythmic Freedom in the Performance of French Music from 1650–1735." Ph.D. diss., Stanford University, 1958.

Pradel, Abraham Du (Nicolas Blégny). *Le Livre commode contenant les adresses de la ville de Paris, et le trésor des almanachs pour l'année bis-sextile 1692*. Facsimile of 1692 Paris edition. Geneva: Minkoff, 1973.

Pruitt, William. "The Organ Works of G. G. Nivers," *Recherches* XIV (1974):5–81; XV (1975):47–79.

————. "Un traité d'interprétation du XVIIᵉ siècle," *L'Orgue*, No. 152 (Oct–Nov 1974):99–111.

Pure, Michel de. *Idée des spectacles anciens et nouveaux*. Facsimile of 1668 Paris edition. Geneva: Minkoff, 1972.

Quantz, Johann Joachim. *Versuch einer Anweisung die Flöte traversière zu spielen*. Third edition. Breslau, 1789. Facsimile edition, Kassel: Bärenreiter, 1953.

————. *On Playing the Flute*. Translation of 1752 Berlin edition by Edward R. Reilly. New York: Schirmer Books, 1966.

Quittard, Henri. *Henry Du Mont*. Paris: Société du Mercure de France, 1906.

————. "Les origines de la suite de clavecin," *Le Courrier musical et théâtrical* XIV (November 1911):675–679; (December 1911):740–746.

————. "Un Claveciniste du XVIIᵉ siècle, Jacques Champion de Chambonnières," *La Tribune de St. Gervais* (1901) I:1–11; II:31–44; III:71–77; IV:105–110; V:141–149.

Raguenet, François. *Parallèle des Italiens et des Français en ce qui regarde la musique et les opéras* and *Défense du parallèle des Italiens et des Français en ce qui regarde la musique et les opéras.* Facsimile of 1702 and 1705 Paris editions. Geneva: Minkoff, 1976.

Rameau, Pierre. *Le Maître à danser.* Facsimile of 1725 Paris edition. New York: Broude Bros., 1967.

Reimann, Margarete. *Untersuchungen zur Formgeschichte der französischen Klavier-Suite.* Regensburg: Gustav Bosse, 1940.

―――. "Zur Entwicklungsgeschichte des Double," *Die Musikforschung* V:44 (1952):317–332; VI:42 (1953):97–111.

Richelet, Pierre. *Dictionnaire françois.* Facsimile of 1680 Geneva edition. Geneva: Slatkine, 1970.

Ripin, Edwin M. "The French Harpsichord Before 1650," *The Galpin Society Journal* XX (March 1967):43–47.

Roche, Martine. "Un Livre de clavecin français de la fin du XVIIe siècle," *Recherches* VII (1967):39–73.

Rokseth, Yvonne. "d'Anglebert." In *Die Musik in Geschichte und Gegenwart.* Kassel: Bärenreiter, 1949–1951. Vol. I, pp.479–480.

Rousseau, Jean. *Méthode claire, certaine et facile pour apprendre à chanter la musique.* Facsimile of 1710 Amsterdam sixth edition. Geneva: Minkoff, 1976.

―――. *Traité de la viole.* Facsimile of 1687 Paris edition. Introduction by François Lesure. Geneva: Minkoff, 1975.

Rousseau, Jean Jacques. *Dictionnaire de musique.* Facsimile of 1768 Paris edition. New York: Johnson Reprint Corp., 1969.

Russell, Raymond. *The Harpsichord and Clavichord* (1959). Second edition, revised by Howard Schott. London: Faber and Faber, 1973.

Sachs, Curt. *World History of the Dance.* Translated by Bessie Schönberg. New York: Norton, 1937.

Sainsbury, John S., ed. *A Dictionary of Musicians from the Earliest Times.* Facsimile of 1825 London edition. New York: Da Capo, 1966.

Saint-Arroman, Jean. *L'Interprétation de la musique française 1661–1789,* vol. I. Paris: Librairie Honoré Champion, 1983.

Saint-Lambert, Monsieur de. *Nouveau traité de l'accompagnement du clavecin, de l'orgue et des autres instruments.* Facsimile of 1707 Paris edition. Geneva: Minkoff, 1972.

―――. *Les Principes du clavecin.* Facsimile of 1702 Paris edition. Geneva: Minkoff, 1972.

―――. *Principles of the Harpsichord.* Translated and edited by Rebecca Harris-Warrick. Cambridge: Cambridge University Press, 1984.

Schneider, Herbert. *Die französische Kompositionslehre in der ersten Hälfte des 17. Jahrhunderts.* Tutzing: Hans Schneider, 1972.

―――. *Die Rezeption der Opern Lullys im Frankreich des Ancien Regime.* Tutzing: Hans Schneider, 1982.

―――. *Chronologisch-thematisches Verzeichnis sämtlicher Werke von Jean-Baptiste Lully.* Tutzing: Hans Schneider, 1981.

Seiffert, Max. *Geschichte der Klaviermusik.* Leipzig: Breitkopf & Härtel, 1899.

Shannon, John R. *Organ Literature of the 17th Century: A Study of Its Styles.* Raleigh: Sunbury Press, 1978.

Snyders, Georges. *Le Goût musical en France aux XVIIe et XVIIIe siècles.* Paris: J. Vrin, 1968.

Somer, Avo. "The Keyboard Music of Johann Jakob Froberger." Ph.D. diss., University of Michigan, 1963.

Stevenson, Robert; Daniel Devoto; and José Castro Escudero. "Notes et documents à propos de la sarabande," *Revue de musicologie* XLVII (July 1961):113–125.

Taubert, Karl Heinz. *Höfisches Tänze*. Mainz: B. Schott's Söhne, 1968.

Tessier, André. "Quelques documents sur les d'Anglebert, extraits du fichier Laborde," *Revue de musicologie* IX (1928):271–272.

———. "L'Oeuvre de Gaspard le Roux," *Revue de musicologie* III (1922):168–174.

———. "L'Oeuvre de clavecin de Nicolas le Bègue," *Revue de musicologie* IV (1923):106–112.

———. "Une Pièce d'orgue de Charles Raquet et le Mersenne de la Bibliothèque des Minimes de Paris," *Revue de musicologie* X (1929):275–283.

Thomas, Michael. "Early French Harpsichords," *The English Harpsichord Magazine* I (October 1974):73–84.

Tiersot, Julien. *Lettres de musiciens écrites en français du XVe au XXe siècle.* Turin: Bocca Frères, 1924.

Titon du Tillet, Évrard. *Le Parnasse françois.* Facsimile of 1732 Paris edition. Geneva: Slatkine, 1971.

Trichet, Pierre. *Traité des instruments de musique.* Facsimile of c.1640 Paris edition. Introduction by François Lesure. Geneva: Minkoff, 1978.

Troeger, Richard. "Metre in unmeasured preludes," *Early Music* XI (1983): 340–345.

Vilcosqui, Marcel. "Une Mélomane au XVIIe siècle: Madame de Sévigné (1626–1696)," *Recherches* XVII (1977):31–93.

Vogan, Charles E. "The French Organ School of the 17th and 18th Centuries." Ph.D. diss., University of Michigan, 1948.

Von Fischer, Kurt. "Variations." In *The New Grove Dictionary of Music and Musicians*, 6th ed. Edited by Stanley Sadie. London: Macmillan, 1980. Vol. XIX, pp.536–556.

Walker, Thomas. "Ciaccona and Passacaglia: Remarks on Their Origin and Early History," *Journal of the American Musicological Society* XXI (1968): 300–320.

Walther, Johann Gottfried. *Musikalisches Lexikon.* Facsimile of the 1732 edition. Kassel: Bärenreiter, 1953.

Weber, Edith, editor. *L'Interprétation de la musique française aux XVIIeme et XVIIIeme siècles.* Paris: Éditions du Centre nationale de la recherche scientifique, 1969.

Wienpahl, Robert W. "Modality, Monality and Tonality in the Sixteenth and Seventeenth Centuries," *Music and Letters* LII (October 1971):407–417; LIII (January 1972):59–73.

Williams, Peter. *The European Organ, 1450–1850.* Bloomington: Indiana University Press, 1966.

———. "The Harpsichord Acciaccatura: Theory and Practice in Harmony, 1650–1750," *The Musical Quarterly* LIV (1968): 503–523.

Wolfheim, Werner. "Die Möllersche Handschrift. Ein unbekanntes Gegenstück zum Andreas-Bach-Buche," *Bach Jahrbuch* (1912): 42–60.

Zenatti, Arlette. "Le Prélude dans la musique profane de clavier en France, au XVIIIe siècle," *Recherches* V (1965):169–184.

Zietz, Hermann. *Quellenkritische Untersuchungen an den Bach-Handschriften P 801, P 802 und P 803 aus dem "Krebs'schen Nachlass" unter besonderer Berucksichtigung der Choralbearbeitungen des jungen J. S. Bach.* Hamburg: Verlag der Musikalienhandlung K. D. Wagner, 1969.

NOTES

1. The Times

1. Robert M. Isherwood, *Music in the Service of the King* (Ithaca: Cornell University Press, 1973), p.250.

2. Jacques Bonnet, *Histoire de la musique*, facsimile of 1715 Paris edition (Geneva: Slatkine, 1969), p.330.

3. *L'État de la France* (Paris, 1686), p.162. For an interesting review of French musical institutions and organizations, see James R. Anthony, *French Baroque Music*, rev. ed. (New York: Norton, 1981), chapter 1.

4. Quoted by Marcelle Benoit, *Versailles et les musiciens du roi 1661–1773* (Paris: Picard, 1971), p.42. Letters of 29 July 1676 and 12 February 1683.

5. Marcelle Benoit, *Musiques de cour, chapelle, chambre, écurie: recueil de documents 1661–1733* (Paris: Picard, 1971), pp.76–77.

6. Benoit, *Versailles . . .* , pp.97–145.

7. Maria Kroll, translator and editor, *Letters from Liselotte* (New York: McCall Publishing Company, 1971), p.40. Liselotte (also called Madame or the Duchesse d'Orléans) was married to the king's only brother (referred to as Monsieur or the Duc d'Orléans).

8. *L'État de la France* (Paris, 1687), pp.232–233.

9. Quoted by A. P. Mirimonde, *L'Iconographie musicale sous les rois Bourbons* (Paris: Picard, 1975), I, p.183.

10. Bonnet, pp.335–339.

11. *L'État de la France* (Paris, 1687), p.201.

12. Ibid., pp.234–245.

13. Benoit, *Versailles . . .* , p.212.

14. Marin Mersenne, *Harmonie universelle*, facsimile of 1636 Paris edition (Paris: Éditions du Centre national de la recherche scientifique, 1965), "Liure troisiesme des instrumens," pp.111, 108. The engravings of a clavecin and an *épinette* appear also in Mersenne's *Harmonicorum Libri XII*, facsimile of 1648 Paris edition (Geneva: Minkoff, 1972), pp.61, 59. Frank Hubbard, in *Three Centuries of Harpsichord Making* (Cambridge: Harvard University Press, 1965), pp.98–99, notes that the keys of Mersenne's *épinette* are mislabeled, and that the range as drawn is perhaps short-octave G or A to f''' at four-foot pitch. The instrument, valued for its portability, is about 2-1/2' × 16'' × 4-1/2''.

15. Jean-Baptiste-Charles de La Rousselière, *Traitté des languettes impérialles*, facsimile of 1679 Paris edition (Geneva: Minkoff, 1972), p.27.

16. The noted builder William Dowd knows of fifteen surviving seventeenth-century French harpsichords, of which only one is a single (personal communication).

17. In C short-octave, the lowest note, E, = C, F♯ = D, and G♯ = E, while in G short-octave, the lowest note, BB, = GG, C♯ = AA, and D♯ = BB; or the split halves of C♯ could furnish GG and AA, and D♯ , BB. Jacques Ozanam, *Dictionaire mathématique* (Amsterdam: Huguetan, 1691),

p.667, describes clavecins with one, two, and sometimes three keyboards, one over the other, ordinarily with two or three choirs of strings. According to Ozanam, the *épinette*, a type of small clavecin with only one set of strings and one keyboard, differs from the clavecin in its shape and in the location of its keyboard.

18. Monsieur de Saint-Lambert, *Les Principes du clavecin*, facsimile of 1702 Paris edition (Geneva: Minkoff, 1972), p.6.

19. Mr Ancelet, *Observations sur la musique, les musiciens, et les instrumens*, facsimile of 1757 Amsterdam edition (Geneva: Minkoff, 1984), p.39.

20. W. J. A. Jonckbloet and J. P. N. Land, editors, *Musique et musiciens au XVIIe siècle. Correspondance et oeuvre musicales de Constantin Huygens* (Leyden: E. J. Brill, 1882), p.26. For further reading about concerts of the period, see Anthony, pp.289–292.

21. Quoted by John Lough, *An Introduction to Seventeenth Century France* (London: Longmans, Green & Co., 1954), p.170.

2. D'Anglebert—Life and Works

1. Auguste Jal, *Dictionnaire critique de biographie et d'histoire*, facsimile of 1872 Paris edition (Geneva: Slatkine, 1970), p.51.

2. Ibid., p.538. "En 1609, Jacques Champion, s^r de la Chapelle, était 'joueur d'épinette de la chambre du Roy'; il avait encore cette charge en 1633, ayant à survivance pour sa charge 'Jean-Henri d'Anglebert,' qui était alors enfant, et que son père fit pourvoir de l'emploi d'épinette, longtemps avant qu'on sût s'il serait un jour capable de l'honorer par son talent, et quitte a l'en demettre s'il ne realisait pas les espérances que Claude-Henri d'Anglebert, son père, avait conçues."

3. Archives nationales, Paris, Z 472 f 207, courtesy of Madeleine Jurgens.

4. François-Joseph Fétis, *Biographie universelle des musiciens*, facsimile of 1878 Paris edition (Brussels: Culture et civilisation, 1972), Supplement, vol. IX, p.17.

5. Information regarding the children is taken from Jal, pp.51–52, and Yolande de Brossard's compilation of Léon de Laborde's records: *Musiciens de Paris 1535–1792. Actes d'état civil d'après le fichier Laborde de la Bibliothèque nationale* (Paris: Picard, 1965), pp.9–10. At the time of his marriage, D'Anglebert, described as a "bourgeois de Paris," lived on rue des Bourdonnais at the Hôtel de Villeroy, but shortly moved to rue Saint-Honoré near Les Pères de l'Oratoire, then to the Hôtel de la Monnoye by the time of Jean-Baptiste Henry's baptism, and to rue de l'Arbre Sec by the time of François's baptism. The title page of the first issue of *Pièces de clavecin* (1689) lists him as living on the rue Ste.-Anne, while the second issue of 1689 gives his address as rue St.-Honoré. The Ste.-Anne address, however, is given at the time of his death. In 1720, Jean-Henry (son) married Marguerite Fournier; the ceremony was witnessed by Jean-Baptiste Henry, François, Magdelaine, and cousin Henri (Archives nationales XVI, 657, 4 May 1720). D'Anglebert's widow died on 27 February 1724, at the age of 84, and was buried at St. Roch in the Chapel of the Virgin. Her property was divided between François and Jean, with Jean-Baptiste Henry, d'Alexandre, and Magdelaine renouncing their rights (Archives nationales LIII, 225, 23 March 1724). Another division of

property among three survivors occurred after François died a bachelor (Archives nationales LIII, 266, 2 October 1733). In a will dated 20 May 1733, Jean-Baptiste Henry left his property to Jean-Henry and Catherine-Magdelaine. A posthumous inventory of Jean-Henry's possessions (he owned a *grand clavecin*) divided his property between his sister and cousin Henry Henri (the priest—presumably d'Alexandre of Bar-le-Duc—having renounced his rights; Archives nationales LIII, 319, 15 September 1747).

6. Archives nationales, Min. cent., LIII, 104 (8 May 1691). Cousin Henry-Henri d'Anglebert, son of Claude-Henri d'Anglebert and Anne Macquart, was born in 1666 and baptized at Notre Dame in Bar-le-Duc. A master of the clavecin, he resided on rue St.-Honoré in Paris. As guardian for the younger D'Anglebert children, he was a representative of the priest of Bar-le-Duc (d'Alexandre-Marie).

7. The godparents of the D'Anglebert children include: for Magdelaine Renée: Guillaume de Botru (Bautru; Count of Serrant, Adviser to the King, and Chancellor of the Duke of Anjou—the king's brother); for Jean-Baptiste Henry: Jean-Baptiste Lully and Charlotte Peston; for d'Alexandre: Alexandre Bontemps (first *Valet de Chambre* of the King) and Marie de Bousteron; for François: François Annibal d'Estrées (Knight and the Marquis of Coeuvres, Lieutenant General of the armies of the King, and Governor of l'Ile de France) and Françoise de Brancas (daughter of Charles de Brancas, Knight of Honor of the Queen Mother); for Nicolas: Nicolas Pinçon, Sr de Villargenne (Con^{er} of the King) and Charlotte Champagne (wife of François Roberday, *Valet de Chambre* of the Queen); for Jean: Jean Champagne Demery (bourgeois of Paris) and Barbe Perier (wife of the Honorable Blaise Champagne, bourgeois of Paris). Listed by André Tessier in "Notes et documents," *Revue de musicologie* IX (1928):271–272.

8. Maria Kroll, translator and editor, *Letters from Liselotte* (New York: McCall Publishing Company, 1971), p.155.

9. This post is presumably the same as the 1633 position of *joueur d'épinette* referred to above, but with a different title to reflect the ascendance of the clavecin over the *épinette*. *Clavecin* and *épinette* appear to be used indiscriminately in the musicians' titles in payment records through the end of the century.

10. Frances Mossiker, *Madame de Sévigné* (New York: Alfred Knopf, 1983), p.371. For musicians' salaries, see numerous listings in Marcelle Benoit, *Musiques de cour, chapelle, chambre, écurie: recueil de documents 1661–1733* (Paris: Picard, 1971). The abbreviation *lt* signifies *livres tournois*, a measure of currency that later became equivalent to the French *franc*. W. H. Lewis gives an approximate value of 1 *livre* (silver) = 1 *franc* (17th cent.) = 1 *franc* (1914) = $.20 (1914). See *The Splendid Century* (Garden City: Doubleday, 1953), p.viii. Three *livres* = 1 *écu*, and 24 *livres* = 1 *louis*, while 1 *livre* = 20 *sous*.

11. Archives nationales, Min. cent. XLV, 213. Reprinted in Michel le Moël, "Les dernières années de Champion de Chambonnières," *Recherches* I (1960):40.

12. François Lesure, "Une querelle sur le jeu de la viole en 1688: J. Rousseau contre Demachy," *Revue de musicologie* XLVI (1960):183.

13. Évrard Titon du Tillet, *Le Parnasse françois*, facsimile of 1732 Paris edition (Geneva: Slatkine, 1971), p.402.

14. Le Moël, pp.41–42. Archives nationales CXV, 183.

15. *L'État de la France* (Paris, 1686), pp.589–590.

16. Ibid., p.529.

17. Marcelle Benoit, *Versailles and les musiciens du roi 1661–1773* (Paris: Picard, 1971), p.198.

18. Archives nationales, O¹80, f° 168, 1736. Quoted by Benoit, *Versailles . . .* , p.199.

19. Archives nationales, O¹18, f. 29v°. Reprinted in Charles Bouvet, "Les deux d'Angleberts," *Revue de musicologie* IX (1928):86.

20. Jal, p.52.

21. J. Henry D'Anglebert, *Pièces de clavecin*, facsimile of 1689 Paris edition (second issue) (New York: Broude Bros., 1965).

22. Nancy Mitford, *The Sun King* (New York: Crescent Books, 1966), p.128.

23. François Couperin, *Pièces de clavecin*, facsimile of 1713 Paris edition (New York: Broude Bros., 1973), Preface.

24. Jean-Henry D'Anglebert, *Pièces de clavecin*, edited by Kenneth Gilbert (Paris: Heugel, 1975), p.vii.

25. Bruce Gustafson, *French Harpsichord Music of the 17th Century* (Ann Arbor: UMI Research Press, 1977), pp.94–95.

26. Ernst Ludwig Gerber, *Historisch-biographisches Lexikon der Tonkünstler*, facsimile of 1790–1792 edition (Graz: Akademische Druck-u. Verlagsanstalt, 1977), I, p.46.

27. Archives nationales, Min. cent., LIII, 104 (May 8, 1691). Reprinted in Benoit, *Versailles . . .* , p.164.

28. Ibid., pp.358–359.

29. Titon du Tillet, p.403.

30. Gustafson, pp.107–109. For a further discussion of this manuscript, see Martine Roche, "Un livre de clavecin français de la fin du XVIIᵉ siècle," *Recherches* VII (1967):39–73.

31. Titon du Tillet, pp.635–636.

32. Antoine de Léris, *Dictionnaire portatif des théâtres* (Paris: Jombert, 1754), p.465.

3. Style and Tempo

1. Luigi Riccoboni, *Reflections upon Declamation*, translated from the French edition of 1738 (London, 1741). Quoted in James R. Anthony, *French Baroque Music from Beaujoyeulx to Rameau*, revised edition (New York: Norton, 1981), p.101.

2. Monsieur de Saint-Lambert, *Les Principes du clavecin*, facsimile of 1702 Paris edition (Geneva: Minkoff, 1972), pp.33–34.

3. Manfred Bukofzer, *Music in the Baroque Era* (New York: Norton, 1947), p.165; Johann Gottfried Walther, *Musikalisches Lexikon*, facsimile of 1732 edition (Kassel: Bärenreiter, 1953), p.189.

4. Demoz de la Salle, *Méthode de musique selon un nouveau système* (Paris: Pierre Simon, 1728), p.172.

5. Material in this section is derived from St.-Lambert, pp.15–25 (my translation). Although Rebecca Harris-Warrick, in *Principles of the Harpsichord*

(Cambridge: Cambridge University Press, 1984, pp.32–45), has rendered a most helpful service by translating this treatise, I believe that she has misinterpreted St.-Lambert's remarks about 6/8 time to mean a doubling (actually half again as fast) of 6/4 time beat in his first manner (two beats per measure) instead of his second manner (six beats per measure). As Rousseau states (see p.34), each half of a 6/8 measure is equivalent to one 3/8 measure. Harris-Warrick also may have read St.-Lambert's remarks about courante tempo to mean three fast beats per measure instead of per half measure. St.-Lambert's pertinent passages follow:

> Aux Pieces marquées du Signe de six pour huit, la Mesure se bat encore à deux temps, tout de même qu'en la premiere maniére de six pour quatre, excepté seulement que les temps de six pour huit doivent aller une fois plus vîte que ceux de six pour quatre, parce que la Mesure n'est composée que de six Croches, au lieu que l'autre est de six Noires; à cela prés, ces deux Mesures n'ont aucune difference.

> Tous nos Maîtres de Clavecin ne mettent aux Courantes que le Signe de triple simple 3, au lieu qu'ils devroient y mettre le Signe de triple double 3/2, puis que la Mesure est composée de trois Blanches, & non pas de trois Noires. Il est vray qu'il y a des Courantes dont la Mesure se peut battre à trois temps legeres en faisant deux Mesures d'une; & il semble que c'est-là ce que ces Maîtres veulent signifier, quand ils ne les marquent que du triple simple; mais de quelque façon qu'ils puissent l'entendre, c'est toûjours aller contre la regle: car s'ils veulent qu'on batte ces Piéces à trois temps legers, ils doivent couper les Mesures en deux; & s'ils prétendent qu'on les doit battre à trois temps lents, il faut donc qu'ils les marquent du triple double.

6. Michel L'Affilard, *Principes très faciles pour bien apprendre la musique*, facsimile of 1705 Paris fifth edition (Geneva: Minkoff, 1971), p.123; Sébastien de Brossard, *Dictionaire de musique*, facsimile of 1705 Paris second edition (Hilversum: Frits Knuf, 1965), p.186.

7. Jean Rousseau, *Méthode claire certaine et facile pour apprendre à chanter la musique*, facsimile of c.1710 Amsterdam "fifth" (actually sixth) edition (Geneva: Minkoff, 1976), pp.35–37, 40, 44–45. The signatures 3/4, 3/8, 6/4, and 6/8 are also found in his 1683 edition.

8. Jean Rousseau, *Traité de la viole*, facsimile of 1687 Paris edition with Introduction by François Lesure (Geneva: Minkoff, 1975), p.82.

9. Étienne Loulié, *Éléments ou principes de la musique*, facsimile of 1696 Paris edition (Geneva: Minkoff, 1971), pp.60–61. Loulié's treatise also describes the *Chronometre*, a large pendulum device that he invented to indicate tempo. His examples of its use include one in 3/2 time (set at "30" = half note) and another in 6/4 time (set at "16" = dotted half note), pp.81–88.

10. Demoz de la Salle, pp.154–158, 161–166.

11. Jacques Hotteterre, *L'Art de préluder sur la flûte traversière, sur la flûte a bec, sur le hautbois et autres instrumens de dessus*, facsimile of 1719 Paris edition (Geneva: Minkoff, 1978), p.57.

12. Michel-Pignolet de Montéclair, *Principes de musique*, facsimile of 1736 Paris edition (Geneva: Minkoff, 1972), pp.116–118, 132–133.

13. St.-Lambert, facsimile edition, p.25.

14. Charles Masson, *Nouveau traité des règles pour la composition de la musique*, facsimile of 1699 Paris edition with Introduction by Imogene Horsley (New York: Da Capo, 1967), pp.7–8.

15. Louis Pécour, *Recueil de danses* and *La Nouvelle gaillarde*, facsimile of 1700 Paris editions (n.p.: Gregg International Publishers Ltd., 1970).

16. Demoz de la Salle, pp.149, 169–170.

17. Nicholas Siret, *Pièces de clavecin*, facsimile of 1710 Paris edition (Geneva: Minkoff, 1982), *Avertissement*.

18. Brossard, p.56.

19. Rousseau, *Méthode claire . . .* , pp.86–87.

20. François Couperin, *L'Art de toucher le clavecin* (1717), edited by Anna Linde (Wiesbaden: Breitkopf & Härtel, 1933), p.24 (translation mine).

21. Bénigne de Bacilly, *L'Art de bien chanter*, facsimile of 1679 Paris second edition (Geneva: Minkoff, 1974), pp.199–200.

22. Jean-Philippe Rameau, *Pièces de clavecin*, edited by Kenneth Gilbert (Paris: Heugel, 1979) p.60. From Preface to *Nouvelles suites de pièces de clavecin*, 1728.

23. Jean Le Gallois, *Lettre . . . à Mademoiselle Regnault de Solier touchant la musique*, facsimile of 1680 Paris edition (Geneva: Minkoff, 1984), pp.55, 68–69, 75–80. The first paragraph from Le Gallois is my translation, while subsequent passages are translated by David Fuller in "French harpsichord playing in the 17th century—after Le Gallois," *Early Music* IV (1976):22–26.

24. Pierre-Claude Foucquet, *Pièces de clavecin*, I and II, facsimile of 1751 Paris editions (Geneva: Minkoff, 1982), Preface to book II.

25. Mr Ancelet, *Observations sur la musique, les musiciens, et les instruments*, facsimile of 1757 Amsterdam edition (Geneva: Minkoff, 1984), p.7.

26. Brossard, p.115.

27. Johann Joachim Quantz, *On Playing the Flute*, translation of 1752 editions by Edward R. Reilly (New York: Schirmer Books, 1966), p.335.

28. François Couperin, *Pièces de clavecin* I (1713), edited by Kenneth Gilbert (Paris: Heugel, 1972), p.xxiii.

29. Rousseau, *Traité de la viole*, pp.56–58.

30. Laurence Boulay, "Reflexions sur François Couperin," in *Mélanges François Couperin* (Paris: Picard, 1968), p.119.

31. French music has a pleasing advantage
    Of never producing a harsh or barbarous sound,
    Sweetness and gracefulness accompany its songs,
    They are tender, pleasing, expressive and moving.

"Musique," quoted by Eugene Borrel, in *L'Interprétation de la musique française*, reprint of 1934 Paris edition with Introduction by Erich Schwandt (New York: AMS Press, 1978), p.149.

4. Ornamentation

1. Marin Mersenne, "Liure sixiesme des orgues," in *Harmonie universelle*, facsimile of 1636 Paris edition (Paris: Éditions du Centre national de la recherche scientifique, 1965), vol.3, pp. 394–395.

2. Mersenne, "Liure second des instrumens," vol.3, pp.79–82, and "Li-

ure troisiesme des instrumens à chordes," vol.3, p.162. For further information, see Janet Dodge, "Ornamentation as indicated by Signs in Lute Tablature," *Sammelbände der Internationalen Musikgesellschaft* IX (1907–1908):318–335.

3. Mersenne, "Liure sixiesme de l'art de bien chanter," vol.2, pp.355–356.

4. Jean Denis, *Traité de l'accord de l'espinette*, facsimile of 1650 Paris edition with Introduction by Alan Curtis (New York: Da Capo, 1969), p.37.

5. Jean Titelouze, *Hymnes de l'église pour toucher sur l'orgue avec les fugues et recherches sur leur plain-chant* (1624), edited by Norbert Dufourcq (Paris: Bornemann, 1965), Preface: "je fais des cadences qui sont communes ainsi que chacun sçait."

6. Mersenne, "Liure sixiesme des orgues," vol.3, p.392.

7. W. J. A. Jonckbloet and J. P. N. Land, editors, *Musique et musiciens au XVIIe siècle. Correspondance et oeuvre musicales de Constantin Huygens* (Leyden: E. J. Brill, 1882), p.23: "apporte des aggreemens qu'on a de la peine à bien exprimer en Tablature."

8. Frederick Neumann, *Ornamentation in Baroque and Post-Baroque Music* (Princeton: Princeton University Press, 1978).

9. Bénigne de Bacilly, *L'Art de bien chanter*, facsimile of 1679 Paris second edition (Geneva: Minkoff, 1971) p.135.

10. Guillaume-Gabriel Nivers, *Livre d'orgue*, facsimile of Preface (1665) reprinted in modern edition, edited by Norbert Dufourcq (Paris: Bornemann, 1963).

11. Denis, p.37.

12. Nicolas-Antoine Lebègue, *Les Pièces de clauessin* (Paris, 1677), Preface.

13. André Raison, *Livre d'orgue* (Paris, 1688), Preface.

14. Monsieur Dieupart, *Six suittes de clavessin* (Amsterdam: E. Roger, c.1702), Preface.

15. Georg von Dadelsen, *Beiträge zur Chronologie der Werke Johann Sebastian Bachs* (Trössingen: Höhner-Verlag, 1958), pp.73–76.

16. Berlin, Staatsbibliothek Preussischer Kulturbesitz, Mus. Ms. 40,644, l43v.

17. Gaspard Le Roux, *Pièces de clavessin*, facsimile of 1705 Paris edition (Geneva: Minkoff, 1982), Preface.

18. Jean-Philippe Rameau, *Premier livre de pièces de clavecin* (Paris, 1706), Preface; and *Pièces de clavessin* (Paris, 1724), reprinted in facsimile (New York: Broude Bros., 1967), Preface.

19. Monsieur de St.-Lambert, *Les Principes du clavecin*, facsimile of 1702 Paris edition (Geneva: Minkoff, 1972), pp.13–14, 61–62.

20. François Couperin, *Pièces de clavecin . . . premier livre*, facsimile of 1713 Paris edition (New York: Broude Bros., 1973), pp.74–75. *Pièces de clavecin*, I–IV, edited by Kenneth Gilbert (Paris: Heugel, 1969–1972).

21. Johann Sebastian Bach, *Clavier-Büchlein vor Wilhelm Friedemann Bach*, facsimile of 1720 manuscript with Preface by Ralph Kirkpatrick (New Haven: Yale University Press, 1959).

22. J. S. Bach, *Clavier-Büchlein vor Wilhelm Friedemann Bach*, in *Neue Ausgabe sämtlicher Werke*, V/5, edited by Wolfgang Plath (Kassel: Bärenreiter, 1962), p.45. See also *Kritischer Bericht*, p.66, for a discussion of the authorship of No.29.

23. Stadt- und Universitätsbibliothek Frankfurt/Main, Mus. Hs. 1538, *Livre d'orgue* of Nicolas de Grigny, manuscript copy in the hand of J. S. Bach.

5. Ornament Performance

1. Monsieur de St.-Lambert, *Les Principes du clavecin*, facsimile of 1702 Paris edition (Geneva: Minkoff, 1972), p.42 (translation mine). This treatise is also available in an English translation by Rebecca Harris-Warrick, *Principles of the Harpsichord by Monsieur de Saint Lambert* (Cambridge: Cambridge University Press, 1984).
2. Ibid., facsimile edition, pp.46–47, 49. A printing error omits the tie of the trill *appuyé* in St.-Lambert's treatise.
3. Frederick Neumann, *Ornamentation in Baroque and Post-Baroque Music* (Princeton: Princeton University Press, 1978), pp.244–286.
4. Bénigne de Bacilly, *L'Art de bien chanter*, facsimile of 1679 Paris second edition (Geneva: Minkoff, 1974), pp.178–179; translated in Neumann, pp.248–249.
5. Jean Rousseau, *Méthode claire, certaine et facile pour apprendre chanter la musique*, facsimile of c.1710 Amsterdam sixth edition (Geneva: Minkoff, 1976), p.54.
6. Jean Rousseau, *Traité de la viole*, facsimile of 1687 Paris edition with Introduction by Francois Lesure (Geneva: Minkoff, 1975), pp.77–79.
7. Rousseau, *Méthode*, p.55.
8. Rousseau, *Traité*, pp.83–84.
9. Rousseau, *Méthode*, p.51.
10. Ibid., pp.56–57.
11. Rousseau, *Méthode*, pp.85–86.
12. Pierre-Claude Foucquet, *Pièces de clavecin*, facsimile of 1751 Paris editions (Geneva: Minkoff, 1982), pp.5–6. M. Bérard's vocal treatise from this period, *L'Art du chant*, also defines trills with and without preparation; facsimile of 1755 Paris edition (Geneva: Minkoff, 1972), pp.114–115.
13. Michel Pignolet de Montéclair, *Principes de musique*, facsimile of 1736 Paris edition (Geneva: Minkoff, 1972), p.82.
14. Jean-François Dandrieu, *Pièces de clavecin courtes et faciles de quatres tons differents* (Paris: Author, Foucault, n.d.), Preface.
15. Jean Denis, *Traité de l'accord de l'espinette*, facsimile of 1650 Paris edition with Introduction by Alan Curtis (New York: Da Capo, 1969), p.xv.
16. St.-Lambert, facsimile edition, p.44.
17. Etienne Loulié, *Éléments ou principes de la musique*, facsimile of 1696 Paris edition (Geneva: Minkoff, 1971), p.70.
18. Carl Philipp Emanuel Bach, *Essay on the True Art of Playing Keyboard Instruments* (1753), translated and edited by William J. Mitchell (New York: Norton, 1949), p.160.
19. James Grassineau, *A Musical Dictionary*, facsimile of 1740 London edition (New York: Broude Bros., 1966), p.99.
20. Sr Perrine, *Pièces de luth en musique*, facsimile of 1680 Paris edition (Geneva: Minkoff, 1982), Preface.
21. St.-Lambert, facsimile edition, p.55.
22. Nicolas-Antoine Lebègue, *Les Pièces de clauessin* (Paris, 1677), Preface.

23. Monsieur de St.-Lambert, *Nouveau traité de l'accompagnement du clavecin, de l'orgue et des autres instruments,* facsimile of 1707 Paris edition (Geneva: Minkoff, 1972), p.62.

24. St.-Lambert, *Principes,* facsimile edition, p.55.

25. Ibid., p.52–53.

26. Ibid., p.54.

27. Ibid., p.51.

28. Loulié, pp.68–69.

29. François Couperin, *L'Art de toucher le clavecin* (Paris, 1716), p.22: "Il faut que la petite note perduë d'un port-de-voix ou d'un coulé, frape avec L'harmonie: c'est à dire dans le tems qu'on devroit toucher la note de valeur qui la suit." Translated by Frederick Neumann, in *Essays in Performance Practice* (Ann Arbor: UMI Research Press, 1982), p.227.

30. Neumann, *Ornamentation,* pp.54–55.

31. Bénigne de Bacilly, *A Commentary upon The Art of Proper Singing,* translated and edited by Austin B. Caswell (Brooklyn: Institute of Mediaeval Music, 1968).

32. Sr Danoville, *L'Art de toucher le dessus et basse de violle,* facsimile of 1687 Paris edition (Geneva: Minkoff, 1972), p.42.

33. Lambert Chaumont, *Pièces d'orgue,* edited by Jean Ferrard (Paris: Heugel, 1970), Preface.

34. Rousseau, *Traité,* pp.85–87, 93–96.

35. Rousseau, *Méthode,* pp.50–53. My translation is a paraphrase of a knotty passage.

36. Ibid., pp.60–61.

37. Loulié, pp.66–67.

38. St.-Lambert, *Principes,* facsimile edition, pp.49–51.

39. Ibid., pp.56–57.

40. A facsimile of the ornament table is contained in the modern edition of Jacques Boyvin, *Premier livre d'orgue* (c.1690), edited by Jean Bonfils (Paris: Les Éditions ouvrières, 1969), Preface.

41. C. P. E. Bach, pp.91–92.

42. Johann Joachin Quantz, *On Playing the Flute* (1752), translated by Edward R. Reilly (New York: Schirmer Books, 1966), pp. 227–228.

43. Jean Jacques Rousseau, *Dictionnaire de musique,* facsimile of 1768 Paris edition (New York: Johnson Reprint Corp., 1969), Table B, Fig. 13.

44. Neumann, *Ornamentation,* pp.54–55.

45. St.-Lambert, *Principes,* facsimile edition, p.48.

46. US-BE, MS 778; in Louis Couperin, *Pièces de clavecin,* edited by Alan Curtis (Paris: Heugel, 1970), p.13.

47. St.-Lambert, *Principes,* facsimile edition, p.56.

48. Ibid., p.57.

49. F. Couperin, *Troisième livre de pièces de clavecin* (1722), edited and translated by Kenneth Gilbert (Paris: Heugel, 1969), p.x.

50. Rousseau, *Traité,* pp.74–75.

51. Michel-Pignolet de Montéclair, *Principes de musique,* facsimile of 1736 Paris edition (Geneva: Minkoff, 1972), pp.86–87.

52. C. P. E. Bach, pp.31, 79.

53. Quantz, pp.113, 162–163.

54. Marin Mersenne, "Liure troisiesme des instrumens à chordes," in *Harmonie universelle*, facsimile of 1636 Paris edition (Paris: Éditions du Centre national de la recherche scientifique, 1965), vol.3, p.162.

6. Transcriptions, Arrangements, and Variations (*Doubles*)

1. Bruce Gustafson, *French Harpsichord Music of the 17th Century* (Ann Arbor: UMI Research Press, 1977), p.139. Some keyboard transcriptions are readily obtained in Almonte C. Howell, Jr., editor, *Nine seventeenth-century organ transcriptions from the operas of Lully* (Lexington: The University of Kentucky Press, 1963).
2. Nos.11, 12, 15, 16, 17, and 18 in the list of transcriptions in Appendix 3.
3. Évrard Titon du Tillet, *Le Parnasse françois*, facsimile of 1732 Paris edition (Geneva: Slatkine, 1971), pp.405–406.
4. Ibid., pp.393–395.
5. On this aspect of harpsichord technique, see Monsieur de St.-Lambert, *Les Principes du clavecin*, facsimile of 1702 Paris edition (Geneva: Minkoff, 1972), pp.28–29.
6. Jacques Hotteterre, *L'Art de préluder . . .* , facsimile of 1719 Paris edition (Geneva: Minkoff, 1978), p.58.
7. Sébastien de Brossard, *Dictionaire de musique*, facsimile of 1705 Paris edition (Hilversum: Frits Knuf, 1968), p.116.

7. The Organ Works

1. Mr Ancelet, *Observations sur la musique, les musiciens, et les instrumens*, facsimile of 1757 Amsterdam edition (Geneva: Minkoff, 1984), p.26.
2. Wilfred Mellers writes that D'Anglebert's "five organ fugues on variants of a common subject show great contrapuntal science, combined with an extremely rich and flexible chromatic harmony; they too must be accounted one of the most impressive examples of this technique in baroque organ music" (*Grove's Dictionary of Music and Musicians*, 5th ed., vol.I, p.158); and François-Joseph Fétis remarks that "les meilleurs organistes allemands et italiens, contemporains de d'Anglebert, auraient pu se faire honneur de ces morceaux" (*Biographie universelle des musiciens . . .* , facsimile of 1873 Paris edition [Brussels: Culture et civilisation, 1972], vol.I, p.109).
3. François Roberday, *Fugues et caprices*, edited by Jean Ferrard, Le Pupitre 44 (Paris: Heugel, 1972).
4. Guillaume-Gabriel Nivers, *Traité de la composition de musique* (Paris: Ballard, 1667), p.49.
5. Given in Marin Mersenne, *Harmonie universelle*, facsimile of 1636 Paris edition (Paris: Éditions du Centre national de la recherche scientifique, 1965), "Liure sixiesme des orgues," vol.3, between pp.392 and 393. See also André Tessier, "Une Pièce d'orgue de Charles Raquet et le Mersenne de la Bibliothèque des Minimes de Paris," *Revue de musicologie* X (1929):275–283.
6. Guy Oldham, "Louis Couperin: A New Source of French Keyboard Music of the Mid Seventeenth Century," *Recherches* I (1960):51–59.
7. Reprinted in Carl Krebs, "J. J. Froberger in Paris," *Vierteljahrschrift für Musikwissenschaft* X (1894):232–234.

8. Johann-Jakob Froberger, *Oeuvres complètes pour clavecin*, I, edited by Howard Schott, Le Pupitre 57 (Paris: Heugel, 1979).

9. Norbert Dufourcq, "Recent Researches into French Organ-building from the Fifteenth to the Seventeenth Century," *The Galpin Society Journal* X (May 1957):66–81 (includes the text of Énoc's contract). See also Dufourcq's *Le Livre de l'orgue français*, III (Paris: Picard, 1978), p.41.

10. Guillaume-Gabriel Nivers, *Premier livre d'orgue*, edited by Norbert Dufourcq (Paris: Bornemann, 1963), facsimile of 1665 Preface.

11. Nicolas-Antoine Lebègue, *Oeuvres complètes d'orgue* in *Archives des maîtres de l'orgue*, edited by A. Guilmant (Paris: Durand, 1909), p.5.

12. Antoine Furetière, *Essais d'un dictionaire universel* (Amsterdam: Desbordes, 1685), p.112.

13. Jacques Boyvin, *Oeuvres complètes d'orgue* in *Archives des maîtres de l'orgue*, edited by A. Guilmant (Paris: Durand, 1905), p.x.

14. Lambert Chaumont, *Pièces d'orgue sur les 8 tons*, edited by Jean Ferrard, Le Pupitre 25 (Paris: Heugel, 1970). Includes reprint of 1695 Preface.

15. William Pruitt, "The Organ Works of G.-G. Nivers," *Recherches* XIV (1974):81.

16. Dom Bédos de Celles, *L'Art du facteur d'orgues* II/III, facsimile of 1770 Paris edition (Kassel: Bärenreiter, 1965), pp.528–529.

8. Classical Suite Order in France

1. According to Bruce Gustafson, external evidence has now established that the Bauyn Manuscript, previously thought to be c.1660, originated after 1676 (personal communication).

2. David Fuller, "Suite," in *The New Grove Dictionary of Music and Musicians*, 6th ed., edited by Stanley Sadie, 1980, vol.XVIII, p.342.

9. The Unmeasured Preludes

1. *Pièces de luth de Denis Gaultier sur trois differens modes nouveaux*, facsimile of c.1670 Paris edition (Geneva: Minkoff, 1975), p.66. See also Denis Gaultier, *La Rhétorique des dieux . . .* , edited by André Tessier, Publications de la Société française de musicologie, vol. 6 (Paris: Droz, 1932–1933), p.112. For further information regarding the lute prelude, see Alan Curtis, "Unmeasured Preludes in French Baroque Instrumental Music," M. Mus. Thesis, University of Illinois, 1956.

2. Thomas Mace, *Musick's monument*, facsimile of 1676 London edition (Paris: Éditions du Centre national de la recherche scientifique, 1966), p.128.

3. The preludes of the Parville Manuscript appear in Louis Couperin, *Pièces de clavecin*, edited by Alan Curtis (Paris: Heugel, 1970); the preludes of the Bauyn Manuscript are included in Louis Couperin, *Pièces de clavecin*, edited by Paul Brunold, revised by Thurston Dart (Monaco: L'Oiseau-Lyre, 1959). The anonymous prelude that Curtis suggests may be by D'Anglebert (p.22) does not resemble his style.

4. Monsieur de St.-Lambert, *Les Principes du clavecin*, facsimile of 1702 Paris edition (Geneva: Minkoff, 1972), pp.12–14.

5. Bruce Gustafson, "A Letter from Mr Lebègue Concerning His Pre-ludes," *Recherches* XVII (1977):7–14 (translation mine).

6. Nicolas-Antoine Lebègue, *Les Pièces de clauessin* (Paris, 1677), Preface.

7. Two variants in Kenneth Gilbert's edition of D'Anglebert's Prelude in D minor deserve mention. The last slur in the left hand (p.47) should extend to the *re* on p.48, thus allowing the *re* to be played as an *aspiration* (see p.94). Continuing with this system at the top of p.48, an additional semibreve *la* in the left hand, found in both the edition and the manuscript, is missing after the fifth note. One might also note that, while the semibreve *la–re–la* of the Prelude in G major (p.2, sys. 4, right hand) lacks slurring in the 1689 edition, each note carries a slur in D'Anglebert's manuscript. The absence of slurs in the edition appears to be an oversight.

8. Elisabeth-Claude Jacquet de La Guerre, *Les Pièces de clauessin* (Paris, c.1687). Not yet published in a modern edition, as of this writing.

9. Jean-François Dandrieu, *Trois livres de clavecin de jeunesse*, edited by Brigitte François-Sappey (Paris: Heugel, 1975), *Avertissement* to *Pièces de clavecin courtes et faciles* . . . .

10. François Couperin, *L'Art de toucher le clavecin*, edited by Anna Linde (Wiesbaden: Breitkopf & Härtel, 1933), p.33 (translation mine).

11. Davitt Moroney, "Prélude non mesuré," in *The New Grove Dictionary of Music and Musicians*, 6th ed., edited by Stanley Sadie, 1980, vol.XV, pp.212–214.

12. Girolamo Frescobaldi, *Toccate e partite* (Rome, 1615), Preface.

13. Moroney, pp.212.

14. L. Couperin, edited by Curtis, Preface.

15. F. Couperin, p.28 (translation mine).

16. Pierre Richelet, *Dictionnaire françois*, facsimile of 1680 Geneva edition (Geneva: Slatkine, 1970), vol.II, p.207; and Jacques Ozanam, *Dictionaire mathématique* (Amsterdam, 1691), p.664.

10. The Keyboard Dances

1. Michel de Pure, *Idée des spectacles anciens et nouveaux*, facsimile of 1668 Paris edition (Geneva: Minkoff, 1972), p.273.

2. W. J. A. Jonckbloet and J. P. N. Land, *Musique et musiciens au XVIIe siècle. Correspondance et oeuvre musicales de Constantin Huygens* (Leyden: E. J. Brill, 1882), pp.23–24.

3. Denis Gaultier, *La Rhétorique des dieux et autres pieces de luth*, edited by André Tessier, Publications de la Société française de musicologie, vol.7 (Paris: Droz, 1932–33), p.112. The other *Allemande grave* markings (pp.9, 16, 67) appear to be Tessier's.

4. Thomas Mace, *Musick's monument*, facsimile of 1676 London edition (Paris: Éditions du Centre national de la recherche scientifique, 1966), p.129.

5. Sébastien de Brossard, *Dictionnaire de musique*, facsimile of 1705 Paris second edition (Hilversum: Frits Knuf, 1965), p.5; Jacques Ozanam, *Dictionaire mathématique* (Amsterdam: Huguetan, 1691), p.665.

6. Jean Jacques Rousseau, *Dictionnaire de musique*, facsimile of 1768 Paris edition (New York: Johnson Reprint Corp., 1969), p.31.

7. Johann Mattheson, *Der vollkommene Capellmeister*, facsimile of 1739 Hamburg edition (Kassel: Bärenreiter, 1954), p.232.

8. Pierre Rameau, *Le Maître à danser*, facsimile of 1725 Paris edition (New York: Broude Bros., 1967), p.110.

9. A detailed explanation of courante rhythmic patterns is found in the Foreword to Jules Écorchville, *Vingt suites d'orchestre du XVIIe siècle français* (Paris: Marcel Fortin, 1906).

10. Curt Sachs, *World History of the Dance*, translated by Bessie Schönberg (New York: Norton, 1937), p.363; Rameau, p.110.

11. Jacques Bonnet, *Histoire générale de la danse*, facsimile of 1723 Paris edition (Geneva: Slatkine, 1969), pp. 125, 133–134, 62.

12. Quoted by Daniel Devoto, "De la zarabanda à la sarabande," *Recherches* VI (1965):45.

13. J. G. Walther, *Musikalisches Lexikon*, facsimile of 1732 Leipzig edition (Kassel: Bärenreiter, 1953), p.189.

14. Mattheson, p.231.

15. This transformation is well documented in Daniel Devoto, "La folle sarabande," *Revue de musicologie* XLVI (1960):145–180.

16. Quoted, ibid., p.161.

17. Ibid., p.164.

18. Marin Mersenne, *Harmonie universelle*, facsimile of 1636 Paris edition (Paris: Éditions du Centre national de la recherche scientifique, 1965), "Liure second des chants," vol.2, p.166; "Liure second des instrumens," vol.3, p.97.

19. Pierre Richelet, *Dictionnaire françois*, facsimile of 1680 Geneva edition (Geneva: Slatkine, 1970), vol.II, p.345.

20. Quoted by Devoto, "De la zarabanda . . .", p.45.

21. Mace, p.129.

22. Brossard, p.300.

23. Michel L'Affilard, *Principes très faciles pour bien apprendre la musique*, facsimile of 1705 Paris edition (Geneva: Minkoff, 1971), p.86.

24. Gaultier, p.28. Other similar references in this volume appear to be Tessier's. For further information about the French duple-meter gigue, see Werner Danckert, *Geschichte der Gigue* (Leipzig: Kistner & Siegel, 1924), chapter 2.

25. S^r. Perrine, *Pièces de luth en musique auec des regles pour les toucher parfaitem^t sur le luth, et sur le claussin*, facsimile of 1680 Paris edition (Geneva: Minkoff, 1973), Nos.3 and 7.

26. Ozanam, p.666.

27. Thomas Corneille, *Dictionnaire des arts et des sciences* (Paris, 1694), p.490.

28. Noted in Bruce Gustafson, *French Harpsichord Music of the 17th Century* (Ann Arbor: UMI Research Press, 1977), pp.408, 418, 420. The Bauyn Manuscript is published in facsimile as *Manuscrit Bauyn. Pièces de clavecin c. 1660*, with an Introduction by François Lesure (Geneva: Minkoff, 1977). No.32 (p.340) = No.66 (p.376), and No.34 (p.342) = No.61 (p.371).

29. *Manuscrit Bauyn*, p.22.

30. Ibid., pp.400, 403.

31. Catalogued in H. W. Hitchcock, *Les Oeuvres de Marc-Antoine Charpentier* (Paris: Picard, 1982), No.545, p.401.

32. M. E. Little, "Gigue," in *The New Grove Dictionary of Music and Musicians*, 6th ed., 1980, vol.VII, p.370.

33. Gilles Ménage, *Dictionaire étymologique* (Paris, 1694), p. 358.

34. Monsieur de St.-Lambert, *Les Principes du clavecin*, facsimile of 1702 Paris edition (Geneva: Minkoff, 1972), p.65.

35. Mattheson, p.228.

36. J. J. Rousseau, p.231.

37. Thomas Morley, *A Plain and Easy Introduction to Practical Music* (1597), edited by R. Alec Harman (New York: W. W. Norton, 1973), pp.296–297.

38. Mace, p.129.

39. Mersenne, "Liure second des chants," p.165.

40. Brossard, p.264.

41. Mace, vol.II, commentary by Jean Jacquot and transcriptions by André Souris (1966), p.32 (compare with my transcription).

42. Gaultier, p.112.

43. For example, see T. Walker, "Ciaccona and Passacaglia: Remarks on Their Origin and Early History," *Journal of the American Musicological Society* XXI (1968):300–320.

44. Brossard, pp.13, 72.

45. Corneille, vol.I, p.184; vol.II, p.175.

46. J. J. Rousseau, p.366.

47. Gaultier, p.69.

48. Ozanam, p.664.

49. Noted by Gustafson, p.368. Modern edition in *Seventeenth-Century Keyboard Music in the Chigi Manuscripts of the Vatican Library*, Corpus of Early Keyboard Music, III, 32, edited by Harry B. Lincoln (n.p.: American Institute of Musicology, 1968), p.60.

50. Brossard, p.45.

51. Ozanam, p.666.

52. Walther, p.398.

53. St.-Lambert, p.19.

54. J. J. Rousseau, p.277.

55. Jean-Henry D'Anglebert, *Pièces de clavecin*, edited by Kenneth Gilbert (Paris: Heugel, 1975), pp.27, 63.

56. Mersenne, "Liure second des chants," vol.2, p.168.

57. Brossard, p.29.

58. Walther, p.274.

59. J. J. Rousseau, p.227.

60. Richelet, vol.I, p.367.

61. For a description and examples of the early and later folia, see Richard Hudson, "Folia," in *The New Grove Dictionary of Music and Musicians*, 6th ed., edited by Stanley Sadie, 1980, vol. VI, pp.690–692.

62. Richard Hudson, *The Folia, the Saraband, the Passacaglia, and the Chaconne*, American Institute of Musicology (Neuhausen-Stuttgart: Hänssler, 1982), vol.I, p.xxvi.

63. Andreas Moser, "Zur Genesis der Folies d'Espagne," *Archiv fur Musikwissenschaft* I (1918/19):362.

64. Sachs, p.408.

65. Raoul Auger Feuillet, *Chorégraphie* and *Recueil de dances*, facsimile of 1700 Paris editions (New York: Broude Bros., 1968), pp.33, 102.

66. Kurt von Fischer, "Variations," in *The New Grove Dictionary of Music and Musicians,* 6th ed., edited by Stanley Sadie, 1980, vol.XIX, p.542.

Conclusion

1. Willi Apel, *Masters of the Keyboard* (Cambridge: Harvard University Press, 1947), p.97.

INDEX

233